BECOMING
ALMOST FAMOUS

MY BACK PAGES IN

MUSIC, WRITING, AND LIFE

BY BEN FONG-TORRES

Backbeat
Books
San Francisco

Published by Backbeat Books
600 Harrison Street, San Francisco, CA 94107
www.backbeatbooks.com
email: books@musicplayer.com
An imprint of the Music Player Group, Publishers of *Guitar Player, Bass Player, Keyboard,* and other magazines, United Entertainment Media. Inc., A CMP Information company

CMP
United Business Media

Distributed to the book trade in the US and Canada by Publishers Group West, 1700 Fourth Street, Berkeley, CA 94710

Distributed to the music trade in the US and Canada by Hal Leonard Publishing, P.O. Box 13819, Milwaukee, WI 53213

Cover design by Richard Leeds—BigWigDesign.com
Text design and composition by Leigh McLellan Design
Front cover photo © David Corio/Michael Ochs Archives.com

Library of Congress Cataloging-in-Publication Data

Fong-Torres, Ben.
    Becoming almost famous : my back pages in music, writing, and life / by Ben Fong-Torres.
        p. cm.
    Includes index.
    ISBN-13: 978-0-87930-880-3 (alk. paper)
    ISBN-10: 0-87930-880-X (alk. paper)
    1. Popular music--History and criticism. 2. Popular music--Writing and publishing. I. Title.
    ML3470.F67 2006
    781.640973--dc22   2006009614

Printed in the United States of America

05 06 07 08 09   5 4 3 2 1

BECOMING

ALMOST FAMOUS

CONTENTS

YOU'RE GONNA HAVE
TO SUCK SOMEBODY

By David Felton

For the 35 years I've known him, Ben Fong-Torres has always been younger and more grown up than me. At first I'm sure I resented him for this. I mean, just take a look at that picture of him on the back of his last collection of work, *Not Fade Away.* He's in his *Rolling Stone* office in 1972, and on one wall hang a dozen clipboards arranged in three neat rows. I don't know if they were for genres of music, months of the year, or hours of the day, but to me they indicated a mind seriously imprisoned by maturity.

And his shirt is tucked in, his hair is trimmed neat, and he's wearing these "cool" metal-rimmed glasses. Sometimes I helped him with headlines for his stories, and I remember for one piece he did on Elton John I gave him "The Four-Eyed Bitch Is Back." I was actually talking about Ben.

I guess I thought of Ben as a grown-up of the '60s, whereas I tried desperately to be a child of the '60s and several decades to follow. Even in the '60s I was too old for the job. I was in my late twenties, living in Pasadena with a wife and child, when I first discovered and covered the Haight-Ashbury for the *Los Angeles Times.* I joined *Rolling Stone* in 1970, and a year later Annie Leibovitz and I were assigned to cover the last night of the Fillmore in San Francisco. When the historic night was over, Annie used up her last roll of film by shooting me alone in the center of the Fillmore floor holding a magnum of champagne.

As it turned out, *Time* magazine asked Annie for the film she didn't use for our story, and a week later they ran my picture alongside an essay about the end of the hippie era. There I was in *Time*—wasted, hair down to my shoulders, and surrounded by Fillmore detritus—an official hippie at the age of 31. I had just made it.

Unfortunately I was not as punctual with my story for *Rolling Stone,* and I vaguely recall an ugly scene days later with the presses stopped, Ben tapping his foot, me hours past deadline, and copyeditor Charles Perry strangling me with his necktie and screaming, "We're publishing a magazine here!" I would have understood if Ben resolved then and there not to trust at least *one* person over 30. But instead he continued to humor me, support me, and—consummate hippie that he is—never lay his trip on me.

Over time, and even though we live on separate coasts, or maybe because we do, Ben has become one of my most cherished friends. I suppose this is partly because time and mathematics have made our differences in age and maturity less pronounced. But mainly because I soon realized that Ben's business-like manner was largely an act, a veneer he put on to get Jann Wenner off his back and onto mine.

It turned out Ben was actually wilder and more twisted than the rest of us at *Rolling Stone.* You just had to wait until the sun went down. Or the weekends. One weekend in the fall of 1975, the staff had gathered at the Ventana Inn in Big Sur for a so-called "editorial conference." These were periodic binges where maybe a speech or two was given, but mostly everyone just lay around getting ripped and ignorant. The Ventana had these modern three-foot-square mirrors hanging in our rooms, and the first thing we all did was take them from the walls and make them into tables, if you catch my drift.

Rolling Stone had just published our first Men's Issue, called "Men on the Ropes," which included, among many droll articles about this sexually paranoid species, a full-page fashion spread of Eldridge Cleaver modeling his latest pants that he had designed in Paris. Eldridge called them "Cleavers," and he apparently felt that if women could dress to highlight their unique protuberances, so could men. Thus the Cleavers featured a long, thick, and, in Eldridge's case, fairly tight sock-like "appurtenance" hanging from where the fly used to be. Available in various colors and fabrics.

So we're sitting around the pool at the Ventana, worshipping ourselves and the California sun, when Ben Fong-Torres suddenly appears wearing a pair of Cleavers that he and his girlfriend Dianne had sewn at home—his handcrafted appurtenance pointing toward the water like a divining rod. I don't recall what kind of chatter was going on inside or outside our heads at that moment, but it suddenly got a lot quieter. And I knew right then, this is a man I'm going to admire for the rest of my life.

And I have, and I do, not least for this incorrigible prankish wit of his. Ben has never called me up without making me laugh and making me make him laugh. When *Rolling Stone* moved to New York in 1977, Ben decided to remain in

San Francisco, his hometown. He and I would now be separated by 3,000 miles, but we got to have one last fling when Jann sent us to Hollywood for eight weeks to join the writing staff on the *Rolling Stone 10th Anniversary Special* for CBS.

Neither Ben nor I had ever worked for network television, a terrifying experience that no person should try for the first time alone. Thank God I had Ben at my side, comparing notes and grimaces, assuring me that I'd actually heard what I'd just heard and seen what I'd just seen. Because the hacks they put us with were truly unbelievable, and Ben, who has this great radio voice to match his wit, nourished me with flawless impressions of them: "You boys go in that room and noodle and gestalt! Go as far out as you want—we'll pull it back!" At one point I grew so frustrated with these network goons, I yelled, "Do you know who you're dealing with? When Ben Fong-Torres jumps, Jann Wenner snaps his fingers!"

Of course, the show was a complete disaster. *Rolling Stone* apologized in print to its readers. One reader actually wrote in, "You probably meant well, but so did Hitler." But like all good wars and disasters, the experience had a brighter side for me and Ben. It cemented our friendship for life and opened our eyes to an uglier and stupider world.

After I moved to New York, the *Rolling Stone* editorial staff organized its first, and worst, house band, the Dry Heaves. It included, among others, me, Jann Wenner, Charles M. Young, Kurt Loder, Jon Pareles, and the late Timothy White. Ensconced in San Francisco, Ben could not help us out of our misery, but he did contribute a song. Dylan had just released his born-again *Slow Train Coming,* and Ben wrote us a parody of one of the tracks. He called it "Gotta Suck Somebody," and one of the verses went:

You may know Paul Simon, you may know Elaine
You may know Jann Wenner, you may even know Jane
You may have home numbers for Ahmet and Clive
You may know the cast of Saturday Night Live
But you're gonna have to suck somebody
(backup singers:)
Suck somebody

The Dry Heaves performed the song, along with classics like "Life During Press Time" and "Hunchback Baby," during a Christmas party at the Lone Star in Manhattan. Mick Jagger attended and made one comment: "You guys should stick to writing."

It's moments like these that make me think of Ben, and Ben who makes me think of moments like these. I'll always cherish his cleverness and outbursts of mock jock mayhem, and I know wherever the Good Lord is keeping him—oh wait, Ben's still alive, right? Sorry. Got carried away.

I guess the point I wanted to make is, as much as I love Ben for his friendship and tomfoolery, what I really admire about the man is his journalism. There is simply no better, more authentic, more astute, or more thorough chronicler of the rock 'n' roll cultural revolution than Ben Fong-Torres. In this one volume alone he covers the revolution from its earliest days in San Francisco to Cameron Crowe's movie valentine decades later in which Ben himself is a character (and to a lesser extent, me, as his effete sidekick).

Rolling Stone was started because no one else was covering the cultural revolution of the '60s in an authentic way. That is largely true today. Most accounts still dismiss the '60s as a time of hopelessly naive dreams squandered by drug-taking crazies. Okay, maybe I was guilty of that, but not everybody. Not Ben.

When *Rolling Stone* was about to celebrate its 25th anniversary, I helped MTV produce a two-hour special marking the event. I got to travel around and interview all my old buddies from the magazine—Hunter Thompson, Annie Leibovitz, Charles Perry, David Dalton, and Ben—and ask them the same question: what did the hippies teach us? I got some interesting answers. Hunter used a homemade bomb to blow up a picture of Jann Wenner. David Dalton passed along some odd racial theories he learned from Charles Manson. But Ben said something that I took right to my heart. He said the hippies taught us that no matter what situation we find ourselves in, we can always start over.

Which, of course, is exactly what Ben did when he left the phone company and joined *Rolling Stone* in 1969. Ironically, he hasn't changed much since then. He's still a rock 'n' roll journalist, he's just gotten better, brighter, funnier, and, like the rest of us relics, more built for comfort than for speed.

On the other hand, Ben has inspired me to start over many times, to quit journalism, get sober, write comedy for television, write promos for MTV, get remarried, and travel to China ten years ago and adopt a baby girl named Grace. I think Ben fell in love with Grace as much as I did. He invited us both to lunch, took her picture, and somehow convinced her that he was her birth father. I've never told her anything different.

Today I'm a minor executive at MTV, I run a lab that produces creative experiments for the people who work here, and I hardly have to write at all—just some memos and occasional dialogue for *Beavis and Butthead.* That's how I solved my deadline problem. For the last few years I've refused to write anything that takes more than a few hours.

Until Ben asked me to do this piece. To tell you the truth, I'm starting to get a little resentful. Of course he wants it on time, the little prig. Well, he'll get it on time. Technically. Okay, it's 1:00 a.m. here in New York, but it's only 10:00 p.m. in San Francisco. He'll get the fucker by midnight.

And don't get any wrong ideas. I'd only do this for Ben.

—*David Felton*
New York
November 2005

TO ELVIS,
FOR STARTING IT ALL.

INTRODUCTION

Left to right: Jann Wenner, Ben Fong-Torres, and Michael Douglas

This is a volume two. *Not Fade Away,* my first compilation of articles from *Rolling Stone* and other publications, was published in 1999. Since then, I've had occasion to teach a magazine editing course at my alma mater, San Francisco State University, and, in fact, to deliver a commencement address to one of its graduating classes. I've moderated and sat on numerous panels attended by people who want to break into writing and other media work. The plain fact is that I like to teach, to share what I know with others.

In my talks to would-be or beginning writers, I encourage them to read as much as they can; to absorb, if not emulate, favorite pieces and writers; to read widely, beyond their chosen or favored fields of interest.

It was in that teach-your-children spirit that I put *Not Fade Away* together. Along with the articles I chose, I added prologues to all and epilogues to some, where appropriate. I wanted to set the scene for each article and take the reader backstage. When I came up with an idea, or got assigned a piece on so-and-so, I wanted to say, here's what was going on in my life. Here's what was happening at *Rolling Stone.* Here's why we wanted this story. And here's how I went after it.

I wanted to show or tell how an article came about and, as best as I could recall, how it got written and how it was received.

I'm doing the same with this volume. In several cases, I dig into the editing process and offer a first draft of a portion of a story along with the published piece—and try to explain why it changed. All articles do change, no matter who the writer, and no matter that the original piece was *perfect, dammit.* Editing— good editing—always improves a work. This is especially true with the articles produced for *Rolling Stone* and, later, the *San Francisco Chronicle,* where I wrote features and a radio column in the '80s and '90s. These are pieces produced on the run, up against not only immovable deadlines, but also the demands of other articles and projects. Those writings, there is no question, needed extra sets of eyes and an unsparing, even brutal, editing pen. Even then, things got through, and I cringe at the way, especially earlier in my career, I toyed with words and phrases, trying to match the laissez-faire attitude of the times, or of the subject, or of *Rolling Stone.* (This collection, I'm happy to say, has been sub- jected to another editor's set of red pencils and scalpels, making many pieces clearer and cleaner than when they were initially rushed into print.) Now, be- cause this is a second volume, I feel strange about introducing myself—and how I came to join *Rolling Stone*—again. So what I'll do is edit down the piece that opened *Not Fade Away,* give you the basics, and let you move on.

It was November 1967 when my roommates Tom Gericke and Doug Leighton came across the first issue of *Rolling Stone.* It was a bracing find, a new high, and it jumped from one set of hands to another around our flat in San Francisco.

For one thing, it came from our own town. But with its correspondents in London, New York, and Los Angeles, it was clearly out to be a national publica- tion. It didn't appear to be either a newspaper or a magazine, but a hybrid. It was printed on newsprint, in black and white, with a splash of a single color on the *Rolling Stone* logo. It didn't even open like a magazine. It was quarter-folded— that is, folded twice. The first issues didn't have covers, but a newspaper-styled front page with several stories.

Those articles were about rock 'n' roll, written in a style that was knowing, critical, good-humored, and hip—neither fawning, like teen and fan magazines, nor crude and condescending, like so much of the mainstream press (that is, when it deigned to stoop to cover rock 'n' roll).

I had covered the emerging rock scene for the *Daily Gater,* the campus paper at San Francisco State, where I was a reporter, a columnist, and, finally, the editor. In the mid-'60s, our campus pulsed with music. Our annual folk festivals, long infused with gospel, country, and blues, were beginning to rock. Musicians like Dan Hicks (later of the Hot Licks) were registered students. And then there were the visitors. One day, it might be Big Brother & the Holding Company, with their new lead singer from Texas, setting up a public address system in the art gallery and running through a few tunes. Another day, Grace Slick and her first band, Great Society, would play a lunchtime concert in front of the men's gym.

To my roommates, I was a natural candidate to write for *Rolling Stone.* Especially since, in early 1968, I was unhappily ensconced in a job writing bits and pieces for a local television station. One of my roommates, Abe, was road manager for several pop acts, including Peter, Paul & Mary and Jimi Hendrix, and one day in February he told me about a free concert in a nearby park. Some friends of his in the Siegal-Schwall Blues Band were playing, he said, and the show was to promote a movie Dick Clark was making about the Haight-Ashbury.

Dick Clark and hippies? "*Rolling Stone*!" I thought. I phoned the office, offered the news tip—amazingly, no one there had heard about the concert—and got the assignment.

I saw *Rolling Stone's* offices for the first time when I delivered my report. They were in a part of town unknown to most San Franciscans. It was sometimes referred to as "South of Market," a region of warehouses, wholesale outlets, and heavy industry. *Rolling Stone's* founder, publisher, and editor, Jann Wenner, had scored free rent in a loft above a printing plant. But, having entered through the lobby and walked along the back wall and up wooden steps to the loft, ink and gigantic rolls of paper weren't the prevailing smell in the air.

The magazine office was just across an alley from a slaughterhouse. That would explain the increasing popularity of incense around the offices.

Rolling Stone had a bare-bones staff: Jann, one other editor, an art director, and a secretary. I handed in my report, looked around a moment, and left.

My story appeared in March, in the issue dated April 6, 1968. Actually, it wasn't even a story. It was just a few paragraphs and ran in a column called "Flashes." I got five dollars and no byline. I had no complaints.

When KMPX, a San Francisco pioneer free-form FM radio station that had been taken over by a band of creative hipsters in spring of 1967, went on strike, I helped cover the story. As the strike dragged over several months, it became my beat. (See "The Night Rock 'n' Roll Woke Nobody" in this collection.)

Covering a long and emotional labor strike called by hippie radio revolution-aries was exhilarating, but the $10 and $20 checks I received were not. So I joined the telephone company, where I wrote for the employee magazine. In my spare time, I was a rock reporter. After helping out on the KMPX news story, I wrote short pieces on Gordon Lightfoot and record producer Erik Jacobsen, then got my first assignment for a full-length artist profile: songwriter Dino Valente, the composer of the hippie anthem, "Get Together."

Thanks to a liberal boss at the phone company, I was able to take the oc-casional day off to fly to Reno to write about Creedence Clearwater Revival, or to interview a young singer-songwriter, Joni Mitchell, at her home in Laurel Canyon. I visited with her, met her boyfriend, a charming Englishman named Graham Nash, and admired a painting of hers, propped on a grand piano, that would become the cover art for her second album.

The story appeared alongside a profile of Judy Collins in an issue that, to my surprise, had Mitchell on the cover. It was my first *Rolling Stone* cover, but it was a momentary high. Someone had left my byline off of the article.

(Speaking of bylines, Wenner wondered what mine was all about, with this fancy hyphenated name, and learned that my father, whose name was Fong, purchased the name "Ricardo Torres" in the 1920s—when Chinese weren't be-ing allowed into the US—and entered the country as a Filipino national. A family friend later suggested combining the two names.)

Rolling Stone was still paying between $10 and $40 for stories, and I was content to straddle the corporate and the rock worlds until early April 1969, when, on the stub of a $30 check for two articles, Jann Wenner wrote, "Call me soon."

I didn't even notice the message for a week or so, and when I called, it was a slightly miffed Jann who suggested we have lunch. We met at an outdoor seafood cafe near *Rolling Stone*.

After asking a few questions about my background, he offered me a job. He was as loose as the phone company had been rigid. "Just come in and, you know, do what you think needs to be done," he said. To me, it was a dream job. Rock 'n' roll—and no more suits. I leaned back, squinted at the sun, and, trying to sound casual, asked about the salary. After all, I was just about to be raised to $730 a month at Pacific Telephone. But Jann knew what he had go-ing, and he could read the interest in my face. He offered me $135 a week, and, without bothering with the math, I accepted.

Rolling Stone operated with only a couple of editors and an art director. They were by no means stereotypical hippies. The art director, Bob Kingsbury, was a bearded, older man—well over 30—who was a sculptor, and who'd never done any graphics design work until he was recruited by his brother-in-law, Jann Wenner. John Burks was a tall, bespectacled man with a Beatle haircut and a jazz jones, who left a job at *Newsweek* to sign up with this music paper. And proofreader Charles Perry, roommate of LSD legend Augustus Stanley Owsley, was semi-bald and wore, as a uniform, mustard-colored shirts and flowery ties. A lover of wine and dead languages, he'd never worked at a magazine before.

The informality of the office setup recalled my college paper. Only here, this was a small group of professionals, taking the best of journalistic traditions and rules, but creating their own, unique publication.

I took on the title of news editor, which made the first few pages of each issue my responsibility. I soon learned two things: first, the news was whatever interested us, whether it came over the phone, by mail, or through an experience the night before at a club, concert, or friend's house. Outside of our network, we relied on the British pop press, from which we pilfered with abandon for the "Flashes" column.

Second, I discovered that titles were meaningless. Whatever we called ourselves, we did a multitude of jobs. We all wrote, we all edited, we all made assignments, we all pitched in with captions, headlines, and story ideas.

Those first months weren't exactly on-the-job training, since I'd written perhaps a dozen stories before getting hired. But I was still learning. Looking back, it's painfully obvious how much I still had to learn. As many of us at *Rolling Stone* were, I was guilty of attitudinizing, of tossing off all those lectures we'd had from our journalism profs about "objective journalism," and siding with . . . well, our side. We were hipper than thou—and than you, too.

It was understandable. We were a downright phenomenon. Wenner had created the most unique new magazine, the most effectively targeted new publication since Hugh Hefner founded *Playboy* in 1955.

Not Fade Away and this follow-up serve as a combined flip side to my memoir, *The Rice Room: Growing Up Chinese-American,* further subtitled *From Number Two Son to Rock 'n' Roll.*

It was the story of how I was born into a rigid Chinese culture and raised in a series of family restaurants and how I broke loose—into the '60s, into *Rolling*

Stone magazine, into free-form FM rock radio, and far, far away from the doctor or lawyer's office my parents had hoped I would occupy.

In the early '60s, a Chinese-American wasn't supposed to be in print or on the air—and they mostly weren't. I had role models, sure, but they were people like Gary Owens, who did the morning show on my favorite Top 40 station (KEWB in Oakland), and Steve Allen, the Renaissance man as comic entertainer.

I was fortunate to have chosen to attend San Francisco State, where racial background was not a factor at either the campus daily or at the radio station. Call me deaf, dumb, and blind, but I enjoyed a similarly smooth ride into *Rolling Stone*. If I could do the job, I had the job. And on the job, meeting with musicians, managers, publicists, concert promoters, and record company executives, I never sensed any surprise on their part as they discovered that the guy from *Rolling Stone* was Chinese. Far more often, I would hear that, from having heard my name on the phone, they expected a Latino ("Torres") or perhaps a Scandinavian ("Von Taurus," maybe?).

Of course, to be writing about pop, rock, and R&B music was to be traveling in relatively loose, liberal, and enlightened circles. But even when those circles extended into, say, the Deep South, there were no problems. That may be, in part, because musicians on tour move in a protected bubble.

The Rice Room (named after a space in our family restaurant in Oakland's Chinatown) covered mostly my coming of age. Readers who'd come of age with *Rolling Stone* told me they wanted to hear more from my rock 'n' roll side, in print and, later, on the radio.

Not Fade Away, by and large, accomplished that. I am happy that, with this second volume, I get to go a little further—to expand beyond the rock world with articles on Carmen McRae and Frank Sinatra; to pop back into that musty old rice room with pieces that deal with being Asian-American; and to revisit my first love: radio.

Life is a circle game. Today, I am back at the *Chronicle,* writing a radio column on a freelance basis, and I continue to contribute to *Rolling Stone.* And, having long ago hurdled the barrier between detached chronicler and out-and-out ham, I'm often found onstage, emceeing fundraisers, making speeches, conducting celebrity interviews at film and music festivals, and even singing. It seems only fitting (not to mention fun) that I experience what so many of my subjects do for a living: perform under pressure.

I'm only glad that I've never had to review myself.

ACKNOWLEDGMENTS

Thanks to *Rolling Stone,* first, because without that magazine, I'd probably be writing those electronics manuals you never read. Instead, I have a second book of compilations and am writing a set of thank yous that may never be read.

Still, I've got to acknowledge Jann S. Wenner and all the people who've populated *Rolling Stone's* mastheads, from then to now.

From those many mastheads, I particularly thank David Felton for agreeing to write the foreword. I'll have to flip back a few pages and see whether or not he turned it in. He was not called "Stonecutter" for no reason. Thanks, too, to Cameron Crowe, who did the honors in my first collection and then made me almost famous. Since Felton works at MTV and has been a writer for *Beavis and Butthead*—well, who knows what might happen?

Another name from those mastheads is Sarah Lazin, who rose from editorial assistant and researcher to become a literary agent. She has also turned out to be an excellent editor in her own right, a savvy mentor, and a dear and valued friend.

I thank the editors of all the magazines and newspapers for whom I have been fortunate enough to write, and, once again, I thank the subjects of my pieces. Without them, I'd be facing a blank screen. (Often, even with them, I was blank, but that's *my* problem.)

This is my third book with Backbeat Books, and I thank the stellar, music-loving team there: senior editor Richard Johnston, marketing manager Nina Lesowitz, production editors Amy Miller and Gail Saari, sales manager Kevin Becketti, and marketing & sales coordinator Steve Moore. I'm also grateful to Matt Kelsey, who guided me through my first two books at Backbeat when he was publisher there. Thanks to Richard Leeds of Big Wig Design for making this look like a book, and special thanks to Julie Herrod, a masterful editor, for hopefully making it read like one. (And, yes, I know there's a misplaced adjective and a misuse of that adjective, "hopefully." We'll make fixes in the second edition. Hopefully.)

I send thanks and love to my family: to our mother, Connie (real name: Soo Hoo Tui Wing); to sister Sarah and her husband, Dave Watkins; to their kids, Lea and Jason; to Lea's husband, John Berlinsky, and Jason's girlfriend, Wendy Todd; to sister Shirley and her daughter, Tina; to Tina's husband, Matt Pavao, and their daughter, Maggie; to brother Burton; to sisters-in-law Robin Ward and Eileen Powers and their husbands, Chuck and Richard, respectively.

As always and for always, this is for Dianne, my wife, who has (voluntarily) read most of what I've written over the years, and has never failed to smile and say, "That was great." She's an excellent liar and an even better wife.

SUPERSESSION

CROSBY, STILLS, NASH & YOUNG

Ben with David Crosby at KSAN, 1970

I **joined *Rolling Stone*** as an editor and writer in May 1969, in time to contribute to its thirty-third issue. A piece I'd done before being hired—on Joni Mitchell—ran in that issue. It was a cover story, but my byline was accidentally left off. Welcome to the big leagues!

For months, I wrote mostly pieces I could handle from San Francisco, by phone or by visiting local bands and Chet Helms and Bill Graham, the two major concert promoters in town. I had done a few feature-length pieces: one on what we decided to call the "third wave" of the San Francisco music scene, one on the singer-songwriter Dino Valente, and one on Jefferson Airplane, one of San Francisco's—and *Rolling Stone's*—favorite bands.

But earlier that year, when I was still freelancing, I'd been in Los Angeles witnessing one of the first recording sessions for a band I noted in my calendar as "Nash-Stills-Crosby." Despite my notation, they chose to reverse the names.

As I wrote in *Not Fade Away*: "All of us in that studio (Wally Heider's Studio 3) were transported—not only by the music, but also by the personalities of these escapees from the Byrds, Buffalo Springfield, and the Hollies, respectively. They were the first 'supergroup,' and they damned well knew it."

CSN (&Y, for Neil Young) were in my first compilation with my report on their 1974 reunion tour. In the five years between their formation and that tour, I wrote about them maybe a half-dozen times. Like the Airplane, they became a beat.

This is my first piece on them. This was my first venture behind the scenes with a major band, following along as they did a recording session, then set up for and performed at Winterland Auditorium in San Francisco. This was the first of the kind of experiences that Cameron Crowe, who would cover later tours of CSNY, would depict in *Almost Famous.*

It's safe to say that I didn't know what I was doing. I just rolled with the guys, taking notes and doing what Jann Wenner had advised me to do when he gave me my first feature assignment: get those details.

As with virtually every piece I did in *Rolling Stone,* this was done on the run—while reporting several other stories, writing much of the "Random Notes" section, and editing other articles.

Reprinting this piece in an anthology of Nash-Stills—er, Crosby, Stills, Nash & Young articles entitled *4 Way Street,* Dave Zimmer noted that I had "an acute understanding of what CSNY was going after and achieving. In this article, he got inside the machinations of the band offstage, on the boards, and in the studio—where the musicians were recording tracks for what would become CSNY's *Déjà Vu* album. Fong-Torres also picked up on the powerful impact the group was having on its audience."

That, frankly, is news to me. But I'll take it.

Behind them, a crew is setting up the curtains that'll hide their electric gear until their acoustic "wooden music" is finished. The curtains are black; there'll be no light show behind Crosby, Stills, Nash & Young. It's Thursday, 5:00 p.m., rehearsal time at the Winterland Auditorium in San Francisco. Four hours before showtime, a guard is already stationed at the old Ice Capades auditorium's doors, brusquely challenging all visitors.

Outside, in brisk autumn weather, a line has already begun, a sidewalk full of hair and rimless glasses and leather and boutique colors. These people know Crosby, Stills, Nash & Young won't go on until 11:30 p.m., maybe midnight. No matter. They'll grab good places on the hardwood floor at the foot of the stage. And they'll wait.

Dallas Taylor, the drummer, is moving along the foot of the stage now, out of view from Stephen Stills, who's on the stage testing out the piano. Taylor is edging toward Stills, a mischievous smile splitting his wide face. Suddenly Taylor springs, with a shout, up behind Stills, his right hand now a pistol, and kills him. Stills stiffens, falls off his seat, and plunges straight into David Crosby and his guitar, causing a crashing cacophony.

Across the floor, in the first row, Graham Nash is stirred alert by the noise. He's trying to put together the order of tunes they'll do that night. He calls out to Taylor, who's scampered off to stage center by now: "Hey, man—not around axes, man! Not when you're near an ax!" Taylor nods, but he knows that any minute now, Stills will have to come back and kill him.

More puttering around the stage, and suddenly it happens. Stills pantomimes the biting of the ring off a hand grenade, waits three seconds, and stuffs it into Taylor's mouth. Taylor dies beautifully, jumping out of his skin at the "explosion," then falling six feet down off the stage, tumbling, landing on his back.

Nash looks up again. No guitars in the way this time. He smiles, shakes his head, and goes back to work on his list.

Crosby, Stills & Nash coasted up the charts effortlessly this summer behind Blind Faith, Creedence Clearwater Revival, and Blood, Sweat & Tears. Then their single, "Marrakesh Express," hit the Top20, then "Suite: Judy Blue Eyes." Then Crosby, Stills & Nash surged up again, past Blind Faith and the others.

And here's Graham Nash, sitting atop a softly vibrating bed in Steve Stills' motel room in San Francisco. "We didn't have a band with just the three of us," he is saying.

Crosby, Stills & Nash was Crosby and Nash and Stills, and Stills on organ, and Stills on bass, and Stills on lead guitar and overdubs of additional guitar tracks.

"We could sing the LP," Nash said, "but we couldn't play it." For their concerts, he said, "we knew we'd have to represent the sound we had on the album. Now we have a whole different band."

Dallas Taylor, with the trio from the beginning—which was a year ago—has been joined in the background by Greg Reeves, a quiet, 19-year-old bassist right out of Motown's studios. And in the foreground—for most intents and purposes—is Neil Young.

Neil Young, composer, guitarist, and singer with Buffalo Springfield, has written a couple of tunes for the next album, "Country Girl" and "Helpless," the latter including a chorus featuring the high, soaring harmonic blend of Crosby, Stills, and Nash—the blend that is perhaps the prime attraction of the group.

But mostly Young is a luxury, a utility man as well as yet another creative force. In the studios, where Stills reigns but shares the reins with opinionated co-producers Nash and Crosby, Young is a solid fourth corner. "We may shape the album," Stills says, "but Neil'll come along and give us that extra thing."

Nash choruses: "He gives us that bit of direction we may need to resolve a question. He's good at making records."

Young was brought in, says Stills, because "we wanted another life force. I always wanted another rhythm section. But instead of a keyboard man, we thought, why not a guy who could do other things, write songs, play guitar, be a brother and stuff."

Here come the life forces into the dressing room at the Winterland Auditorium. It's 1:30 a.m. Sunday now, and they've finished their third of four nights. Dimly lit in red, the room is small, attic-like, but serves as an adequate shelter. Crosby, Stills, Nash & Young and Taylor and Reeves want some quiet. David's voice is out, and he's slumped into an old couch, his doctor standing over him.

David had had a sore throat since midweek and that day, Saturday, had wrecked it at the Vietnam Moratorium rally in Golden Gate Park. "He got carried away a bit," Nash had explained that evening backstage. "After the first thing he yelled he realized he'd gotten carried away." By the time he'd reached the stage at Winterland, with each of the 5,000 onlookers able to shout louder than him, he knew he'd paid the price. He could talk best by nodding, smiling, and crinkling his 'stache up and down. At the mike, Graham explained David's ailment, and the crowd cheered at their disabled compatriot.

Stephen, seated with an acoustic guitar on his lap, and facing David, went into "Suite," and the audience, just itching for the group to justify the adulation they'd already poured onto them, whooped it up. Slowly, surely they galloped through the number, until the verse beginning, "Chestnut brown canary, ruby-throated sparrow." And when David reached the high note (. . . "thrill me to the MARrow"), he couldn't make it, and the crowd applauded, anyway, while he grinned sheepishly and held his throat.

From that point on—what, five minutes into the set—Crosby was pretty much out of it, and the program had to be overhauled. David's usual solo, "Guinnevere," was dropped, along with a couple of duets with Nash. Young stepped in to sing a medley of Buffalo Springfield tunes, on acoustic guitar, with Stills. Later, during the electric half of the set, David came back to spend the remains of his voice on a hoarse facsimile of "Wooden Ships," and Steve substituted for him on "Long Time Gone," a song clearly Crosby's.

The audience, like the ones in New York and Los Angeles and Big Sur, cheered everything they did, of course, but Crosby, Stills, Nash & Young knew better. The night before, they had done their now-standard encore number—a brief, softly sung, untitled Stills composition about freedom, once submitted to *Easy Rider*—and gone offstage and around the rim of the old Ice Capades rink and settled into their dressing room and lit up a snack, and those 5,000 freaks on the other side of the curtains were still stomping on the floor, in their seats high in the distant balconies, scream-ing for MORE! MORE!

Now, tonight, it was pretty quiet by the time they'd reached the room, and Steve Stills is looking up. "Hey, you should have been here last night," he says, clear eyes dancing. "Tonight was okay, but it was nothing. You know, we were bored out there."

And you know he's being straight. "Down By the River," the Neil Young composition used as the set-closer, seemed interminable, with Stills and Young trading lead guitar runs and strums as laconically as two men lob-bing a medicine ball back and forth. Graham Nash, he of the high, silken voice, sang out a trade-off riff of his own and knocked Neil out for a second, but that was a second out of 30 minutes. Still, the audience went crazy.

Crosby, Stills, Nash & Young can do no wrong.

It could be the flawless harmony—tight as the Everly Brothers, soft as Simon and Garfunkel, melodic as the best of the Springfield. It could be reports, words-of-mouth about the mini-Woodstocks they'd created wher-ever they performed, sending out those effortless good vibes and coming off like "gentle free spirits." It could well be a mass appreciation of their aversion to the kind of hype that flooded Blind Faith, making them an instantly high-priced, out-of-reach act.

Crosby, Stills, Nash & Young

Young speaks: "See, the thing is, everybody, especially David, is a controversial character. Everybody has an opinion. Like, I like to watch David just to see what he'll do next." Crosby is, of course, the Byrd who was canned because he wanted to speak and live, as well as sing, his political piece. He was deeply hurt when Roger McGuinn fired him, and over the months since his departure, Byrds interviews seemed to build a picture of Crosby as a huffy, moody, intolerable, hard-to-work-with sort of man.

Crosby loves Stills, Nash, and Young, and these days he and Nash play cheerleaders at recording sessions, conducting playback parties for visitors and heaping mountains of praise onto their colleagues. "This is the best music I've made with other people," old folkie Crosby beams. Away from the microphones, he spends his time behind and to the side of the control board, hand-cleaning future refreshments or bouncing up and down, his jacket fringes dancing to the music of the band.

"Don't ask him about Christine," someone had suggested, thinking of David's fragile shell, so badly cracked when his lady of three years was killed in a bus collision on a road near his Novato home. David had been spun nearly out of his mind. The group cancelled what would have been a wonderful stay at the Winterland with John Sebastian on the bill with them, and David took to the water, to a schooner, to escape. He and Graham went to England to stew and unwind some more, and when he returned, he dove into the task of keeping himself busy, keeping up the happy front—so that even his close friends would say don't ask about Christine. But David, knowing he can't, doesn't try to suppress the memories.

"Man, you know how hard it is to find a good woman, a woman who's just right—who's with you on every single level. Every step of the way, it was right." And Crosby's looking straight at you. "But you know," he says, "at least you know that it can happen."

And David knows that, just as he is not alone in his joy over his music, he is not alone in his sorrow over lost love.

Stills lost the love of Judy Collins and let his broken heart dictate the words: "Listen to me baby—help me, I'm dyin' . . . it's my heart that's a sufferin', it's a-dyin' . . . that's what I have to lose . . . ."

Graham recently parted from his lady of the island, Joni Mitchell, and bassman Reeves "had a slump," as Stills puts it, over a chick. Both Dallas and Neil are married, Neil to a lovely girl with Judy Collins eyes, named Susan.

"We've canceled a lot of studio time because of women troubles," Nash says matter-of-factly. "Women are the most important thing in the world next to music."

Lament Over Lost Love provided the theme—if anyone ever listened to the words—of the first CSN LP. But where "Suite: Judy Blue Eyes" opened and paced that album, a song called "Carry On," written by Stills, will set the tone for the second: "Rejoice! Rejoice! We have no choice!"

Stills, for what it's worth, is apolitical. In that song, written when the war was still largely confined to Sunset Strip, he wrote of pickets proclaiming nothing stronger than "Hooray for our side." In the song he wrote for *Easy Rider,* he encapsulated the movie with the line "Find the cost of freedom buried in the ground." But it was a synopsis, rather than any analysis.

And at the Vietnam Moratorium rally at Golden Gate Park, he pounced on the piano to pound out a searing, machine-gun-paced version of "For What It's Worth," but only after shouting to the 125,000 marchers: "Politics is bullshit! Richard Nixon is bullshit! Spiro Agnew is bullshit! Our music isn't bullshit!"

Music, by a wide margin. Or as Neil put it: "Steve's trip comes to its head when he sings."

Stills is the one most intensely involved in the group's music. Onstage he bounces from acoustic guitar to piano to organ to electric lead. In the studio he directs most of the 16-track traffic, writing and singing the most songs, overdubbing the most tracks, staying the longest time. On several occasions, working on the second LP, he put in 16-hour days at Wally Heider's studios, located on the fringe of San Francisco's greasy Tenderloin district. He stayed at a motel a few blocks away. It was like he was on call to the burgeoning music, constantly in labor, in his head.

"We—Dallas and Bill [Halverson, their engineer] and I—spent last night till six doing this," he said one evening at Heider's, holding up a stack of one-inch tapes, "drunk out of my head playing the piano," on a backing track for one of the tunes on the new album. "That's what you can do when you've had a gold record." Beaming like a newsboy who's just won a trip to Disneyland and gets a day off school.

In the studios, Stills is a man of restrained excitement, of quiet pride, of nonstop devotion to the task of making records. "Steve's whole thing right now is the group," Young says. "It'd be impossible to have everybody into it as much as him. It'd be complete bedlam."

In the studios, Young, who so often clashed with Stills in the illuminating but frustrating Springfield days, generally stands back with his scowling demeanor, big-eyed, glowering stares shining out between messy black curtains of hair. He seems content in the shadows, thrashing his guitar mercilessly, like a country bluesman possessed. Young is a satisfied man—secure with his own band, Crazy Horse, on Reprise Records, as well as this insane, perfect gig with this superb, if not "super," group.

While Young and Reeves work out their backing for Young's "Country Girl," Stills hovers over engineer Halverson, and he and Nash act as unofficial conductors. Nash picks out the slightest flaws in tuning, pacing, whatever—and relays his thoughts to Stills. Then the group works it out, a team considering each member's errors as remorselessly as a mistake in mathematics. It's a stop-go-stop-go process, of course, but somehow a song flows, maintaining its vitality and spontaneity, through the constant self-interruptions.

Neil, the fourth corner, is wandering off from the control room following a playback on the track he and Reeves have just done. "What we've got to do is listen with an eye to simplicity," he says. "Think how we can make it bigger by simplifying it."

Steve Stills was the leader of Buffalo Springfield, but Neil Young stood out the most—tallest, darkest, fringiest, flashiest writer of some of their best songs ("Nowadays Clancy Can't Even Sing," "Expecting to Fly," "Flying on the Ground Is Wrong"). And he was the most desultory and uppity, quitting the band twice before they folded, saying he never wanted to be in a group anyway, just like you wouldn't have Dick Nixon to kick around anymore.

But this is different. Young is in two groups, right, but, as he explains, "Before I joined Crosby, Stills & Nash, I made it clear to both sides that I belong to myself."

First, there was Crazy Horse, who'd backed him up on his excellent second LP, *Everybody Knows This Is Nowhere,* and who're working with him now on his third album. They're also setting up a concert tour beginning in February, with Neil, of course, in the lead.

"I didn't want Crazy Horse to die just as we were getting it together," he says. Crazy Horse is important to Young as a counterbalance to the tight, structured kind of music Crosby, Stills, Nash & Young put out. "Crazy Horse is funkier, simpler, more down to the roots." Young has production control with Crazy Horse. "I dig a lot of bass and drums, man. To my mind, the bass drum should hit you in the stomach. Listen to *Nowhere* at the same volume as *Crosby, Stills & Nash* and you'll know what I mean."

Neil will do Don Gibson's country classic, "Oh, Lonesome Me" on the LP with Crazy Horse. He couldn't hope to do that kind of thing with CSNY. "But then, see, I have another side to me, and it's technically too far advanced for Crazy Horse, so the other band plays that. They complement each other inside me."

Young is contracted to Reprise and has a "temporary contract" with Atlantic, the remains of his five-year pact as a Buffalo Springfield. Hassles are few since both companies are under the Warner Bros. umbrella. Neil works out his tour schedules so that both bands know when they can have him.

With Crosby, Stills & Nash, Young sings lead on his numbers—with the three others building waves of smooth harmony behind his high, hard-edged voice. He does very little harmony singing himself. "I don't consider myself to be a background singer."

Away from either band, in what he calls his own scene, Young is getting into the movies, writing a song for Strawberry Statement and doing the score—with Crazy Horse—for *Landlord,* "a racial comedy about a white guy who buys a tenement house in Brooklyn and kicks out the floor to build a New York City-type townhouse out of it and gets into all kinds of shit . . . voodoo fights and things—with the neighbors. I think one of the stars is Pearl Bailey."

Young is also getting into filmmaking, beginning with a brand-new Beaulieux Super 8, which he coos over like a newborn baby. He and Susan (who he met last year at a Topanga Canyon cafe she ran) are planning to move slowly toward "the big time," when they'll blow their scored films up to 16mm and have showings at the Topanga Community House, where the local women's club usually meets. Married for a year now, they plan to stay at Neil's redwood, hillside Topanga Canyon house, their home since August 1968. He's even building a 16-track recording studio under the house.

Crosby has settled into a ranch in Novato, in north Marin County, and Stills is looking for a house in Marin County. Reeves lives about 90 miles north of San Francisco, in Guerneville. If Young moves, he says, it'll be to either Big Sur on the Pacific Coast or back to Canada.

Whatever the specific moves, there is a migration, of spirit, at least, to San Francisco. Stills and Crosby are close friends of Jefferson Airplane and the Grateful Dead family. Stills joined the Dead at the Winterland at one of Bill Graham's San Francisco Band nights and he and Garcia got it off for four or five numbers. And Garcia, in return, is now an unofficial member of CSNY. Garcia dropped by a session at Heider's one night and ended up playing pedal steel guitar on Nash's light, once only slightly country tune, "Teach Your Children."

"We just sat down and fiddled awhile," Stills said, "and we got an incredible take. The opening lick will just curl your whiskers."

Jerry Garcia and Neil Young, and young Greg Reeves, cool, half-black/half-Indian bassist, and Dallas Taylor, all in addition to Crosby, Stills & Nash. If the first LP was a milestone, this new one should be an event.

The first album hid the words, lovingly intertwined harmonies and impeccable instrumentation shading out most attempts at verbal communication. David's song of political strife and personal anguish, "Long Time Gone," written after the Robert Kennedy assassination, came out of the speakers like a celebration, an orgy of joyous voices. So did Stills' "Suite." How can you cry when you sound like a sparrow?

The words are on a separate sheet and you can read the poetry of Crosby's "Guinnevere" (which he has difficulty singing, remembering Christine) and the unrhymed agony of Still's two paeans, any time.

Back when the LP was being recorded, Stills, the construction engineer, had said, with tongue only slightly in cheek, that all he wanted to do was produce "the best album of the year." He and his friends put out one of the best, certainly, and they all had a right to float through the spring months, as they did, waiting for the LP's release. Now, Nash says, "Our main complaint on that LP was that it sounded so constructed. This will change with Dallas and Greg, and with Neil and me branching out more." Still, "it's all one man's opinion, whatever's said. So we have three one-man's and that's it."

Next time around, Nash says, it'll be the same as before: "Our main thing is to set some kind of a mood; our only rule when it comes to choosing our music is to pick something that gets us off."

At this point, Crosby, Stills, Nash & Young are coasting. Their next album is pre-sold gold, judging by their success across all fields of music—Top 40, "underground," and "middle of the road" (their LP even reached No. 35 on *Billboard*'s Soul chart). Their concerts, stage-managed by Chip Monck Industries, are near-perfect, the group relaxed in subdued light, making love with their soft, bluesy, acoustic music, slapping palms soul-style after a particularly well-executed number, then charging on with a full load of amps and speakers, and collapsing in a circular embrace at the end of it all.

And their heads are straight. Stills, aglow with recognition as some sort of musical genius after those two years with Buffalo Springfield ("A sheer case of frustration," he calls them), won't play huge arenas where sound is sacrificed for a bigger gate. "And we won't have any ball-busting, one-night tours. So you make your million dollars in 30 days instead of 15, right?"

Money, and lots of it, right. But not so fast that the music, or the mind, is sacrificed. "The important thing," Graham Nash says, "is to make people happy."

"The good thing," Stills says, "is to do a concert and instead of giving them one big flash, leaving them with flash after flash, and people come up and say—softly—'Thank you . . . thank you, man.'"

—*Rolling Stone*, December 27, 1969

▬▬▬▬▬▬

As I said, this was my second piece on Crosby, Stills & Nash. The first was for a Los Angeles-based magazine edited by the late Judith Sims, who I met through the fabled photographer Jim Marshall. The magazine was called *Teenset* when Judy took it over. Under the influence of *Rolling Stone,* she changed its name and began employing writers and photographers from publications like *Rolling Stone. Aum* didn't last, but I was able to hire Judith as our Los Angeles correspondent a few years later. She did excellent work for us and, later, for the *Los Angeles Times,* and she is missed.

JOE COCKER
IS NOT
A MAD DOG

By spring 1970, *Rolling Stone* had been around for a couple of years, and it was a certified media phenomenon. "*Rolling Stone* is where it's at," the *Chicago Daily News* gushed. "It digs deeply and writes vividly." The magazine, the *Washington Post* said, was "the best rock and youth culture publication in the country."

But, being a startup, we didn't have much in the way of a cash reserve, and we didn't throw around what money we had. Except for the occasional run down to Los Angeles, I stayed in San Francisco, relying on correspondents in London, New York, Boston, Memphis, Austin, and L.A. for our news and feature articles.

It also happened that, especially with Bill Graham and Chet Helms producing major concerts every weekend at the Fillmore, Avalon, and, increasingly, other facilities, all the major acts came through San Francisco anyway. As tour producers became more sophisticated, they often plotted tours to begin on the West Coast and make a big finish in New York.

And so Joe Cocker and his band, which grew to circus or commune proportions and became known as Mad Dogs & Englishmen, came to town. As with the Crosby, Stills, Nash & Young piece and one I did about Sly & the

Family Stone, my job was to penetrate the inner circle and, in this case, tell how Cocker—a shy, seemingly meek young man—allowed things to happen to and around him. Ultimately, Leon Russell took over the show and used Cocker as a springboard to his own stardom. Not that Cocker didn't enjoy the music that Russell and his many fellow Los Angeles session players brought to the stage. And it's not as if his career suffered for it. Russell's Mad Dogs & Englishmen tour became a documentary film, and Cocker has maintained a career for 30-something years.

At *Rolling Stone,* we were encouraged to participate in a story if we thought the article would benefit from it. It wasn't like we were aping any of the writers who'd come to be known as practitioners of the "New Journalism." It was just that, growing up in the business in the '60s, we knew that objective journalism was little more than an ideal, and an antiquated notion at that. A reporter can't help but be subjective in one way—or in many ways. We are who we are, and, try as we might for equal and balanced quotes and presentation, we do make judgments by the facts and quotes we choose to present, and by the way we structure leads and depict the people in the stories.

But participating can also mean bringing in past experiences relevant to the subject at hand. I had seen Joe Cocker before—before the madness—and placed my memories of that event into the story. It would, I hoped, offer a more vivid picture of Cocker, before and now.

Long before Joe Cocker and his Mad Dogs & Englishmen had begun their procession to the stage, the Fillmore West was a ballroom filled with talk about what a knockout evening it was going to be, with both Van Morrison and Joe Cocker on the bill. Now, as the 42-member troupe carved out places for themselves on the large platform, the talk was about how crowded it was, about the fire hazards, about Bill Graham's uniformed rent-a-thugs rousting people from cramped aisles. Even locked on the floor behind a huge concrete post, you couldn't lie down without a flashlight coming down on you, and a barked command to "Sit up, sit up!" At one break, one cat shouted at Graham, who was onstage, "Hey, Graham, there's still standing room in the bathroom!" and got an ovation from that sector of the ballroom.

And Graham was on his king-of-the-mountain riff again, raging and pushing people off the stage, pushing them like dominoes that ended up piled against the walls. Bill Graham/jam session time again.

But when Cocker and Leon Russell and their traveling soul commune swooped into the first song, even Graham was diminished, a pencil-thin flashlight beam to Cocker's writhing presence bathed in spotlights. Cocker was top of the bill. And even if it took fighting through the arms and legs of stoned neighbors to get up, 3,000 (or however many there were) persons got up to hail this white Manchester king of soul when he'd finally finished his set.

Joe Cocker, outstanding among the sea of faces and instruments and clapping hands, sometimes mild and meek among the wildness, had arrived. And Graham, who can always be counted on to come to his business senses, had him at the larger Winterland the next two nights. Cocker Power, as Joe's family calls it.

But just a year ago—less than a year ago—you didn't go to no ballroom to see no Joe Cocker.

A blast from the past: it's June 1969, and the Fillmore West is, typically, crowded. The Byrds, after all, are in town, and they're billed with the up-and-coming PG&E. And third on the bill is this cat with the funny name who'd had this Top 40 hit, "With a Little Help from My Friends," this singer named Joe Cocker. The first stories about him—in the British trades—had surprised me. I'd thought he was black, a man just lucky enough to latch onto a Beatle tune and make it work.

And when the Byrds had finished their set—mostly a workmanlike medley of old album tunes and a number of countryish songs (they were into "Wheels of Fire" and "You Ain't Goin' Nowhere" at that time)—at midnight, at least half the crowd straggled up and split. That left Joe Cocker, bottom of the bill, with maybe 500 spectators.

But he had it all down. Just like a soul revue, the Grease Band came out first and warmed up. Wispy Chris Stainton, old buddy, on organ and ready to shift to piano; Henry McCullogh, ghostly pale with dark eyes, on guitar; Alan Spenner, chubbier, naughtier-looking, on bass; and Bruce Rowlands on drums. A couple of catchy tunes, yes, but the reaction was, who's this Cocker think he is, getting the stage set for him, man?

Then Joe came on, eyes dazed, chunky in an orange T-shirt and bells, medium-long hair resembling a well-used SOS soap pad. He picked up a Styrofoam cup, drank, and, with a whipping motion from his right hand, spun the Grease Band into frenetic motion and proceeded to show that he could do it all alone.

It didn't matter that people discussing his first LP would invariably talk about the use of Stevie Winwood and Jimmy Page and Matthew Fisher to help grace and sell the album; it didn't matter that the critics seemed engrossed by the Ray Charles influence in Cocker's voice and phrasings; and it didn't matter that so many spent so much ink discussing his spastic stage style. Nothing mattered then as nothing matters now.

Or, as his producer Denny Cordell says today: "Joe is a strange guy; he has no ambitions at all. He just likes to rock 'n' roll, and he has no dreams about how he could do it, because he could rock 'n' roll any way he wants to."

That June night last year, Joe kept his right foot planted and contorted everything else, bare hands playing lead guitar licks while McCullough picked out the notes; rolled up T-shirted fat boy's arms fluttering around playing themselves, then breaking at the wrist to allow the fingers to glide up to the high notes of his invisible electric organ, then crash, and both elbows swoop down to turn the body into a baton, stopping the band. Then a half motion pitcher's windup, and Stainton glides in again, and all through this, Cocker is dreamily laying out this sandpaper/soul voice, distorting words, "What do I do when my love *airs* away," or, months before *Abbey Road*, "Something in the way she moves . . . 'tracks me like no *otha* lover . . .".

And my god, the light show! With that foot planted and the rest of the body lost in smokey space, Cocker is some kind of a pub-fighter surfer, swirls of blue and green sailing behind his flowing visage. Rippling undercurrents of music by the tight Grease Band, little flashes like McCullough and Spenner singing falsetto to cover the parts sung by Madelene Bell and Su and Sunny Wheetman on the first album.

Fillmore West never felt so good. Just 500 of us scattered around the floor in front of the stage, a fan (a fan!) blowing a gentle breeze down from the high ceiling while Cocker surfed and washed and rapped stoney little raps. Five hundred people discovering something truly incredible. We leapt up to an ovation for the band, forced Joe back for an encore, jumped up and down while he sang that last song, and pretty much forgot what the Byrds had done—something about a medley of old album tunes. . . .

It was no fluke. Later that week, A&M records did a press party for him, putting him in one of the most wretched places one could find in San Francisco—Arthur's Discotheque—blinking colored lights and knee-high, drink-sized tables all lined up neat like personal mini-bars. Cats in fresh Sebring hairdos and women in high heels and tinted round glasses and Top 40/mod clothing. And Cocker didn't care. He rocked and rolled and stoned that cliquish gathering, got them standing up and swiveling in their bright coats, putting down their drinks to clap hands. One just hoped that Joe'd make it big—and soon—so that he could avoid the prisons that can be set up for artists by the narrow, mindless forces of press agentry. Of course, the media, convinced, helped to release Joe. They started talking about him and playing his records. Through their inebriated, Max Factor enthusiasm, they'd caught on to some of Cocker's gospel. They, too, had made a discovery.

Cocker is a quiet man. Just as he doesn't write a whole lot of songs, he doesn't talk much, absorbed more by questions than by any answer he might give.

"I don't know what I'm trying to do, really," he said the first time we met. "Things just sort of evolve."

Back in Manchester, and around London, Joe had been trying music since 1963, playing the pubs by night for the pipe fitters he worked alongside by day. He was called Vance Arnold, and his band was The Avengers.

Joe was into Ray Charles by then, having found Charles' *Yes Indeed!* album when he was 14. ("It was a cosmic buzz; I thought it was another Little Richard at first.") And he was into the very physical stage style. "Back home, it used to achieve a communication thing," he said. "It also keeps things together more." But where last year he turned one woman spectator in a Hollywood club into a groupie, her hands slithering up towards his crotch while he sang above it all, back in Sheffield and Manchester, among the men, the style brought him mostly empty beer bottles heaved up by irate laborers.

"Well, I don't blame people for being cynical about it," he said, shrugging away any further discussion. Asking Cocker about his movements is like asking any head about the length of his hair. The righteous answer is obvious; no answer can ever satisfy those that don't seek satisfaction.

Back then, Cocker caught on to the Beatles and recorded "I'll Cry Instead" as a single for Decca. It was the earliest—and worst—Joe Cocker record ever. It earned him $1.21 in royalties and a dissolution of the Decca contract, but it also hooked him up with Jimmy Page, back then also on Decca, and with Winwood, a teenager scouting his way through Island Records.

With a Little Help from My Friends was no contrived supersession, no great plot to make it by using Dylan and Beatle and Traffic songs. "Page had just finished with the Yardbirds, so he was free," Cocker said, "and Winwood—he wanted to play on the whole next album before Blind Faith came along."

Winwood played bass on "Dear Landlord" on the second LP. "He just wanted to play. He's such a tasty musician; he just rolled along. Every take he played was different . . . but so good."

As for his choice of songs—before Leon Russell popped onto the scene—Joe had said: "Over the last year I started liking less and less. About the only people who are still buzzing me are Dylan and the Beatles."

Cocker has never needed either charging or recharging jobs, but Russell has played a huge role in establishing Cocker as an almost American product. He was never really at home at home. "A lot of people in Britain are suspicious of me," he had said. "There's this big boom in soul music, and the fact is, I'm white. Also I'm not teenybopper, and like on TV there all you have is Tops of the Pops, and the new records are all the things I hate, like Tommy Roe. England hasn't buzzed me for a long time."

Last year he discovered Russell, longtime L.A. musician by way of Oklahoma who wrote a tune called "Delta Lady" that Cocker and his producer Denny Cordell liked. They recorded the tune at Russell's studio/home and Russell became part of the crew, helping to produce the second album, *Joe Cocker!*, in Los Angeles.

Now, Leon Russell is head of Mad Dogs & Englishmen, and what a scene: a full horn section made up of musicians who'd just split from Delaney & Bonnie and Friends; Chris Stainton, surviving the split-up of the Grease Band and staying on; Russell himself on guitar and piano; two drummers; bongo and conga drums; and a chorus of men and women numbering between six and 11, all of them capable of solo spots.

Plus their various families—old ladies, a child or two, and a spotted dog that looks like a squished-in dachshund. All together, about 21 in the band and another 21 in the family, and, all together, they travel from town to town in a private plane, a Martin 202, four-prop.

Plus: A&M is tagging along for the entire tour, filming and taping everything that's going down. A live album is almost finished, taken from stops at Fillmore East, at Santa Monica Civic in California, and at the Dallas State Fair. The film crew trots in and out of motel rooms, shooting interviews, listening in on group meetings, talking to members about any problems that pop up, hoping to get enough out of the 52-date tour to weave together a full-length documentary on Joe Cocker.

All this because Cocker stumbled into Los Angeles a few months ago without the Grease Band and with hopes of scotching a planned tour for a vacation.

"I wanted to blow it out because we weren't doing anything new," Cocker said to explain the breakup of the Grease Band.

But, as Cordell explained, "Immigration said he couldn't just cancel his tour or they wouldn't let him into the musicians' union or something, and all the promoters threatened to sue, so it was a question of force."

Cocker and Stainton—who'd been with him since his scuffling days in Sheffield—went to Russell, and Leon made a few phone calls.

"Not only did all of them want to join," Cordell said, "but each one knew another one, and so they all came along. When the time came to see who was capable, these were the ones who were capable: all of them."

Leon's first calls went to percussionists Jim Keltner and Chuck Blackwell; then, he said, "members of the old Delaney & Bonnie band called up and said they were quitting and did we have anything?"

Leon, who, with Cordell, has started his own record label, Shelter (the first artist was Leon Russell with all-star session men from the Stones and Beatles), holds the band together on stage. While Cocker still conducts things with fingers and body, Leon is the magical, Mad-Hatter Mitch Miller of the troupe, arms flying out from behind the piano to guide concluding bars of a song; lurching around the stage, looking maybe like Chet Helms doing a Chuck Berry impression, long hair prancing along with him, carrying the energy on his shoulders and in his machine-gun ax, able to chop short, whole passages from choruses with a single stroke. A powerful figure, a star-like bottom to Joe Cocker's top.

"There's no leader or arranger," he says. "The leader leads and the follower follows. Any arrangement is based on the premise that everyone involved in this thing knows what the fuck he's doing."

Rehearsals went on five days a week, 12 hours a day, at A&M's sound studios, the site of the old Charlie Chaplin movie lot.

The scene in Hollywood must be changing. Once, not long ago, it was superstars and a big fence around them, leaking out nothing more than streams of hype. With the Cocker sessions, "Everyone was welcome with open arms," Cordell said. "In fact, we picked up about 30 percent of the people at the rehearsals, and even some on the road."

As for the selection of songs, it was Leon Russell, chief among the brainstormers but not as a composer, arranger, conductor, or band member. "I'm a Joe Cocker fan," he said, "so I represent the Joe Cocker fans and say, 'We'd like you to sing this song. Do you like this?'"

Cocker liked "Honky Tonk Women," and that now opens the set. He liked "The Weight." He liked "Cry Me a River," the song made famous by torcher Julie London some 15 years ago (a long gestating idea inside the head of Russell, who always thought of the song in a gospel form).

And, of course, he likes "Help from My Friends," the most wretched blues of all, each tortured word squeezed out of a strain on the face or a tightening of fingers. The sad song he'd taken and made better.

Now, with Russell and what appears to be a spiritual as well as a physical family, Joe seems content, mixing in some jazz and Ray Charles and Leon Russell along with his Grease Band songs. The sound is more varied than the first two albums might suggest, and that's about the only improvement anybody around can think of right now.

But that's right now, and who's to say what's next? The band, as Cordell said, "is as permanent as today." Five dates were added to the original tour set up for Cocker and the Grease Band. "If we could add a few more every week, maybe we'd just keep on going."

That's not likely. As Joe himself said: "I don't know what I'll want to do after the tour, let alone what Leon and Chris and the others feel like. Maybe we'll keep the core and do some recording. I don't really know yet."

Mad Dogs & Englishmen happened, and it may never happen again, not even on film, just as *Woodstock* didn't really happen again, with split screens and the focus on close-ups of the musical acts. But when the A&M film comes out and fails to re-create the family scene, Joe may be back where he was in that Woodstock film, pretty much alone. And that's the way it is—with a family.   **—*Rolling Stone*, June 11, 1970**

JANIS

THE SCENE
IN LARKSPUR

Rolling Stone, in the early going, was a patchwork of professionals and walk-ins. One editor had logged time at *Newsweek;* another was a dope dealer who specialized in dead languages. I was somewhere in the middle, having served as editor of the campus daily at San Francisco State, and then working a year each at a radio station (as an announcer and writer of copy for local advertisers) and an employee magazine (as an editor and writer).

Our story-gathering methods were also a mix of original ideas and reporting, and outright stealing stories from other publications, usually the pop press in England. We also used the *Paris Review* and *Playboy* as models for The *Rolling Stone* Interview.

We also did a lot of learning on the job. As one of the first serious rock publications around, we had few models for profiles and reviews. We had no problem with news stories, but I don't think we were ready for the frequency of obituaries we'd have to write. After all, we were part of the youth culture.

In the issue dated April 6, 1968, the first issue in which I had a story—actually, just an item for the "Flashes" column—there was the news that Frankie Lymon, a teenager who'd had several hit singles in the late '50s ("Goody

Goody" and "Why Do Fools Fall in Love") had died of a drug overdose. Six
—issues after I joined as an editor, I wrote the obituary for Brian Jones of the
Rolling Stones. And in 1970, I wrote about the deaths of Motown singer Tammi
Terrell and Al Wilson of Canned Heat.

And then, in October, Janis. For her, we did our version of blanket cover-
age, the way we'd attacked Woodstock and Altamont. Different editors took
on different assignments, reporting, writing, editing, and calling on Joplin's
fellow musicians for comments. I engaged Nick Gravenites, who'd worked in
one of her post-Big Brother bands, to talk at length about Janis, and drove up
to Larkspur, 40 miles north of San Francisco in Marin County, to take a look
at Janis' home.

I filed a memo to the editor who was putting the main story together and
went back to work on the Gravenites piece and the rest of the music section
for that issue.

As things worked out, my memo became the end piece of the obituary.

Last December Janis had finally escaped her adopted city, where she'd
lived in the Haight-Ashbury across from Buena Vista Park and Hippie Hill
and, later, on Noe Street. She found a hideaway home in Larkspur, across
the Golden Gate Bridge, three or four towns into Marin County.

Larkspur is one of those pleasant little places. The freeway leads com-
fortably into a small shopping center; the homes are respectable, middle-
class. Then, somewhere, you make a left turn and several roads take you
into the woods. Baltimore Avenue is one of those roads, its width narrowed
by huge trees that block its way now and again. Janis' house was at the end
of Baltimore.

It's hidden away more by its appearance than by its location. It's right
there in front of you, behind the rounded off end of the road. Short,
A-framed, shingled, modern, comfortable in a forest of tall trees that keep
everything but the wind away. You can't even hear the sound of kids at
Larkspur School, just up the road and a few blocks over.

The house is unidentified. A Yuban coffee can is nailed to a front post.
"This is a temporary mailbox," it is labeled, and someone has added, "Temporary Hell." Near the adjacent garage, two dogs are wandering around.
A TV cameraman waves his light meter at the air, then pans his camera
from the wooden stairs near the garage that lead into the woods. He pans

across the house, to the fence Janis had had constructed to keep burglars away.

This wasn't a very private or a very quiet house for Janis and the girl-friends who stayed there. The place was burgled several times, and Janis and her clothes-maker friend, Lindall Erb, lost furnishings, jewelry, and other valuables. Several months ago, Janis had a party there that resulted in complaints from the neighbors. Cars clogged the road all the way up Baltimore Avenue, and the music blared out of that shingled megaphone as far as the cars went.

Now the TV cameraman is back in his car—one of three cars parked facing the house. A high school girl is seated 100 feet away, watching. "I came here from Mill Valley to pay my tribute," she said. "I'm just an acquaintance. I came by once and gave her a bottle of tequila and it got her off."

Up the road, two neighbors, grandmotherly women, are talking. They're saying something about "overdose" to a couple of kids on bicycles. One of the women talks with a smirk. "Oh, did she have parents? . . . There was a lot of noise when the band was practicing—if you call it a band. . . . We never talked to her. She just ran down and ran up again in her car."

"I don't think we'll make the seven o'clock news," the other, named Betsy, says with a laugh.

Inside the house, it's quiet. One man, a member of Janis' second band—the one after Big Brother—steps out to get something from his car. Lindall is in L.A., he says. She left the night before, when she heard the news. The people in the house are friends of Lindall's. And no one wants to talk.

The two old ladies have stopped looking at the TV man, and they're discussing reupholstering an old couch sitting in Betsy's front yard.

—*Rolling Stone*, October 29, 1970

THE ROLLING STONE **INTERVIEW**

GRACE
SLICK
& PAUL
KANTNER

Left to right: Norton Buffalo, Sammy Hagar, Ben Fong-Torres, Craig Chaquico, and Paul Kantner. Back: Miles Hurwitz.

A **week before** Janis Joplin died, I had visited Grace Slick and Paul Kantner of Jefferson Airplane. This was on September 25, 1970, a week after Jimi Hendrix had died in London. I'd been covering for Charles (Smokestack el ropo) Perry, our chief copyeditor, while he was on vacation, and wrote the Hendrix obit. It was kind of a busy month, but, in retrospect, typical of my time at *Rolling Stone.* According to my calendar, and I have no reason to doubt it, I went to Los Angeles twice and interviewed John Kay, Leon Russell, and Ry Cooder. By phone, I did interviews with Edwin Starr, Dave Mason, Little Richard, Mary Travers, the great record producer Jerry Wexler, and David Kapralik, Sly Stone's manager. Those were most likely for various "Random Notes" and short news stories. Wednesday nights, whenever I was in town, I went to Chinatown to do some editing and writing for *East-West,* the first bilingual newspaper in America.

In July, I'd been called by KSAN, the pioneer free-form FM rock station, and invited to do some fill-in DJ work on weekends while some of the station's regulars went off with "Big Daddy" Tom Donahue, DJ and rock entrepreneur, to make a rock-on-the-road movie, *Medicine Ball Caravan.* I did four four-hour shifts in September. Some of those DJs never returned, and my temp gig extended to about ten years.

And to think that it could have been even crazier. Jackie DeShannon, the wonderful singer-songwriter, had invited me to join her in Las Vegas, where she was going to see her friend, Elvis Presley, in concert. But I had that John Kay interview to do, so no go. They wound up staying up all night in the kitchen at the International Hotel, eating and chatting.

I'm still so upset about missing that shot at the King, that I'm going to introduce the Grace and Paul piece with the same comments I made when the article appeared in a book entitled *The* Rolling Stone *Interviews:*

> Of all the *Rolling Stone* Interviews that I did, this was the least like an R.S.I. This one, with Grace Slick and Paul Kantner, was more like a stoned rap session, as we called them back then.
>
> With Slick and Kantner in the fall of 1970, none of us expected anything else. Jefferson Airplane was the one San Francisco band of the '60s that maintained a high drug and political profile while enjoying consistent commercial success. Grace Slick, at age 31, was the Acid Queen of outrageousness, and Kantner, 29, was her calm, dry, sardonic flip side.
>
> In 1970, Marty Balin, the group's founder, was making moves to leave the group, and Grace and Paul were assuming the stewardship of what would become Jefferson Starship. Slick and Kantner were expecting their first child, and there was talk about the band starting their own label and breaking away from RCA. It was time for a sit-down. Airplane members were never more than a phone call away, and this interview would become one of a dozen stories I did on the Airplane and its various parts. I just called up and dropped by the Airplane House in midtown. The entire interview was done with all three of us in their bed upstairs. And, as I recall, a joint or two got to be part of the afternoon.

Grace Slick and Paul Kantner have unofficially assumed the leadership of that San Francisco rock 'n' roll starship, Jefferson Airplane.

They hadn't planned on it. Members of the Airplane foresee very little of what happens to them. But Marty Balin, who put together the first Jefferson Airplane (including Kantner, Jorma Kaukonen, Skip Spence as drummer, Bob Harvey as bassist, and Signe Toly Anderson as second lead vocalist behind Balin) in the summer of 1965, has stepped back behind

Grace. For years and two or three albums, their soaring vocal trade-offs have been a mark of the Indian/jazz/mechanical/blues/rock sound of the group. But now Kantner is writing and singing more and more, he's been busted again and again for dope and other extralegal activities, and he's hanging out with people like the Dead's Jerry Garcia, and CSNY's David Crosby and the Airplane's Grace Slick, who in December will be the mother of his child, to be named god. ("Just god," said Grace. "No last name, no capital G. And he can change his name when he feels like it.")

When Grace and Paul speak for the Airplane, they're representing a haphazard community of people who've set some important paces for San Francisco, for the elite of the hip scene and for rock 'n' roll bands everywhere. Sure, it's "gotta revolution," but it's still "Jefferson Airplane Loves You," the slogan for their first promotional button in 1966. The Airplane still plays free park concerts. They still battle their record company on behalf of the people (RCA recently re-released *After Bathing at Baxters* with a reduction on the original $5.98 retail price, which had outraged the Airplane in early 1968) and their own aesthetics and politics.

From the very beginning, the Airplane has been short and terse, their humor simple and unanswerable—unlike their music. In the very first story of the band, in the *San Francisco Chronicle,* August 1965, the writer described Balin's newfound base, the Matrix nightclub. "One wall is a huge collage," he wrote, adding Balin's explanation: "We call it the huge collage wall." Grace, for an interview for a women's page feature, explained her housekeeping: "Yeah, we try to keep the house from falling down."

But the anti-norm, anti-intellectual, anti-art stance isn't an obligatory posture. That's just the way they choose to live their life, in line with or despite what the media has forced upon them. And there is that aristocratic air about them as they sit in their bed in their overwrought Tiffany mansion/ rehearsal place. The room is just naturally littered, just as the second-floor office is filled with whimsical art, Jefferson Airplane's anti-idea of what's funny. (That ten-inch-square color photo of the peanut butter and jelly sandwich that surprised you when you opened up the *Volunteers* album— that was funny, see?) And downstairs, instead of furniture, there's a pool table and a torture rack, the rack occupied by a stuffed walrus.

It all fits if you and he and she are all together in that aristocratic circle that moves between the mansion across from Golden Gate Park down to the studios in the whorehouse district and out to Marin County where the Dead and Quicksilver live. One musician called it a "booster club" in *Rolling Stone.* And Kantner explained: "Well, he doesn't get off in this situation." And Garcia would add: "Of course, it's our situation."

A couple of weeks ago—after Jimi, before Janis—Annie Leibovitz, the photographer, and I went to the Airplane mansion for the interview, waited half an hour while they were waking up, and retreated briskly up the stairs as the office was invaded by a suntanned promotion team from RCA.

I remember once you were talking about why Signe Anderson left the Airplane, and you'd said it was because she was pregnant and couldn't handle all those things—touring, recording, having a baby, hanging out—all at the same time. And that's what forced her out. How does that compare with your situation now?

Grace: Well, people all around me have been trying to force me out. . . . It's been going on for five years now. But I think there were other pressures on Signe that made her leave. In my case, there are a whole lot of different chicks around, and everybody is sort of helping each other out with various different things, and they can take the child for a while and I can theirs at the house at the beach, and we can trade off.

That kid's going to get mixed up.

Grace: Well, not really. Some of the most interesting and happiest kids I've seen have lived with a lot of different adults, because a kid can go up to one guy and wear him out. And as soon as the adult gets tired, there are five other guys, or five other chicks to go and wear out, and the kid gets to be very bright—and tolerant, you know, with that many kinds of people around.

Why did you decide to have a child?

Grace: Oh, it's just a small person, and they expand more than animals do. Some people have animals around. I like animals, but I thought I'd try a human being because they have more happening. I think it's partly an ego thing; you get an old man that you like or dig a lot of qualities about, and you have to like yourself to a certain extent, and you want to see what the combination of those two minds and bodies will turn out like—you're really curious.

Your contract with RCA is going to be up in November. Any idea who you'll go with?

Paul: Whoever gives us what we want most.

Bill Thompson mentioned the possibility of forming a record label of your own, and just finding a distributor.

Paul: Yeah, it's not too hard, and it doesn't involve too much, other than having them print your names on the album—if we wanted to get into it on just that level. We'd just get that much more control over everything.

How much control do you have now?

Paul: Almost total.

That's from fighting over five years . . .

Paul: It has a lot to do with the fact our contract's up and they really want us to sign again. So they'll do almost anything.

It seems that with every album you've done, there's been a clash. For the cover, for the lyrics, for whatever . . .

Grace: Well, you know, when you come in late at three o'clock in the morning, a 14-year-old kid knows he's going to have to say something about it. It doesn't matter that it's right or wrong, he knows that that's going to have reprisals. So we know that every time we put something out, there's going to be something, even if it isn't the stuff we assume we're going to have hassles with. We put out some word and everybody thinks, "Oh, god, we're gonna have to hassle with them on that," and they'll pick out something else. Like that cupcake thing. We were in the studio doing the musical end of it, and Thompson comes in and says, "Hey, how about everybody drawing a little something on this piece of paper, whatever you feel like," and everybody's doodling on paper. And Paul's eating a cupcake. He put, you know, one of these fluted things that are around cupcakes—he just put it down on the paper and drew around it. And passed it off and went on with what he was doing. RCA said, "You can't put it out; it looks like a psychedelic cunt. *"How did RCA know what a psychedelic cunt looks like?*

Grace: So it's actually just silly. You just hand it in and wait for them to worry about it, and then talk to them. And they usually manage after a while to understand some of the proportions.

Was there any problem with "Mexico" before it came out?

Grace: No, 'cause nobody's ever in the studio.

Paul: We just told them, here's a new single, and didn't get any hassle. All very simple. Of course, there was nothing dirty in it.

What about Dick Cavett? "Mexico" was banned there, too. To you, privately, did he say, "Hey, I really want you to be able to do this song?"

Paul: Oh, yeah, he held up the show for an hour and a half—it was taped late—with all the audience sitting there, 'cause he was upstairs with the executives arguing with them, telling them what assholes they were for not having us play the song. So they finally still said we couldn't do it, and he came down, all pissed off. Said, "Sorry, man, I really feel like an asshole to have to tell you . . . " And ABC had censors there waiting with scissors to cut out "motherfuckers" from "We Can Be Together." But they had fucked the sound up so much when we did it that we spent a whole night in New York blasting at them and telling them how shitty they were and they'd better fucking get the sound together or we'd blow your radio station up or something. So they spent the whole time—see, it's like taped a day in advance—and you have to get a certain amount of time filled, so if they were to snip four or six minutes, they'd have to find something else to fill. So they spent a good deal of time trying to work with that, and they didn't have time to look at it for censoring or anything.

Thompson was talking about instead of going with a particular record company, to form your own company—and it could go beyond rock 'n' roll and records and get into the future of the media: videotape, cassettes, holograms.

Paul: I'm going to try and get my Starship thing onto videotape. That's a song, side two of my album. It's about us—me and Jerry Garcia and David Crosby stealing a starship—hijacking a spaceship, going where whoever comes along wants to go.

It's my answer to the ecology problem. It's the only way it's all going to get together and work. Unless we have a war or a big disease or a famine, there's just too many people, and they're gonna have to get off the planet. This is my way of starting to get off a little earlier.

We don't have to stay anywhere; we'll land wherever we want and then take off again. The sun is only one solar system out of millions of solar systems. The orbit of Pluto is probably a speck of tiny dust in the whole universe. There's millions of other whole planetary systems. It would be interesting to just keep going till you stop, to see what stops you, until you run into the side of the bowl or something and see this guy out there looking at you.

That's what old Owsley could do, is to make a machine that would go that far that fast. He'd just read some books for a couple of weeks and get it down. That's how he made acid. Just went out, got some chemistry books and decided to do it, and did it. He does it with sound systems; he's been doing the Grateful Dead sound from one aspect or another for five years. He fucks up at it a lot because he doesn't have great equipment or enough money to really get it together. I mean, if you give him $50 billion and an island and a machine shop, he'd have the starship together in less than a year. . . .

I have a song called "To Diana," the chick who got blown up in New York with the Weatherman. For the woman Diana. "Crazy Miranda" is the Women's Liberation freak.

Grace: It's more or less pathetic. The whole song is actually the second line, which is, "She believes in anything she reads." And the rest of it's more or less superfluous. There's a lot of information coming in; it's the inability to make up your mind as to what part of that information applies to you. And I think a lot of chicks who are into that are having trouble figuring it out. What they're supposed to be doing. Well, should I sit back and let it happen or go out there and grab that guy by the balls? And they sort of do a little bit of each of it and look and sound confused.

I mean, brassieres and stuff; if you don't want to wear one, just take it off. But burning it . . . I think a lot of street theater is fun, but like anything else I'd also like to see people who are good at it. It's preferable to see people who are capable of getting together more or less what they've decided to do. Like I prefer Abbie Hoffman to Richard Nixon simply because he's more entertaining, more interesting to listen to. I don't care what the two of them are talking about, they could be talking about toothpaste, and Abbie's gonna come out hands down because he's just a more entertaining guy. And if those chicks were to send out their best representatives—figure out who is good at those various things, instead of just sending out anybody and it looks dumb and makes them look stupid.

I'd like to see Bobby Seale doing his nightclub comedy relating to what's going on today.

Paul: I'd like to see Bobby Seale out.

Grace: I think that kids are the reason all that flamboyant stuff is going down, because you realize after a while that there is little to distinguish yourself from animals except entertaining other human beings. I mean, we all essentially do the things animals do—shit, fuck, sleep, and eat. And art is the only thing that separates us at all. Science, art—those two things, being together or apart.

Paul: When they're together, it's called Magic.

People are calling you and the Stones the rock 'n' roll bands most outwardly calling for violent revolution.

Paul: Violent in terms of violently upsetting what's going on, not a violence of blowing buildings up or a violent "shoot policemen" or violent running down the street with an AR-18 shooting everything you can see. But violent shit, changing one set of values to another.

Or something violent in the eyes of the establishment.

Paul: Oh, yeah, just a whole turnaround of values. That's violent to them. It's extreme.

I like, "It doesn't mean shit to a tree."

Paul: It doesn't. Don't get serious about it at all. 'Cause it's not serious.

So this whole conversation is just a gag.

Paul: There's no real importance to attach to it in the general scheme of the universe.

So what's the importance of what you do?

Paul: Important's a shitty word.

What's the reason for it?

Paul: Trying to make consciousness. Pointing things out. Just make people enjoy themselves. We didn't even know what we were doing when we started doing it. Looking back, all we were saying was, "Look, we're having a good time." And nothing else. Just sitting around having a good time with all this shit going on around us. Pretty soon people start filtering in, saying, "Hey, they're having a good time." David calls it "egg snatching." Kidnapping children.

It's also very safe to be in a rock 'n' roll band if you want to smoke dope. You have a lot of shield between you and the gun folk. People get uptight at us riding a Cadillac when we're in New York, but it's the single most effective weapon against getting busted in the world. It's the one thing they recognize. We're driven through New York with police leading, in front of us.

But outside of that shield, aren't you more liable to be busted because of the things you say or promote?

Paul: No . . . it's very hard to bust people these days.

Another shield, I suppose, is to have people around you who know what's going on in any situation and know how to handle it.

Paul: Well, it's like they know if they bust us it's going to involve a lot more shit that they're going to have to do right up front, than if they bust some kid out in the street and has no lawyer in back of him. . . . It almost feels like Al Capone or the Mafia or the Untouchables, 'cause you get down there and a lawyer will come and [fingersnaps] pick you out. When they busted me in Hawaii I even got another guy out of jail, a spade cat they'd busted the night before and beat the fuck out of, and we just bailed him out, and they were really pissed off, 'cause it was easy to do. It was pleasant to do, just to get them uptight, 'cause they did a bad thing to him in front. It wasn't a bad thing they'd done to me—more inconvenient. Humorous inconvenience.

I want to know how you got into rock 'n' roll . . .

Grace: Rock 'n' roll, rock 'n' roll, rock 'n' roll. I think it was just I went down to see Jefferson Airplane because there was an article in the Chronicle, and there was a picture of Marty, and he looked sort of like he was Japanese or Filipino or something, with a Prince Valiant hairdo, which nobody had at the time, and underneath, it said, "He's got a rock 'n' roll band," and it sounded very weird, and I went down to see it. And I said, "Hey, that looks great, let's do that. Those people are having fun; let's do one." So that's the Great Society thing. But that's not rock 'n' roll, it's kind of electric, folk-freak stuff.

That's a story you've given out several times, and several times you've also said you're not a singer, that you're just talking. But obviously, you're developing or sharpening some kind of technique.

Grace: Well, I don't think you can get away from yourself. I mean, you have a certain kind of nose; I mean, unless you go in for plastic surgery you got a certain kind of nose that distinguishes you and the same thing with your voice and the way you pronounce words, it's going to come out a certain way so anybody essentially that sings is going to sound the way they sound, unless you work on sounding like somebody else or changing it. So it's not a singing style; it's just the way my nose looks or the way my fingers feel.

You still learn about phrasing, learn about breath control . . .

Grace: Hmm, yeah, more or less. It's nothing compared to people who actually study singing four or five hours a day and all kinds of tiny little things that they learn but are actually worthless when it comes to singing over 115 db, because you have to be able to hear yourself to do the correct pronunciations and all that kind of stuff. So, you develop something else and there's no name for it as yet; it's like trying to tell a classical guitarist I want you to do one of those high, whining woooows, and that's all you can do; you can't give him notes to have him reproduce the sound, and there's nothing you can tell Jorma except with your hands and with your mouth kind of trying to duplicate the kind of sound you heard him make that you want him to make again. And I watch Paul in the studio, and he'll go out there and he looks like an airplane going out of control, you know; he'll be directing because you can't write it down. There are too many names for whatever it is.

It seems like most of your professional life is entwined with your personal life, that it all comes out of what you need or what you want. Convenience defines your singing, or why you're a singer, why you're doing a book, why you're having a baby. Everything's a principle.

Grace: Chaotic circumstance—I was on that corner at that time. A lot of it. And it depends on what you do with the corner when it presents itself to you.

I remember a story about Sly Stone being producer of a single you were trying to record when you were with Great Society . . .

Grace: He's incredible. God, the guy—he's amazing. He went around to each instrument and played—we watched him—from instrument to instrument, played really well, and sang, and produced.

How did that affect your group?

Grace: Oh, we were so . . . people had picked up their instruments two weeks before—you know, like, "why don't we start a rock 'n' roll band? Jefferson Airplane looks like that's pretty much fun." So there was no professional hassle at all. I think now if someone comes up to Jorma and says, "Jorma, let me show you how to play that," that's a little different, 'cause he's been playing for a long time.

Paul: But even in the beginning, who was it, Bernie Krause, was hired by Matthew Katz to try and orchestrate the band while we were at the Matrix. And he had a shattering experience for himself, trying to direct Jorma . . . saying, "Guys, if you could just play, dom-da-de-da-dom . . ."

Grace: You guys were different, though; you weren't ever really children, and I've told people before, like the Airplane was the top money-maker in San Francisco, and all the rest of us were on sort of the underneath level, and they were always the star billing, and all the other bands—Great Society, Big Brother, Charlatans, Marbles—we were all underneath them. And at the time you didn't have the individual dressing rooms; everyone just piled into one room, and the Airplane would come in and they wouldn't talk to anybody; they'd just come storming in with this really arrogant attitude, carrying their guitars and kicking things over and stuff like that, and we used to laugh at them—"Lookit those big shots, they think they're such hot shit," and they never really were a young group; they started out being arrogant like that and have not finished with it yet.

I wonder why. Well, I know why. Marty owned the Matrix where you started.

Paul: Yeah, we had it pretty easy for a group starting out.

Pretty good timing . . .

Paul: I got into it when I saw the Byrds doing it. I got into making a rock 'n' roll band on the same level that she's saying how the Great Society started. You know, from being David (Crosby)'s friend . . .

Grace: Well, you guys weren't my friends. They weren't anybody's friend. They were their own friends. Gosh, you guys were arrogant. Except

Casady. Everybody liked Jack. But they didn't like anybody else in the band. I think it was 'cause he was kind of shy, and he was the only member of the band that wasn't a superstar at age three.

How'd you meet Crosby?

Paul: When I was in school, he came to me and said, "Hey, have some of this. The first one's free." Then I was hooked, and I could never get away from him after that.

Grace: Yeah, he's just the old dope pusher.

Paul: I met him in L.A. Me and [David] Freiberg and a couple of other people went down there to achieve stardom and all that, and we got together and got a little house in Venice on the beach, and we'd practice every day and night, and spend every day on the beach incredibly fucked up on grass that Crosby'd get for us.

Did you do that trip of having a guitar on your back and going from coffee club to coffee club?

Paul: Just mildly.

Grace: Marty said that's how he got you for the band. You walked into the club with your cap on and all this hair sticking out and a banjo on your back, and it sounded like the ethnic folk story of all time. "I saw him, and I knew he had to be a member of my band!"

"You play drums, kid?"

Grace: Right. "No, but I play banjo." "Learn the drums. We don't need any banjo." He still plays banjo.

[To photographer Annie Leibovitz]: *Annie, did you have any questions?*

Grace: My favorite color is black.

Annie: Yeah, I wondered how you saw yourself in a photograph?

Grace: Oh, being pregnant. All I see it as is a very large stomach . . .

Annie: Would you like to be photographed with a very large stomach?

Grace: No, for some reason I don't . . . it's not the large stomach, it's the posing that I don't like, and my old man figured that out. He tried for maybe two weeks as a young fledgling photographer to position me, and living with me he finally got real good at candid photography. Because if he ever said, "Move your arm a bit," I'd say, "What for? It's not real." The arm's there.

Boy, you'd be a good model, wouldn't you?

Grace: I hated modeling. I did it for two or three years. It's also a matter of a personality flaw, of being almost totally stubborn. I don't like to be told what to do at all. That's unfortunate because a lot of people come up with good ideas and can direct you . . .

Do you mind being advised?

Grace: Yeah . . . I don't like it at all. And I think it's wrong sometimes because I lose out in that process. I feel really restricted if someone says, "I want you to play that faster." And I think, well, I won't play it at all. Like a kid. "I don't wanna do it! I don't wanna do it!"

Are you also very insistent, then, when you direct others?

Grace: No. I don't care what they do. All I do is get someone who's a real good musician and I can trust him, and they always do come out with something good.

The phone's going to ring.

[Two seconds later, it does. It's a special, super-compact Trimline that Grace calls "the Ferrari." She answers:]

Grace: Yes? You have a very direct voice today, whoever you are, Abbie.

Paul: Where's our tickets to the show, you fucker?

Grace: When do you spreck? [Abbie Hoffman was in town for a speech, later canceled.] You all by yourself? Come on by. . . . Yeah, we talked to him for a couple of hours . . . good stuff. Just a second, I'll give you the man. [Kantner gets on the phone with Hoffman.]

How was your date with Abbie at the White House?

Grace: Oh, it was funny. God . . .

Did you see Tricia?

Grace: No . . . I suppose it could've been done because the White House didn't know who we were until the reporters let them know because the reporters were taking pictures, so the guard said, "Sorry, you can't come in," and I said, "I've got an invitation." "Don't care if you've got an invitation. Guards say you're a security risk." "Hey, man, I'm a singer." "Well, sorry, you can't come in." If Abbie hadn't been there I think it would've been smoother. But I preferred that silly business. I always like that.

We got the invitation. It said, "Mr. and Mrs. Gerald Slick." And I showed it to Jerry, and he was lukewarm about going. So I called Abbie and he got this flag together and slicked his hair back—he looked like a pimp, you know. Greasy hair and this funny suit that didn't quite fit. Draped a flag that his old lady, Anita, had made over the fence.

They were right, though, 'cause I had acid powder in my pocket and I don't know that I would have used it, because I don't know the setup of the White House or how it would've gone down, but in case everything would've been cool, they would've had good reason to keep me out. You see, it was a tea, and what I'd envisioned in my head was White House and Finch College and all that junk, those formal teas, they have a table, 'cause you're taught that, that's one of the things a finishing school teaches you—how to serve tea. The usual setup is a long table with two silver-encrusted large teapots, and the hostess and whoever she figures is the maid of honor serves at either end, and you each get cups and stand around like at a cocktail party.

And the amount of acid that I could have just in the sweat on the end of my finger could have gone by just like that [flick] and nobody would've even noticed it going into a cup. And I was thinking of talking to Tricia and saying, "Thank you for a nice tea, and I think you're probably going to enjoy the rest of the afternoon considerably," dump, and she'd be thinking about that remark for a while . . . and that's the only reason I was sort of disappointed at not getting in; otherwise it was just great fun.

I see you're starting to get a few gray hairs. You must be over 30!
Grace: I wish it was all the way out to here. It's only about five inches long because I used to dye it black, and it's been there since I was about 24, but I'm just starting to let it grow out, and it's five inches of gray hair and five inches of red.

How's your throat now? It sounds like the nodes are something that'll keep recurring. . .
Grace: It'll probably keep doing it. I've got a stupid throat. I enjoy singing, but it's not strong, so that's it.

It's like Crosby said, I don't think it'll be too much of a problem because I don't plan to be singing that long. There's nothing more ridiculous than old people on the stage. And it's getting to be so that the level ought to come way down as to who ought to be cavorting around on a stage. When I was young, around ten, and my parents' friends would come over and try to be real chummy, like be your, friend or peer, and you just thought they were assholes. And people who continue to perform on stage figure everybody really thinks they're neat, and they don't. They think, "Look at that old jerk." There's a time. And also there's a matter of your head wanting to do a number and being able to handle a number of other things. You start out performing because it's fun; then you learn more things and you want to do more than go "Na-na-na-na" on a stage. The production end is interesting, writing is interesting, and you learn to coordinate all these things.

So in later years you may see your role not necessarily as an entertainer singing rock songs, but maybe as a communicator . . .

Grace: Yeah, there's just a certain appearance and attitude with rock 'n' roll—like the guy Alice Cooper—and stuff like that, and I enjoy that, young kids goofing around and making a lot of people uptight about it. There's no reason to be uptight, it's like that reviewer in New York who got really upset with Jagger's film *Performance*, and he just laid himself all out in this review by making these incredibly stupid statements. . . . You just make statements to amuse people, and you wear certain colors just to make people laugh, and there's no big deal about it—and he has lipstick on, all right, it's just not that big a problem. And people get excited by Alice Cooper because he's got false eyelashes on. Well, that's for your amusement, you just go, "Ho! Ha! Look at that guy with false eyelashes on." But that's good stuff, and I think a 35-year-old person still having the mentality or the desire of a 20-year-old is sad, actually.

I don't think so.

Grace: I don't mean to close yourself up and become conservative. I mean by that time it would seem that you would have learned enough to extend yourself further than that. It's hard to say what will happen to this whole scene in ten years, though. Like you might grow with the audience while they grow with you, and you'll probably move to a different place and still be valuable in some kind of communications role.

Paul: We seek to eradicate that audience/performer relationship as much as possible. That's not really valid anymore, for us. Just don't like it.

Well, whatever you do, whether it's film, TV, records, you're still performing on some form of stage, and they're receiving it.

Paul: I like a live stage.

Grace: All I'm talking about is being a huge, fat, full person as much as you possibly can, and it doesn't necessarily mean that you have died because you're not prancing around on a stage. Prancing around on a stage is not the entire purpose of my life.

—*Rolling Stone*, **November 12, 1970**

Grace never named her child god; she opted to call her daughter China, who would have a brief run at show business herself, as a VJ on MTV. The Starship never split from RCA. Grace, however, split from Paul, and finally from the Starship. But the band, with Kantner its most stable force, closed out the '70s with several hit records. With constantly varying personnel, it survived the '80s, even welcoming Grace back for some background vocals. But, unlike a certain Rolling Stones lead singer, Slick stuck to her pledge not to prance around on a stage when she got older.

Jefferson Airplane were inducted into the Rock and Roll Hall of Fame in 1996. These days, although Slick has moved to Malibu and is an accomplished painter, Kantner, along with Balin and whoever's available among Casady, Kaukonen, and others, continue to play occasional dates.

As for the Airplane House: it's occupied by a single family. The mother told me she used to see the Airplane at the Winterland. And that she had a thing for one of the band members.

CRUISIN' WITH

CHEECH
& CHONG

It's been said that I was the first Chinese-American to have a regular byline in a national magazine, and to be an editor of a major general-circulation publication. In 1971, only a couple of years into *Rolling Stone,* I was certainly not thinking about that as anything near an interesting fact. I was just doing my job, with a vague awareness that it was one hell of a gig. And when I doubled up with the weekend shifts on KSAN, I was again aware that I was being paid to have fun, and not that I was the first Asian DJ on a major rock station.

But I had daily reminders of my ethnicity, whether it was from my ongoing work at *East-West,* the Chinatown weekly, or from the way much of my mail was addressed. I'd say "Fong-Torres," and they'd type out their mailing labels to "Mr. Fonturas," "Ben Fond Torres," the musical "Ben Song Torres" and "Ben Fong-Tones," and, my favorite, "Mr. Bob Fongatorres." It got to the point that I created a montage of all the misspellings. It should be on eBay any day now.

My first chance to say, outright, that I was Chinese came in this piece on the first, and perhaps last, Mexican-Chinese comedy team. Since most people thought I was also Mexican and Chinese, if not a comedy team, I drew the assignment to go get 'em. (Oh: I'm 100 percent Chinese. My father, wanting to come to America from China, and needing to circumvent the Chinese Exclusion Act in force in the 1920s, got the "Torres" name through devious means and entered the United States by passing himself off as a Filipino.)

This was one of *Rolling Stone's* first profiles of a comic act. Later came stories about Monty Python's Flying Circus, Martin Mull, Robert Klein, and Albert Brooks. And in 1974, David Felton, direct from the *Los Angeles Times,* began a brilliant series of funny pieces on funny people, including Lily Tomlin, Richard Pryor, Steve Martin, and Bill Murray.

But Cheech & Chong were the first comedians who got the rock star treatment. And boy, did they lap it up.

San Antonio—When he first lighted from the jet and looked down the stairs, Slim Pickens must've thought it was all for him. Nice first-class breakfast, a little stereo music with Dave Dudley and Bobby Bare, a friendly chat with these hippie fellers from Hollywood. And now, down below, a battery of cameras and cocked elbows. Right nice.

But wait. These are just kids, high school kids, holding the cameras. And over there, just outside the cluster, Santa Claus, only with a clearly Mexican face and grin. Four cheeky, mascaraed little Chicanas here in the 40-degree Texas nip, respective full right breasts swelling under red and green award ribbons, dime store cutout letters identifying each of them as a TACO BELLE, here, on behalf of the National Taco Council, to welcome the dignitaries with "the world's largest taco"—only a foot in diameter, actually, much smaller than the 45-pound number they sent to President Kennedy, as a Taco Council official will point out later. But that taco got lost somewhere in the caverns of the White House, while here, mouths agape, come the targets in the brown and yellow flesh, the world's foremost Chicano-Chinese comedy team, Cheech & Chong.

Slim Pickens will get his later, as he always does. One of the cameras there does record the cowboy star's arrival for the evening news. But for the moment, it's Cheech & Chong's moment.

Which one's Cheech? Which one's Chong? No matter; they both get engulfed by eager-to-smile strangers and trained-to-smile Taco Belles. They are guided to yet another surprise: a 1957 Chevy wagon, a junk heap realization of the "Cruisin' with Pedros de Paca" cut off the Cheech & Chong album, all primer paint and masking tape on the windows, mounted atop a set of Goodyear rally tires, Cheech & Chong lines slapped all over the body . . . EVIL WAYS . . . MAN THAT'S SOME GOOD STUFF . . . LA BAMBA . . . COME ON BETO (from their new single, "Santa Claus and His Old Lady") . . . a set of bongo drums on the dash, and cutout reindeer and Christmas party-deco in the back . . . "This is really Cheech & Chong country, huh?"

"No shit," says Cheech, drinking it all in.

At the welcoming pep rally at Holy Cross High, they will be greeted with jubilant raised fists. They will learn that they are doing a benefit for a very special kind of a parochial school. Holy Cross, on the rough west side, the Chicano side, of town was ordered shut down three years ago when the local archdiocese could no longer provide funds. But the brothers decided to stay open—to provide the kind of environment, if not education, that the regular schools couldn't afford. One brother talked about "the development of the whole man. I teach them not to let others look down on Chicanos." But to stay open, the school slides into a $75,000 annual deficit. Singer Vicki Carr has made Holy Cross a pet project and does an annual concert to raise $30,000. To get the rest, the whole school hustles.

And when KTSA announced a youth voter registration contest, with the winning high school getting a Cheech & Chong benefit concert, Holy Cross amalgamated into one brown fist, and its tiny student body of 550 gathered 3,800 registrations in three weeks. The whole city gained 15,000 new voters, and Cheech & Chong were on their way back, the last time being a triumphant first appearance in September at La Semana de La Raza festival, a youthful alternative to the traditional celebration of Mexican Independence Day. San Antonio, 51 percent Chicano, nine percent black, became Cheech & Chong country. No shit.

Now, at KTSA, they learn that their Christmas record—a Chicano's explanation of the rather far-out Santa Claus legend to a red-freak rock musician—is No. 20 and the most requested record in town, way out in front of No. 2, who else, the Osmond Brothers. And at the concert, where they headline over the native Sir Doug, 4,000 cheer them as if they were the town's creation, and they pick up on the first words of bits the way sane people pick up on the first notes of a pop star's goldie, and they rock with laughter and nod ain't-that-the-way-it-is appreciation at Cheech's command of old Tex-Mex stereotypes. Chong portrays "Blind Melon Chitlin'," the archetypal, dug-up old bluesman being revered by even blinder white kids, and when Chitlin' finally gets his left leg stomping the audience joins in, clapping and stomping. Mirror, mirror, on the stage.

There are plenty of simply outrageous, hip burlesque costume changes and voices: Cheech, wondering about what's being sold on TV these days, turns into a TV DJ ten years from now: "Hey! All you groovy chicks out there, now you can get it together with all-new! tie-dyed! Tampax!" The audience screams its laughter out, and Cheech wraps it up: "Up tight, and out of sight." Later, he's the Pope, receiving a message from the Mafia demanding that he, as head of the Church, must make love to a beautiful woman if the Church is to stay intact. The Pope is horrified but, finally, agrees, under four conditions, which he states with petulance. First, the woman must be blind, so she can't see the defilement. Second, she must be deaf, so she can't hear the file. Third, she must be dumb, so she can't talk about it. And fourth, she's gotta have the big-a tits, and Cheech's eyes and tongue pop out. "You can get the big-a tits for me, boom-boom." And the audience damn well knows the punch line, having heard it, even on AM radio in San Antonio, but they roll with it.

Still, Cheech & Chong's main themes are dope and one of the prime results of smoking it: incoherence. Chong, as "Laid-Back Lenny," is always short of grasping, and he neither knows nor cares that he never connects. He is the classic stoned-out red freak stumbling through a dope trial, hitching a ride from the short-chopped cruisin' Chicano, or watching TV and wondering why the picture's so fucked—until his friend shows up and turns the set on. "Oh . . . far out, man," but he really didn't mind those hours of silent gray, you know. . . . "The red freak is the modern-day wino," says Cheech. "We don't say it, but we just show it as we see it. Wherever you find something funny, you find something that's true." Chong, guest DJ on KTSA: "Here's a public service announcement. Anyone who knows or has had any contact with Debbie Hempseed, go directly to the free clinic."

The most-played sketch from the four-month-old first album is a sharp yet subtle portrayal of all the twisty weavings of paranoia and incoherence that surround the doped. Chong is in his own reverie when a friend, who's just scored some dope and fears he's been tailed, knocks on the door.

"Who is it?"

"It's Dave. Let me in."

"Dave's not here."

"I know. I'm Dave. I've got the stuff and I think someone followed me. Let me in."

"Dave?"

"Yeah, Dave. Now let me in."

"Dave's not here."

Cheech & Chong play on stereotypes, they revert to naughty shocks for laughs, they use the blackout technique of the well-established Committee, they use the ghetto voices of Richard Pryor, they use parody more than satire, and they rarely do one-liners. To slip across a point on drugs, Chong asks the audience: "How many of you smoke grass?" A majority. "How many of you sell it?" Maybe a dozen, half of them joking, probably. And Chong observes: "There's a difference, isn't there? Like 20 years."

And people are listening to this Chinaman and this beaner, like they aren't listening to the rest of the crop of "hip" humorists catering to the rock audience. The Firesign Theatre are a recording, studio-to-inner-head phenomenon. Lily Tomlin and George Carlin are TV and nightclub acts. The Congress of Wonders do great radio bits, the Credibility Gap are best doing radio news, and the Conception Corporation conceive mostly clichés. But Cheech & Chong have won out wherever they've performed— in New York at the Bitter End, in Chicago and Detroit, most certainly and clearly in Texas, and at home in L.A., where they'll soon top the bill at the Troubadour. Also, on the eve of the New Year, they'll be at Carnegie Hall with Sha Na Na.

"We said, basically, 'What can two heads do for a living without having to work?'" said Chong, who had owned a plush topless club called the Shanghai Junk in Vancouver and turned it around with his stage show. "Lots of sex and dope, and a mime artist and four topless chicks. Not that kind of 'topless,' but we did skits, like a hip burlesque. And you know how, say, the Committee will simulate taking clothes off for a skit? Well, ours did it."

Before Shanghai, Chong, 32 and from Alberta, Canada, had played guitar with Bobby Taylor and the Vancouvers, the first nonwhite act on Motown. Among other things, he co-wrote "Does Your Mama Know?," a precedent for the Supremes' ethnic nod, "Love Child," and, on tour, he took notes on two of the best improvisational comedy revues in the business: The Committee (San Francisco) and Second City (Chicago).

"The people I played for never went to the Committee. But there was never any question about a market. Like a kid would throw a Frisbee and hit someone and everybody fell down. But there was nobody doing humor. Cheech and I took the essence of all that insanity; he knew the concert field, I knew the staging." So after the improvisational hip tease folded, Cheech & Chong did a concert on their own, confirmed the reaction with a coffeehouse job, and decided to hit L.A. That was two years ago, and it took two years, working discotheques, doing a talent night show at Red Foxx's, going through would-be managers like Sally Marr, who is Lenny Bruce's mother, playing to black audiences at the Climax, and standing in front of the Troubadour on Monday mornings so they could be first in line and get to audition. Finally, the word began to get around. A Chicano-Chinese comedy act. Far out. At the Troubadour they were spotted by Lou Adler, and he signed them for his Ode label and cut their first record. Now they're being booked by William Morris, and for Richard Cheech, what a homecoming!

Cheech, real name Richard Marin, was born in Watts, California, 25 years ago, raised in the middle of a huge family "with a lot of funny relatives," went to college and got an English degree, and left for Canada, a mistaken draft classification the chaser. As a kid, he lived in white suburbia, sang folk by himself and R&B with all kinds of pick-me-up bands like Rompin' Richie and the Rockin' Rubins and Captain Shagnasty and His Loch Ness Pickles. He worked his way through school at a liquor store, and as a dishwasher and a janitor. In Canada he was a potter, a carpet delivery-man, and a cook at a big hotel in Banff, a ski resort in Alberta's Canadian Rockies. He'd bullshitted his way into the job. "I couldn't fry water, man, and they found me out when I got a Denver sandwich order and sent out a ham and egg. I didn't know." At one point, he met Frank Zappa, who was looking to form an oldies band and was enchanted by this authentic L.A. Chicano. The Rockin' Rubins? Zappa settled for his album *Cruising with Ruben & the Jets,* and Cheech proceeded to meet and join Chong in Vancouver.

Cheech & Chong agree that the timing is right for them, right down to their very names, and with appropriate nods to the Committee, Bill Cosby, Richard Pryor, and, most of all, Lenny Bruce.

"Lenny was funny," says Chong. "He got bitter when he got busted, and then he started a whole new style of comedy. We're doing sort of early

Lenny Bruce, with the emphasis on the young and the doped more than the ethnic and the ghetto, more on the times than on topical matters and personalities.

"Nixon makes a fluff and a million lives are lost," says Chong. "Nixon and hunchbacks are taboo. It's a bad trip, and we forget about it on stage. It's not funny. There's nothing ridiculous about it."

Tonight, Cheech & Chong will gross more than $5,000 for Holy Cross High, and they'll proceed to Chicago to perform for a growing youth coalition aimed at registering young voters and dumping Nixon.

"I *love* the power structure that's going on now," says Chong, tall and assertive with a full, low voice. "It's impossible to keep that image—they're doomed—'cause a lot of guys like to get laid. That's part of why they have long hair, 'cause that's what the chicks dig. Man, only if you're a fanatic Christian can you remain a bigot till the day you die."

At the end of a weary day and night and morning, Cheech shakes his round, happy head. "This trip just blows my fuckin' mind—the incredible acceptance."

Cheech & Chong's fans came in all forms. There were the cops who tailed them to the nightclub off the San Antonio River to tell them how much they dug them, even if the arena manager had threatened to shut off the power because of the language. "Them boys can't go around saying 'motherfucker' and 'son of a bitch!'" And the friendly cab driver, the hotel clerk, the all-night waitress, all laughing along. And backstage at Municipal Auditorium, Sir Doug Sahm's kids sped around the dressing rooms and corridors, mini-Dougs. Ronnie, eight years old, asked if I was one of them, because I look twice as Chinese as Tommy Chong, whose mother is white. Her favorite line from the album, Ronnie said, is "Whack his pee-pee," the judge's order of punishment for a child molester.

From the first, Cheech was overwhelmed by the reception. Well, maybe not "over." Riding into town, a DJ from KTSA asked him, "See, didn't I tell you you'd come back in style?"

Said Cheech, straight-faced: "Screw that, man, I want some bread."

—*Rolling Stone*, January 6, 1972

AL GREEN

"I'VE GOT
TO BE FREE,
AND THEN
I CAN SING"

By **1973,** I'd done a few more cover stories—on Leon Russell, the Jackson 5, Ike & Tina Turner, Marvin Gaye, Three Dog Night, Santana, and the Rolling Stones. Sadly, I'd had to write a few more obituaries as well—for Jim Morrison, Clyde McPhatter, and Danny Whitten, Neil Young's guitarist. Some of those pieces are in *Not Fade Away.*

The list indicates that I ranged widely at *Rolling Stone.* All of us did. But coming from a childhood marked by a love of Top 40 radio, I was a lover of all kinds of music, with a special affection for R&B. I wound up writing about so many Motown acts that when the editors of a book about Motown Records found themselves without a writer for the main text—the history of the fabled label and biographies of all of its major stars—and needed both items in about two weeks, I got the gig. I always get the easiest assignments.

At the magazine and through the radio station, I got more new music than I needed. Most of the albums and tapes I received had to go unheard—unopened, even, in some instances.

But when Al Green came along, it was clear that we were in the midst of stardom. This was one of those voices that, like Ray Charles, Otis Redding,

Van Morrison, or Aretha Franklin, could sing just about anything and make it musical bliss. I played him on KSAN, and when he hit the Bay Area for his first big concert, I had to be there.

The following piece led to others. Al Green was one of those rare stars who enjoyed making themselves accessible to the press. We like that. Especially when they make real news, as Green did—unfortunately—when he experienced a horrific incident in which a woman who wanted to marry him confronted him at his home in Memphis and, spurned, attacked him and then killed herself. Around that same time, he'd been born again and would start a local church of his own. There, he seems to have found peace. And it was there that I visited him in 2005. That article, "Al Green, Soul Savior," appears later in this collection.

First, here's Al—pre-Rev.—in my backyard, 30-something years ago.

<hr>

"I never did get to meet Otis Redding," says Al Green, answering the inevitable question. "I liked his material. I saw him just once, in Chicago at the Regal. I was 16, 17, and I said, 'Whoa! When I grow up, I'm gonna do that, too!' He had this long black Cadillac outside, which I just looked at."

Oakland—It's a big, long, cream-colored Continental Trailways bus, repainted and redone so that the destination, it says over the big front windshield, is AL GREEN. Point of departure, it says by the side of the front door, is AL GREEN. Company name, in big red letters along the sides: AL GREEN AND THE ENTERPRISE ORCHESTRA. It sits here backstage at the Oakland Coliseum Arena, which is just now being emptied of 14,000 people. The bus is accompanied by a pair of black limousines, also Al Green's. And it is being studied by four dozen people. Two dozen can barely see the bus, stuck as they are in the balcony behind the stage, leaning their Afroed heads down over the railings as far as they can, looking at the limos and the bus, hoping for one more look at Al Green, seeing, mostly, the two dozen other people.

The other people are the requisite ornaments of overnight pop success. London Records, a quiet, white company (Ronnie Aldrich, Engelbert Humperdinck, Mantovani) whose rock roster has been mostly British and blues (Savoy Brown, John Mayall, Rolling Stones, Ten Years After, Moody Blues, Gilbert O'Sullivan), and whose soul label, Hi, is respectable but minimal (Otis Clay, Syl Johnson, Ann Peebles, trumpeter/vice president/producer Willie Mitchell), suddenly finds itself with the country's number one R&B/pop artist. Al Green is so much a star that his James Brown/Little Richard/Ike & Tina/Ray Charles-styled, drum-rolled introduction, teen-aged as it sounds, doesn't go too far. Listen—and remember to imagine Apollo Theater screams at *each* and *every* pause:

It's SHOWtime! Here's a young man's GOT to be solid gold! The prince of peace! The god of love and happiness! Because without them, how can you mend a broken heart! For the good times! . . . and the music as innovation . . . he's got the driving wheel! But he can't get next to you! Why! 'Cause I'm tired of being alone! So let's stay together! 'Cause I'm still in love with you! Sit right down and talk to me. CALL me! Four gold singles! Two gold albums! That makes you the world's greatest superstar! Here he is: Al Green!

So here is white and quiet London Records, along with other VIP fans, here to press Al's flesh, to just wish him well as he takes off on his first major US tour, from February through April, headlining the big coliseums from Oakland and L.A. to Richmond, Virginia, with a stop at New York's Philharmonic Hall March 18 and two weeks at the Latin Casino in April. Then, in May, Europe.

This, then, will be Al Green's most important tour since he joined Willie Mitchell at Hi Records in Memphis two years ago and funked through "I Can't Get Next to You" and "Driving Wheel" before he got his first major hit, "Tired of Being Alone," then busted through to the top with "Let's Stay Together." By last spring he was a certified idol, headlining the Apollo for a week and getting held over for two more. There's a story going around about how this skinny Harlem girl shimmied down a furnace pipe to sneak into the theater to see Al Green. And yet last summer he was still second-billed at the major, big auditorium concerts. At the Cow Palace, he casually stole the audience of 14,000 from a retiring Smokey Robinson, but that sleek limo huffing away at the back door, that driver and those guards—they were for Smokey.

Just before the Coliseum concert, despite SOLD OUT signs posted at 2:00 p.m. at the freeway on-ramps and announcements by all the radio stations, ticketless kids milled around the Coliseum, desperately wanting in. An hour into the revue—Bloodstone, Spinners, Al Green's comic and intro man, then Al Green—a crowd of kids tried to push their way in, through a window, and failed. Young men sauntered up to the black guards, nose to nose, not too proud to beg—come on, brother, you can *lemME* in!—and failed, flash-cussing as they walked away, their whole night now fucked.

David Jefferson, promotions coordinator at the Coliseum: "Most of the audience for the big soul shows, their buying habits are such that they buy their tickets on the night of the show. But Al Green appeals to the young white audience, too, and they bought their tickets beforehand, at the agencies, so we were sold out. And for a soul show, that's rare."

So, after the show, with everybody lingering around, waiting for this man's sweat glands to slow, Al Green has just about 12 minutes to talk before they open him up to the next press of flesh.

"The crowd was extremely warm, very loving, completely understanding," he begins, at ease in this room crowded up by his entourage, including Shirley Alexander, his secretary (and an ex-Ikette) and a bodyguard-sized bodyguard named Curtis. Green had come onstage, arms raised, like a middleweight champ, except all dressed up in white and headed for vases of long-stemmed roses at stage left and right, to hand out to the audience, ensuring a show-stopping onrush of fans even before he'd hit his first high note.

"They seem to be so serious about it," he says, looking innocent. "This little girl, right after the show, actually jumped on the stage. That's unusual for a girl, being able to jump onto that high stage." Green is amazed at such moments, but not surprised by the idolatry.

"See," he says, searching for the words, "I'd contemplated it first, I'd figured it out . . . it's really personal, but it was something that was pre-planned . . . preset in my mind, or preregistered—in my head, so that when it comes off I'm just happy about it."

The Al Green show is slicked up now from, say, last summer, when his set was shorter and more jittery. His presence then was undeniable, and the girls were already screaming at this synthesis of Gaye, Brown, Redding, and Mathis. But without the confidence that has sprung the red roses, the extended dancing, the more generous doses of his falsetto squeal, the looser interweaving of songs, he was more open to straight vocal comparisons to Redding.

The comparisons still work. There's that Memphis oomph to the sound, that freedom on the stage, that eclecticism, magnetism . . . with an extra taste of romanticism. Backed by the nine-piece Enterprise Orchestra—three horns, two guitars, congas, drums, organ, and bass—he does a couple of bars of "Alone Again Naturally," then breaks into a spoken bit about a Friday morning in Memphis when he felt bothered and picked up a pen to write, "I'm so tired of being alone . . ." A few bursts from the horns and the audience screams, recognizing "Look What You Done."

The horns get into a little shuffle step while Green stalks the stage. He goes into "How Can You Mend a Broken Heart" and switches, halfway, into "For the Good Times," moving over to sit on a monitor speaker during the break. "Love and Happiness" finally snaps the languid beat, the bedrock of most of Green's songs, and he skitters across the stage, loosely, in command. The coat comes off, exposing a white shirt with a netted bib. Kids begin moving toward the stage again, and guards repel them, like insects, with sprays of flashlight.

"Choreography," Green says, "would hang me up, mess my head up. I can't perform if I've got to do something. I've got to be free, and then I can sing."

As for that high wail that he has made a trademark, that sends him to a glass of water after every couple of songs, he explains: "I started tampering with it at an early age. I liked Jackie Wilson, for one thing, that high voice, and Sam Cooke, for the smoothness and control he had." Visiting Dusty Street at KSAN-FM the night before the concert, Al said the falsetto was for accent, and he said he achieved it through training. In his younger, gospel days, he said, he was singing even higher.

The afternoon of the concert, he was at *Rolling Stone,* bearing champagne, to pick up his "Rock & Roll Star of the Year" award and to flash the press. Someone asked him to sing bay-beh, and, without a break in conversation, he smiled and hit the peak.

Cocktail-talking with everybody, searching out people to wave to as he left the offices, Al Green came across as a star trying hard to keep his feet on the ground. He proudly showed off his electronic Pulsar digital watch, and when a staff member noted his gold chain bracelets and a huge diamond ring in the shape of a wedding cake (which he designed) and joked, "I see that success has gone to your wrists," Green just smiled again.

In his dressing room, crowded in by his entourage, he discussed success. There's less privacy now, he says, and the company wants more product than he has time to write and produce (another album remains a few cuts from completion), what with the tour and TV shots.

"The only problem is the money," he says. "The money changes the way your friends feel about you, the way people act toward you. If it wasn't for the money, it'd be really out of sight."

—*Rolling Stone*, **March 15, 1973**

THE BAND WITH DYLAN

"IT'S RIGHT
ON THE DOT"

Bob Dylan and The Band, 1968 (Photo by Elliott Landy)

The year 1974 began with a trip to frigid Chicago, where I'd be tracking Bob Dylan's first tour in too many years—eight, if you want to get exact about it.

By now, *Rolling Stone* had mastered the craft of covering major rock tours and events. For Dylan, the plan called for me to tackle the first concerts—in Chicago, Philadelphia, Montreal, and Toronto—and then pass the baton to other reporters in New York and the South. We also figured on grabbing Dylan for an interview early on, but that depended on my ability to lasso him, as his publicist guaranteed nothing. Over the three issues that spanned the beginning of the tour, I filed a report on the first couple of concerts and audience reaction to them, lucked into an interview with Dylan in Montreal (published in *Not Fade Away*), and then, the day after talking with Dylan, flew back to San Francisco where I deciphered notes I'd taken from chats with members of The Band, who were opening for and then backing Dylan on the tour.

Those notes became this piece, which also served as a breather before I caught up with The Band and Dylan again. My reports, along with those from New York and Atlanta, would be packaged as a paperback book, called *Knockin' on Dylan's Door.*

"See the man with the stage fright . . ."

The Toronto crowd whooped in approval. After all, Bob Dylan had just finished his sixth number, "The Ballad of a Thin Man," had offered a quick bow, had moved down the stage steps and into his modest backstage quarters, leaving The Band on its own. Now Rick Danko marched up to the mike, past the booming guitar intro, and sang about the "lonely kid who suffered so much for what he did."

"It's accidental," said Robbie Robertson, The Band's lead guitarist, spokesman, and composer of "Stage Fright."

"I mean, it was not put there because [he whistled a brain-stormed, what-a-clever-idea whistle] 'If we do this *here!* . . .' at all. The key that 'Stage Fright' is in, coming after the song before it—it's a nice lift. It's picked musically and for its tempo. It's not necessarily picked because it's relevant to this or that."

"Stage Fright" is, in fact, "about ourselves," said Robertson. "We're those kind of people—not outgoing, basically shy. We've never been very comfortable showing off. We play music, write songs, and like to play them, but we have never and will never really have it in the palm of our hand. And we don't want to. We enjoy that rush of being scared. A lot of people I've gone to see, it just seems to roll off their tongue. They don't seem to sweat. You see no pain in them whatsoever. It's just a wonderful evening of entertainment. It's not for us. It's turmoil. It's pulled out like a tooth."

But the music is at least as painstaking as it is painful. Doing ten songs of their own each concert and backing up Dylan on another 13 each show, The Band is winning over each audience it faces. And that is not an easy achievement, given the complete absorption by each audience in the anticipated presence, the overriding mystique, of Dylan.

One critic of The Band complained about their "blasé professionalism." Others hear it as a precise execution of some of the best, most thoughtful and picturesque American rock 'n' roll ever, mostly by Jaime "Robbie" Robertson. And The Band (Robertson on lead guitar and vocals, Levon Helm on drums and vocals, Rick Danko on bass and vocals, Richard Manuel on keyboards and vocals, and Garth Hudson on organ) is not and cannot be a machine, as it has to roll with Dylan's musical changes of mind almost every show.

We are at the Inn on the Park in Toronto. On the way here to this hotel in Don Valley, we passed through a part of town, hidden by snow in the night, that got Robbie smiling: "This is Cabbagetown," he said. "You know, on the cover of *Moondog Matinee*? I described the feeling of the place to the artist, and he got it just perfect." Robertson and all of The Band, except Levon, are from Canada, and he's quite at ease, talking with a low voice, at a slow gait.

The touring history of The Band, since their emergence in 1968 from the big pink house in Woodstock, is a simple one: they've done as little as possible, taking a year and a half off between the recorded concert in New York, December 31, 1971, and a Watkins Glen appearance in July 1973. Then nothing until the Dylan tour. The Band prefer to stay home with families—all are now in Malibu, along with the Bob Dylan family—and work on albums.

And, as Robertson repeated several times, in various contexts, The Band are not "very in-touch people," and they don't relate to much of the current rock scene. There is more than a touch of elitism when Robertson states: "We don't have fancy outfits or sparklers on our eyes, and we don't cut off our heads."

But even the albums come hard. After *Rock of Ages,* the live set from New Year's Eve at the Academy of Music, Robertson considered a few sound track offers, then decided to do another album of original songs. He'd written a few tunes, he said, and The Band began the album; then he shifted into another gear. He had been listening to the avant-garde classical music of Krzysztof Penderecki.

"I bought one of his albums a few years ago because I liked the album cover: it was a guy holding a candle. Very spooky-looking cover. One day I put it on and I thought, 'My god. That's terrific.' I think he is the contemporary classical writer of this age.

"He doesn't just use strings or orchestras. He uses very unorthodox techniques. He uses guitars and 30 men singing at half an octave below their range. It's incredible, what he reaches for, and I like very much the lyrics that he writes and I find his music haunting. Other people's music I can shake off very easily. His music I cannot slough off like that."

Robertson's own writing, however, is not outwardly changed by his admiration for Penderecki. "Just like you could be influenced by Leadbelly; it doesn't mean that you'll write Leadbelly tunes. It just means you like him, but you don't necessarily do anything similar to what he does at all. But Penderecki is who I've listened to, to get where I am now musically."

So Robertson and The Band began putting together a new, more ambitious album. "More of a 'works' than just some songs," he said. "But after getting into it for a while I realized that it was much more involved and advanced, that it took a whole other kind of writing and attention. You couldn't knock them off the way you could other things. So after about halfway into it we said we got to do something. I mean we got to do something to just say hello to everybody again. We were fooling around one day and we played a couple of tunes that we used to play years ago, and it was really fun, and we said, 'Gee, why don't we do our old nightclub act?'

"It seemed like people wouldn't object to that at this point because a lot of people feel nostalgic, because what's happening now is kind of watery and they're picking the past apart again, so it seemed to make sense.

"It wasn't as easy as I thought. A lot of the tunes were hard to get into seriously. I mean, to do 'Bony Maronie'—you listen to it and you say, 'Whew!' It was fine, but we don't mean it. We can't mean 'Bony Maronie.' So the ones we picked are the ones we believed the most."

The result was *Moondog Matinee* (named after Alan Freed's Cleveland radio program of 1951, *The Moon Dog Show* on WJW), featuring tunes like "The Great Pretender," "I'm Ready," "Mystery Train," "Holy Cow," and "Share Your Love."

Next would be the album with Dylan, cut in three days in November at Village Recorders studio in Los Angeles. Robertson, who supervised the sound on the album and mixed it, with Village chief engineer Rob Fraboni, was enthusiastic: "Oh, man, what a record! And it just gets better and better and better. The more you live with it. It happened so quick and it's great. It's just right on the dot."

Why did it happen so quick?

"We were not going to play around," said Robertson. "Drive it into the ground." Fraboni, 23, had previously worked with Dylan in 1971—at the Record Plant in New York on the Allen Ginsberg album with Dylan as backup. It was never released, said Fraboni, because "it wasn't on the commercial side."

Robbie had heard about the studio, which included a new room and monitoring system put together by Fraboni. "He heard it was tight," the engineer said. "And it's out of town (in West L.A., near Westwood). When the Stones were there it was comfortable for them; they had security." (Dylan and The Band were booked under the names "Judge Magney," a name picked by studio general manager Dick La Palm and, coincidentally, a rest stop on Highway 61 along the Minnesota border). The only visitors to the sessions were Cher Bono (friend of Elektra/Asylum head David Geffen), Geffen himself, and Jack Dishonor and Donna Weirs, who sang backup on one track. "It was good," Fraboni said, "but it had a different feel, and wasn't left in."

Only three songs required overdubs, Fraboni recalled: "Going Going Gone," "Never Say Goodbye," and "On a Night Like This." Two of the songs, Fraboni said, were worked out completely in the studio: "Dirge" and "Wedding Song."

"One Saturday afternoon, after the cutting with The Band was finished, we were putting together a master reel. Dylan was writing 'Wedding Song.' He told me he wanted to record. So I set up some mikes, and we let it roll, and that was the take. You'll hear some noises on the track; those are from buttons on his sleeve hitting the guitar."

Next for The Band, according to Robertson, will be either a live album from Watkins Glen, the "works" album, or another record with Dylan.

Finally, The Band is yet to decide its business future. David Geffen, the man who brought Dylan into Elektra/Asylum, had told me he's also signed The Band. Robertson denied it. What about after their commitment to Capitol, consisting of two more albums?

"Hmmm . . . I'm not sure," he said. "I think we have our hands full with other things. I'm not thinking about that too much, really. It's not very interesting to think about. And it will just kind of take care of itself in the next few months."

—*Rolling Stone*, **February 28, 1974**

LOUNGING

WITH THE

WICKED

MR. PICKETT

Las Vegas in the Seventies was nothing like what it is today, but it was still a whole lot of something. Elvis had opened its grandiose doors to rock music in 1970, and the hotels began booking younger pop, rock and R&B acts.

I first visited, according to my trusty calendar, on February 15, the day after Dylan and The Band's last concert in Oakland. I was there to see the Pointer Sisters. I returned in early May to profile Gladys Knight and the Pips, and it's amazing. Maybe it was Vegas' energizing force, but Mr. Calendar tells me that I flew in from New York, where I'd appeared on Geraldo Rivera's show, *Goodnight America*, where I sat with Grace Slick and Jerry Moss, the "M" of A&M Records, to talk about the drug scene.

After two nights in Vegas, I was back in San Francisco on a Saturday and, after a weekend that no doubt included a DJ stint on KSAN (they'd become so regular that I no longer entered them in my calendar), I began writing. My entry for Tuesday: "Finish." Six thousand words in a couple of days. That's how many of us worked at the magazine. Today, a 6,000-word profile would take—I dunno, three days. But we were all multi-taskers, and we were always on the move.

On another visit to Las Vegas—this time in late 1975, this time for Olivia Newton-John—I popped in on another show. In the old days, Las Vegas had what were called lounge acts, lower- to medium-level entertainers who played smaller rooms, shorter sets, and later hours. The idea, I suppose, was to offer visitors yet another reason to stay conscious, and to do more drinking and gambling. But this show featured no lounge act. Wilson Pickett was one of my all-time favorites. I identified myself to the host and asked him to get word to Pickett that I'd like to meet him. Our visit became a short piece, and, perhaps because it happened on the spur of the moment (not unlike my accidental happening upon Jim Morrison and the midnight call from Janis Joplin, both of which are covered in *Not Fade Away*), it's one of my favorites.

———

Las Vegas—In the city without clocks, it is 2:15 a.m.—showtime at, among other places, the Casino Lounge at the Las Vegas Hilton. For Liberace in the main showroom, you have to stand in line and pay $15 (plus tax) a head to get a good chance of being squeezed tighter than the headliner's teeth.

At the Casino Lounge, there's no cover, no minimum (drinks are $2.50), and you can stagger in without a reservation and, depending on your timing, see any of three rotating shows: Kenny Rogers and the First Edition, the Kim Brothers, or—of all the names to pop up in Vegas—Wilson Pickett.

We time ourselves to see the wicked one.

He is introduced by one of his nine Midnight Movers as "The Dynamic . . . Soulful . . . Legend in His Own Time," and he comes bouncing out, glowing like a bruised but unbowed champ in a simple black tux, a long white scarf tied around the neck.

He is facing a third of a house—maybe 36 occupied tables—but he performs main showroom all the way. He joins his horn players in a few easy shuffle steps, lets out his patented, leathery scream and rolls into and through "Funky Broadway," "Get Me Back on Time, Engine Number Nine," and "I'm in Love." It's hits all the way. With "Mustang Sally," he moves into the crowd. One woman jumps up to bump with him; another offers a taste of wine. Wilson turns his attention back to the stage for a lengthy workout on "Don't Let the Green Grass Fool You." Pickett the producer/songwriter picks the song apart, scats a bassline, makes childlike percussive sounds at the drummer. His back is to the audience—he seems oblivious—and as the congas rev up, a party of four ups and leaves.

In Ghana, West Africa, for the "Soul to Soul" show in 1971, part of the Independence Day crowd of 100,000 charged the stage and had Pickett dancing all the way to his dressing room. Here, the applause from 35 tables died down long before the music. The soul was all onstage.

Pickett didn't care. The 34-year-old native of Prattville, Alabama, has been working Vegas (16 weeks a year, four weeks at a time) for four years—or since Ghana. By 1971, his greatest hits were mostly behind him, and in early 1973 he left Atlantic Records, his label for eight years, to sign with RCA. At RCA, he got the financial guarantees he said he couldn't get from Atlantic, but no hit records. Atlantic's Jerry Wexler and Tom Dowd were the music men behind Wilson in the early days. Of RCA, Pickett himself said, "They were just too busy . . . I've always felt that their biggest clientele was in electronics anyway."

He found Vegas an easy way to cushion his already cushy income. ("He's one of the highest-paid performers in certain areas—like Vegas and Japan," said an RCA publicist. "I hear he was making $17,000 a week in Vegas. And RCA paid him a lot of money, too." Pickett himself agreed that he had a "great guarantee" at RCA, and laughed. "I mean, I didn't have to do any more work!") Except for a tour through Japan last spring, he gave up concerts and road work.

But Pickett is tiring of Vegas now. "It's the type of gig that you can neglect the rest of the music world," he said. "I don't think it's a place an artist of my caliber should just stay. I had a four-year contract here, I honored my contract, and I'm finished. You see, I got to go back out there now."

Wilson had shaken us out of a five-hour sleep with his return call. At ten in the morning, he sounded anxious to talk. In his large but simply appointed "San Franciscan" suite, he greeted us in a blue robe, took a corner sofa, and got to the point: "See, I've just been given my own record company, and I've left RCA. T.K. Productions—Henry Stone—has given me my own label, and I have a single coming out next week called "The Best Part of a Man," and then I have an album out in January called *Chocolate Mountain*. So things are beginning to change for me. I was kind of missing for a little while there."

"Maybe I can put the blame on myself," said Pickett. "I probably just neglected the fact that I'm supposed to cut this kind of record. I went into material that was so personal to me, and I had forgotten about the outside world that really wasn't that deep into this kind of thing, that seriousness.

They want to hear a fuckin' beat, man, and 'sock it to me' with the *Soul Train.*"

Other artists, we ventured, had succeeded with "statement" albums, Marvin Gaye and Stevie Wonder among them. And sometimes, we added, the best material is the most personal. Pickett was quick with his answer:

"They ain't gonna buy it. Matter of fact, they never gonna buy it any more by me 'cause I'm not gonna make any more." A *humph* of a pause. "So—they can forget about that!"

Pickett has his own label—fittingly called Wicked Records—because "I wouldn't sign ever in my life again my name to any contract for any record company as an artist," but has no immediate plans to build its roster. "First of all," he said, "I want to get *me* going."

After Vegas, Pickett was planning to hit the road, first to Zambia, Africa, then that other exotic town, Denver.

The stage show, he promised, would be more than greatest hits. In Vegas, he had been working around the corner from the Thunderbird, where "Dick Clark's Good Ol' Rock 'n' Roll" revue was packin' them in. Most people, we told Pickett, were not ready to see him on that road. The president of Wicked Records straightened up on the sofa:

"I ain't goin' with no fucking Dick Clark," he said, a snort on his face. "I ain't no oldie but goodie—nowhere near me, man. Don't retire me now!"

—*Rolling Stone*, **December 4, 1975**

Wilson Pickett did not retire for almost another 30 years. Amazing. He continued to be in demand—especially after he was inducted in the Rock and Roll Hall of Fame in 1991. It took ill health to slow him down, in 2004. In early 2006, at age 64, Wilson died of a heart attack. He was, as Aretha Franklin said, "one of the greatest soul singers of all time." He set high standards. In fact, he sang them: "Ninety-nine and a half just won't do. Got to have a hundred! . . . Lord have mercy!"

EMMYLOU HARRIS

WHOLE WHEAT HONKY TONK

Here's one I debated with myself about including, and all because of one paragraph.

But that one graf—as it's called in the business—illustrates a minor issue that turned into a nagging headache, and one that nagged for years.

Other than that graf, this piece is a straight-ahead visit with a celebrity. Well, Emmylou Harris has never been your typical "celebrity." But in 1978, she was one of those artists who'd put out a couple of albums and showed promise of a career of purity in her music. It was not only honky tonk, as the title suggested, but also country-rock, alt-country—the results of Gram Parsons' and others' pioneering work.

I loved Emmylou's music and thoroughly enjoyed our visit in Los Angeles. But while writing the article, I succumbed to something I rarely did. I looked at other profiles in *Rolling Stone* and let them influence me. Writers, I thought, were increasingly crossing the line between reporters and critics. While essaying a profile of a performer, they seemed to be commenting on that artist's work as well, proffering critical opinions.

OK, I thought. I'm no critic, but I'll give it a shot. Thus, that graf.

I stand by my opinion. I mellowed about the album as time passed, and as I played it more and more. But what I wrote is what I thought at the time.

Well! The Harris piece turned into another reminder of that axiom I'm just now making up: that artists don't care about 1,000 positive words. The 25 or so less-than-laudatory ones are all that matter.

And so, over the months and years, I heard that Harris was upset with me. And when, in 1990, I was working on *Hickory Wind,* my biography of Gram Parsons, and wanted to interview her (Emmylou having been his partner in music), it was not possible. I would have to make do with what she'd said when we were still speaking.

In recent years, I had opportunities to write about Harris, primarily in entries for various music books. In *The Encyclopedia of Country Music* I wrote Emmylou's entry, noting: "Long before artists were being called 'New Traditionalists,' Harris was stretching boundaries—and succeeding on her own terms, introducing traditional country to a wider audience while helping to redefine country music itself." (Ironically, the foreword to the encyclopedia, produced by the Country Music Hall of Fame and Museum, was by Emmylou Harris.) And in a column I did about Parsons for the music site allmusic.com, I wrote about Emmylou: "With her instinctive and intricate harmonies, delivered in a jewel of a voice, she brought Parsons' songs—and Parsons himself—to greater heights in their short time together. Since his death, she has carried the country-rock, "Cosmic American Music" torch Parsons first lifted, and has carved out a stellar career—one that, in its adventurousness and its passion for music, wherever its roots, often draws on lessons learned from her time with Gram."

That wasn't an attempt to get back—or to get—on her good side. That's just how I felt when I wrote it.

And that's how I still feel about her.

Dolly Parton had surprise in her eyes when she invited Emmylou Harris into Porter Wagoner's Fireside Studios in Nashville in the spring of 1976 to listen to the final tapes for Dolly's *All I Can Do* album. See, Dolly had cut "Boulder to Birmingham," Emmylou's beautiful paean to the late Gram Parsons, without telling her. And now, in the darkness of the studio, the tape was rolling. But Emmylou was suddenly distracted. The song before "Boulder" was a Parton composition called "To Daddy," which seemed at first to be just another of those pretty/sad country tunes about the self-sacrificial mother. Just when she expected to learn how Mamma died, Emmylou heard Dolly singing the words of a note that Mother had left "to Daddy," saying she was leaving to search for some love she needed badly.

Emmylou was devastated. "That song had my lip trembling," she remembers now. "I was afraid I was gonna make a scene . . . and 'Boulder to Birmingham' came on, and it was so anticlimactic because I was so wrapped up in this song." She remembers thanking and hugging Dolly, but her mind was on "To Daddy." "To me, it's like an O. Henry short story because she sets you up. You're expecting the woman to die, but Dolly just comes back with the old whammo and turns it all around."

"That's about my mamma," Emmylou recalls Dolly saying. But "To Daddy" was left off Dolly's album, and Emmylou immediately added it to her own repertoire. Now, it's the first single from her new album, *Quarter Moon in a Ten Cent Town*. And, as with "If I Could Only Win Your Love," "Together Again," "One of These Days," "Making Believe," and "(You Never Can Tell) C'est la Vie" from her previous three albums, "To Daddy" is a hit on the country charts.

This past New Year's Eve, Emmylou was off to Nashville again, flying from L.A. with Linda Ronstadt for a working holiday at Dolly Parton's home. The three are doing an album together and spent four days trying out songs, singing solos, duets, and three-part harmonies, while Dolly's mother cooked and brought over the traditional New Year's food of the South, black-eyed peas.

In a time when women dominate the top of the pops, and almost ten years since Crosby, Stills & Nash first got together at Mama Cass' house in Laurel Canyon, it's Ronstadt, Parton, and Harris. RP&H. Or, as Emmylou said, kidding (maybe): "How about the 'Queenston Trio'?"

Not long ago, Nashville, to Emmylou Harris, was not much more than an escape from New York, itself an escape from home in Virginia and college in North Carolina. It was 1970, she'd just had a baby, her short-lived marriage had shorted, she'd given up on music, and she and her two-month-old daughter had to leave the house they were staying in "because I couldn't afford the rent." She took jobs as a model in an art class ("Fully clothed—I didn't have the nerve to do it nude. I had on this long gown and I was holding an umbrella for some reason.") and as a cocktail waitress "serving pu-pu trays" in a Polynesian restaurant. But the money was so bad ("I never got any tips anywhere I worked in Nashville") that she had to get food stamps.

She recalls that on her first shopping trip while on food stamps, all she bought was baby food.

Emmylou only spent eight months, from May to December, in Nashville in 1970. From there she went back to her parents, who were living near Washington, D.C. She put together a small band and renewed what until then had been a casual musical career. She sang six nights a week at various clubs and lounges, was discovered by members of the Flying Burrito Brothers, hooked up with country-rock pioneer Gram Parsons, and fell apart after his death in 1973.

She slowly picked up the pieces, put a new band together, was signed by Warner Bros., moved in with her producer, Brian Ahern, and found herself an extremely popular solo artist, not only with pop, rock, and country audiences, but also with her peers. She has not only recorded with Ronstadt and Parton, but also with Bob Dylan, on the *Desire* album. Her own records sell well upward of 300,000 each. Brush Arbor, a country group, wrote and sing a song called "Emmylou," which chronicles a groupie's attempts to catch her attention all the way from a hotel in Houston to the Palomino Club in Los Angeles. It concludes: "Well, I love Olivia's eyes/And Ronstadt's really nice/But heaven is a girl named Emmylou!"

And, now, she is part of the "Queenston Trio."

So the Emmylou of not long ago, who spent most of her interviews sounding haunted by Gram and uncertain about being on her own, has come back with the old whammo and turned it all around. Now, at age 30, she is married, mother to two girls (her own eight-year-old Hallie and Ahern's ten-year-old Shannon) and settled into a new house in Studio City near Hollywood.

It's an unassuming little house, the kind any upwardly mobile young couple in California would be happy to snag these days. She and Ahern are beginning to fix it up and fit in furniture—a somehow harmonious mix of Danish and Italian modern and Art Deco antique.

Emmylou is in a red T-shirt (advertising the now-defunct Smiling Dog Saloon in Cleveland) and rolled-tip jeans, red tennis shoes, and white socks. Her fabled good looks—I've heard of DJs who've kept her *Luxury Liner* album cover in front of them for entire shifts to keep themselves inspired— are not played up offstage. Her long, dark hair has an instantly noticeable amount of gray strands, and hers is a commune-sweet-commune beauty. She is soft-spoken but not fragile, quiet but not shy. As onstage, she seems eager to please. And soon after meeting her, one realizes that the name Emmylou fits.

"I've been real fortunate," she says, "in being able to do exactly what I want to do, the record company being supportive of that and the public being supportive enough to where nobody decides that anything should change. I've done it without having a pop hit"—she spreads her arms on the two words, as if to capitalize them—"'cause all my hits have been country, and there's been no crossover. At the same time, I feel like I'm sort of out in the middle there, somewhere, without any category."

This, however, has its cost. "We do have trouble, like my road thing. You want to go on the road and pay your band enough money and not come out in the hole. Unless you're a really big act, it's hard to go out and headline, take your own sound and lights and have the show exactly the way you want it. It came down to me realizing that I want to play with this band, and if I have to open, I'll open. I don't care."

Emmylou sketches in some pieces of her convoluted biography: the daughter of a Marine officer, she was born in Birmingham, Alabama, and raised in Woodbridge, Virginia. In high school, she was always studying and became known as an oddball. She wanted to be "hip and cool" and began singing at parties because it attracted attention. She was a cheerleader, won beauty contests (one of her titles was "Miss Woodbridge"), and was class valedictorian. But, she says, she was never popular. Hoping to be a majorette, she wound up playing alto sax in the marching band. "Boy, the rejects of humanity are the members of the marching band," she says. "That's just the lowest thing on the social climbing ladder." She played sax for two reasons: she was interested in music, and her fingers were too little to close the holes of a clarinet ("I was always squeaking").

She entered the University of North Carolina in Greensboro in 1965 and studied drama, but quit after a year and a half. She discovered that she "was a pretty lousy actress and that I loved music and wanted to do that more than drama."

While in college she had begun performing with other musicians at a club called the Red Door, but she didn't really know what she wanted to do. "At one point I thought about switching over to something like nursing, just because if I was gonna be in college, I didn't want to come out with a degree that said, 'You have a degree in nothing.' I had had enough of all this nebulous shit, and also, I suppose, there was the element of being a young woman: what do you do? Everybody else is getting pinned and settling down and getting married, and you're looking at all that stuff and saying, 'That's pretty silly.'" So, because "there was nothing else to do," she went to New York, where she stayed at the Y, hung out in the Village, and began singing again, having been introduced to country music by new friends Jerry Jeff Walker and David Bromberg. She got married. She made an album for a small label. (She is happy to note that the company went under, so that the record—"a disaster"—is no longer available.) She discovered herself pregnant—"the worst thing any girl could do to her budding career"—and, even worse, she began to feel that her marriage was a mistake. After having the baby, she and her husband left New York for Nashville. "And Nashville, of course, is where we broke up."

A large, curly bearded, serious-looking man in a white T-shirt and overalls enters the living room. Emmylou introduces Brian Ahern, her producer and, since January 1977, her husband. Born in Nova Scotia, he was a rock guitarist in his teens and produced Anne Murray's first string of hits before meeting Emmylou in 1975. His initial impression of Emmylou as a performer: "I thought she had a really good instrument and understood it."

They decide to play her new album for me, and since their stereo gear isn't all set up yet, we drive over to the Enactron Truck. That's the name of Ahern's studio, a converted mobile videotape trailer parked outside a rented house in L.A.'s Coldwater Canyon. Ahern found the truck in New York five years ago; it'd been wasting away in a shed. "I was in a nomadic state of mind," says Ahern. "I wanted to be able to take the studio where the music was." He picked up the 16-ton truck for $3,500, put in a 36-input, British-made board and a pair of 24-track tape machines, and has done all his recording here. (Aside from Harris, he has recently produced Jesse Winchester, Mary Kay Place, Billy Joe Shaver, and Jonathan Edwards.)

While Ahern conducts a quick tour, Emmylou sits at the console and writes out a check, and then, when the tape is ready to roll, she ducks out. "The sound is so true on these Klipsches [speakers]," she says, "it's hard for me to listen."

From the first lines, it is clear that Emmylou is retaining the spare, down-home country feel of her previous albums. She is true to the bluegrass territory of the Louvin Brothers and to good-time, hard-drinking songs (this time it's Delbert McClinton's "Two More Bottles of Wine"), combining pure, sweet country and rock 'n' roll. And her soprano voice sounds thicker; on "Two More Bottles," it even takes on a choked, Teresa Brewer quality.

But *Quarter Moon,* in the end, lacks luster. There are few grabbers, no old chestnuts, and, aside from "To Daddy" and a couple of other ballads, Harris is rarely challenged or inspired enough to do more than the expected capable reading.

But Emmylou seems totally satisfied (even if, as she says, she can't listen to it). The songs, she is pleased to say, "came from left field." Having no familiar material "wasn't something I sat down and planned. However, I was glad it strayed. I've been accused of formula. I really feel good about getting into newer material."

Besides including a familiar tune on every album, formula—in the case of female country-rock performers like Harris and Ronstadt—means lost-lovesick blues and an image of "weaker-sex" vulnerability. But Harris argues that her songs speak of strength and determination as well. And, she adds, "I don't think vulnerability is a negative thing. There're two sides to it. I don't know what else people want people to sing about other than the same old things, because basically that's what we all deal with. I don't know. I heard a song about a dancing pizza man the other day, so I suppose there are other things to sing about. But I never get tired of singing about the same old shit."

But Emmylou's first love was country-blues—à la Robert Johnson and Mance Lipscomb—and folk music, the songs of Seeger and Guthrie. These had an "intense emphasis on lyrics. I never got into making a political statement, but I was influenced by the importance of words. At first I did country music because it had feeling, and then I realized how much the lyrics meant. Country music uses incredibly simple lyrics to put across strong basic emotions and feelings. It's like walking that tightrope between the real maudlin and banal and the real honest and truthful. An example: 'Together Again' [which Harris recorded on *Elite Hotel*] obviously is a happy song because it says, 'We're together again.' But it intimates so much heartbreak. Let's say a situation like my mother and father went through when my father was a prisoner of war for 16 months [in the Korean War]. For most of that time my mother didn't know whether he was dead or alive. It's the kind of song that says nothing else matters, we're together again. That really means something. And then you have what I really love about country music—the harmonies and phrasing. There's a certain stateliness and gracefulness to it."

Before her work with Gram Parsons, Emmylou rarely sang harmonies—some Ian & Sylvia and Hank Williams stuff in college was about it—and to this day, she has trouble. "If somebody's doing three parts, they say, 'Okay, you sing the tenor and I'll sing the baritone,' and I go, 'Well, wait a minute now, show me the part.' If somebody's singing a melody, I consider the harmony to be another melody and I just sing along with it. Gram and I seemed to sing together. I wasn't aware that I was following him. It was always a matter of just singing together. It was always very natural."

She also simply fell in when she was hired to sing harmonies on Bob Dylan's *Desire*. "I didn't give much conscious thought to what I was doing because it all happened so fast, and he's really a dramatist in his singing, and I didn't think of myself as doing anything other than just singing with him and trying to follow him."

Emmylou's work on *Desire* is outstanding, to the point that Dylan allowed it to stand out in the final mix. On "One More Cup of Coffee" her miming is particularly accurate and effective. "I am real familiar with the way Dylan sings," she says. "I get familiar with the way people sing. And the way people pronounce words and syllables is so important to me—even more important than the parts. It's a matter of that feel."

Although Emmylou has done some of her best work in harmony with other artists, she is now at ease on her own. But that doesn't mean she's forgotten Parsons, although stories about her no longer take on soap-operatic tones, with headlines like GRIEVOUS ANGEL and EMMYLOU HAUNTED BY GRAM.

"It was the kind of thing I tried to stay away from, but at the same time I couldn't, because obviously what I was doing musically had a lot to do with him, and I did have a lot of feeling for him. I still think back on that period of time as probably my happiest time, as a performer, or my most . . . I don't know what the word would be, because I enjoy being on the road now and singing. But working with him . . . I got something out of it that I just have never gotten again and probably shouldn't.

"I will never forget him. I suppose I think about him as much and still care about him and love him just as much. We were very intense friends, and I know that I loved him very much. I came into his life very late and

I regret that I never got to spend much time with him. But he did come into my life and affected it, and no matter how much pain is caused by the loss of that, what do you say? I wish it would have never happened? You never look back and think that way."

Back at home, Emmylou makes dinner but burns it, so what had been promoted as lamb stew becomes goulash. At the table, the two girls, Hallie and Shannon, talk about how Parker Stevenson, Shaun Cassidy's mate in the Hardy Boys, needs a record producer. "How about B.A.?" asks Shannon, looking eagerly at her dad. B.A. manages to look horrified and paternally friendly at the same time.

Later, in the living room, Bob Hunka, Ahern's business partner, points out a small metal sculpture atop a speaker. It depicts a thin, long-haired horn player. "It's by a Dutch sculptor who gave it to Emmylou in Holland," says Hunka. "It looks just like her, but he had no idea Emmylou played sax in her high school marching band."

Harris is big in Europe, and she was looking forward to her five-week tour, now under way. Although she is still an opening act in the US, she has headliner status overseas and can finally do shows just the way she wants them. The two-hour concerts, called "An Evening with Emmylou Harris," are divided into an opening acoustic set and an electric set . . . just like CSN ten years ago.

"I can't play enough," Emmylou says. "I feel like after the first or second show I'm just getting warmed up. I guess I'll never get over my honky tonk syndrome."

—Rolling Stone, **February 23, 1978**

STEVE MARTIN

MORE THAN

JUST A

PRETTY FACE

Magazine ad for
Pennies from Heaven

Almost immediately after it was known that I'd left *Rolling Stone,* I got a call from Walter Anderson, editor of *Parade* magazine. He wanted to know whether I might be interested in writing on oc-casion for him.

As with anyone who ever read a newspaper, I was familiar with *Parade,* which was inserted into hundreds of Sunday newspapers around the country. Because of the way it was distributed, and perhaps because it came out weekly, and was on newsprint, it struck many people, both in and out of the business, as something other than a real magazine. Which, come to think of it, was how a lot of people saw *Rolling Stone.* We first appeared on newsprint, and we ap-peared every other week. But, unlike *Parade,* we weren't all that easy to find, as some distributors balked at the language and some of the photographs in *Rolling Stone.*

Parade was strictly mainstream—almost too strictly, I thought. But Ander-son said he was trying to get the magazine to appeal to more young people, and that I could help him do it.

I don't recall talking money early on, but I'm sure Anderson didn't shy from the subject. In the early '80s the big national magazines were paying as much as $2,500 for substantial feature articles that might run 5,000 words or more.

Parade's articles generally topped out at about 1,500 words. For such a piece, an established writer could expect to earn that top rate of the other magazines—and more.

We soon agreed on a first assignment, on a comedian I'd gotten to know in San Francisco, one I'd had on my radio show on KSAN whenever he was in town, playing nightclubs. He was one wild and crazy guy.

———

Steve Martin—wearing red tap dance shoes and white socks and blue shorts—is twirling a lasso in the middle of a large, mirrored room. With a flick of the wrist and a jump, he's inside the rope and watching the dancing circumference he's created. A moment later, he effortlessly skips out of the circle and lets the rope rest.

"This is the way I started," he says. "Twirling rope at Disneyland. Johnny Carson told me one time, 'Anything you've learned as a performer, you'll use it all.' And it's true."

Steve is at Danny Daniels' Dance America, a studio in Santa Monica, California, for his daily tap dance lesson. It's part of his preparation for the film *Pennies from Heaven,* which begins rehearsals tomorrow in Illinois.

Steve's instructor is D.J. Daniels, son of Danny. As a pianist pounds out rinky-dink show tunes, Steve begins to hoof, doing toe-tapping exercises while D.J. counts off the rhythm.

Steve watches his shuffling feet intently. He moves from single-foot exercises into double, and then into different rhythms.

Suddenly he's out on the floor, skipping the length of the room, arms shooting out. Soon he's swaying his body casually while executing elaborate steps and stomps. He dances with ease—sideways, then backwards, occasionally putting on a mock-frightened look.

Steve works on combinations of steps. Then he takes a cane and holds it in front of him, horizontally, while moving from side to side. He walks and dances with the stick. He bounces it against the floor and catches it behind his back.

D.J. is in awe: "He's incredible! He's got a fantastic sense of rhythm. Usually it takes someone a lesson a week for two to three years to learn this. He's taken two to three weeks."

After the session, Steve says he's never taken dance lessons. All the things he's done onstage—the scatter-limbed "Happy Feet" outbursts, the Fred

Astaire dance routine with Gilda Radner on *Saturday Night Live,* the Egyptian moves to go with his hit, "King Tut"—have been made up "as I go along." Steve recalls a comment by Carl Reiner, who directed his movie *The Jerk:* "Your act is a guy who watched other people and said, 'I can do that.'"

It's more than that, of course. By now, the 34-year-old Martin's characters are familiar: the good-looking, well-dressed, all-American jerk who'll do anything for a laugh. The smug Continental man whose opening line to women is: "Was it good for you too?" The hardworking show businessman who's mad at his 102-year-old mother because she asked to borrow $10 (Steve's face twists with disgust) "for some FOOD."

The wild and crazy, banjo-playing "Ramblin' Guy." The orange-juggling, animal-balloon-blowing mix of intellectual and idiot.

Since the early '70s, when Martin—eyes bugged out and mouth tugged wide by his index fingers—leaped into the national consciousness through TV (*The Tonight Show* and *Saturday Night Live*), he's attained a popularity untouched by any other contemporary comic and equal to the biggest rock groups. His three albums have gone gold or platinum, and one earned a Grammy. His "King Tut" record sold a million copies. His book, *Cruel Shoes,* was a bestseller. He's performed in front of audiences of 25,000. He's headlined in Las Vegas. And with *The Jerk,* which grossed $75 million, he's become a movie star.

He has spawned a nation of imitators, from white-suited grown men yelling, "I am a wild and crazy guy!" and "Ex-CUUUSE ME!" to 5-year-olds memorizing entire routines from his albums. A nation, in short, that has watched him and said, "I can do that."

Sure. Anyone can wear a fake arrow-through-the-head and act silly. Anyone who's had a drink, a smoke, a snort, or a visit from Out There can sound spacey. But how did Steve Martin, who after a brief hitch as a hippie (in the late '60s) has given up drinking and drugs, doesn't eat meat, and swims almost every day—how did he get so weird? And make it work for him?

Steve blames college.

He went to Long Beach State in 1964. By that time he had put together a magic act, had learned to play banjo, and had done some acting. In college, he connected comedy to philosophy.

"College totally changed my life," he says. "It changed what I believe and what I think about everything. I majored in philosophy. Something about non sequiturs appealed to me," he says. "In philosophy I started studying logic, and they were talking about cause and effect, and you start to realize, 'Hey! There is no cause and effect! There is no logic. There is no anything!' Then it gets real easy to write this stuff, because all you have to do is twist everything hard—you twist the punch line, you twist the non sequitur so hard away from the thing that set it up, that it's easy . . . and it's thrilling."

Steve majored in philosophy because he thought he might become a professor. "But then I thought, 'I can't give up show business.' I'd studied philosophy and realized the only true value was accomplishment. So I changed my major, transferred [to UCLA], and went into theater."

He began writing comedy essays and caught the attention of Mason Williams, who was looking for young writers to join him on the staff of TV's original *Smothers Brothers Comedy Hour*. But while writing for the Smothers (and, later, others), Steve was putting together his own act.

"I said, 'I'm not going to be political. People hate it, there's nothing you can do about the government, you have no voice.' So I internalized everything. There was no government; it was just a guy who had to distort the world in order to make sense out of it. That was my philosophy.

"And I felt like there'll be a time when people are gonna get sick of this 'love everything.' I think things move in cycles. That's why I can predict and live with even my own demise. Knowing I can come back."

I first saw him in 1972 at the Boarding House nightclub in San Francisco. He was the opening act for various folk, country, and rock bands and was going nowhere slow with his mixed bags of strangeness.

I liked the way he went against the grain. At a time when young people were long-haired, political, and activist, Steve—the clean-cut native of conservative Orange County, California—had cut his hair and was doing nonsense.

I invited him to my Sunday radio show. On mike, he was goofy, quick-witted, and inventive, always looking for the twist, the punch line. Away from a performing situation, he was friendly but quiet, serious, and seemingly distant.

He's much the same today, though more settled. He occupies an expansive, well-planned house in Beverly Hills. The house reflects Steve's intense interest in, of all things, nineteenth-century American art. He is turning one bedroom into a gallery. Still-packed artworks await hanging. The dining room, though still missing chairs, is decorated with several paintings—winter scenes and such—in ornate gold frames.

"Art is so complicated," Steve says. "Beauty is only a part of it. It's from 'Gee, that looks like my grandmother' to 'Will that fit over my sofa?' to 'It really moves me' to 'I like the color blue.' That's why it's so big. If an idiot can like the *Mona Lisa,* and a genius can like it—that's why it's popular."

On weekends he drives to his house in Santa Barbara, 50 miles out of town, where he relaxes by swimming, reading scripts, writing, sometimes calling friends to drop by.

"I like to work with people," he says. "Get a friend over, we'll talk about things. It's such agony to sit there by yourself without a sounding board. You don't know what's funny anymore."

Steve keeps his personal life private. His girlfriend for three years has been singer-actress Bernadette Peters. "We see each other and we don't see anybody else," Steve says flatly. As for having a family someday, he's even flatter. "I'm not partial to having kids. It never even occurs to me." And how does Bernadette feel? "Bernadette and I get along great."

Steve and I are in the dining room of his house in Beverly Hills. He's just had a writing session with Carl Reiner and George Gipe. They're working on a movie called *The Three Faces of Steve* and are secretive about the nature of the film.

He talks about success, its costs and effects. "In my wildest fantasy," he says, "I would think it's impossible for a comedian to draw more than 3,500 people. My envy was for rock stars like Mick Jagger. They'd stand up, and the place would go crazy. I didn't think a comedian could have that."

Steve got it. But with success came restrictions. For one thing, he could no longer ad-lib. "The feeling was that, 'Well, there's 15,000 people out there. This better be good. Better be tight and great.' You just couldn't afford to disappoint these people. Also, the size of those halls doesn't allow for any intimacy, for experiments. My act got so broad. It was really fun, like a big dance for an hour." But, he adds, "you lose the art. You lose the style 'cause it's so grand. It became operatic. At the Boarding House it was funny. In concert it's 'popular.'"

And with success came criticism. Steve sounds philosophical: "When you're small, they're discovering you," he says. "When you're big, they have to explain why you shouldn't be. It's the natural flow of things. I knew it ahead of time. Pretty soon it'll be hip to praise me because everyone will have criticized me.

"The thing that's wrong about reviews is that they try to make you ashamed of your work. And nobody has the right to do that. I mean, we do this out of . . ." Steve suddenly stops then, slowly: "Oh, I can't say why . . ." He begins to chuckle. "I was gonna say 'love,' but I know that's not true. It's almost lust."

Although he's made plenty of money, Steve says he's not in show business just for that.

"The desire to do these things is part ego, part challenge, part the fact that you can do it. It's fear of failure. There's so much involved. It's like I said about art—there's so many reasons to like it." Once Steve compiles enough new material, he'll be back on the boards. "Once you lose that contact with live performing," he says, "you've lost something real important." But—to borrow from one of his best-known bits—he'd like to get small. "I'd like to start from the bottom again. Start at the smallest club, then expand it again. To get that feeling again of . . . funny."

These days, whatever Steve wants, Steve gets. Which is another problem. "The movie studios are lined up," says his longtime friend and manager, Bill McEuen. "We could make any deal we want. We could say, 'How about two guys in a jeep?' and they'd say, 'Great, as long as one of the guys is Steve . . .'" "That's what's so hard about it," adds Steve. "You start questioning—are they just doing it to get a movie, or do they give a damn?"

But the latest breakthrough in Martin's career is different. The lead role in *Pennies from Heaven* is something Martin had to go out and get.

"*Pennies from Heaven* is the biggest challenge of my life," says Steve. "And I've never felt better. I feel alive again."

The MGM movie, to be directed by Herbert Ross (*Play It Again, Sam, The Goodbye Girl, The Turning Point*), is an adaptation of a six-hour BBC production broadcast here on Public Television. Set in England in the 1930s, it is a hybrid of drama and musical, with the main character dancing and lip-synching to popular records of the period.

"I couldn't believe it," says Steve. "I'd sit there and go, 'This is the greatest thing I've ever seen!' I watched it religiously. And then the script falls in my lap. From the first page I'm going, 'I'll do it!'"

But it wasn't quite that simple. The producers had a few other, slightly more seasoned, actors in mind—among them Richard Dreyfuss, Jack Nicholson, and Al Pacino. "I had to earn it," says Steve. "It's a great second [starring] movie. For me, it was like, 'What's your next movie? Is it an inane comedy—a sideways step to nothingness—or an up move, a *Pennies from Heaven*?.'"

Pennies, as Steve tells it, "is about a guy who's a song-sheet salesman in the 1930s. [The story has been reset in the United States, in southern Illinois.] He's got this dream: he wants to go into records. He thinks that's where the big money is. He's real down and out, he's got a wife who's frigid, and he sells these songs and has these fantasies.

"It's just like me when I was a kid: the rock 'n' roll songs told you about life. He had a romantic link with these songs. They're so powerful, so concise, and they give you simple answers to life. So he goes into these reveries. He breaks into songs right in the middle of a heavy dramatic scene—and everybody goes along with him—and when it's over, it goes back like nothing happened."

Steve remembers his own years of dreaming, remembers his manager setting up an office on Sunset Boulevard in the late '60s. "None of us knew what we were doing, and we pretended like we were in the business." He laughs. "But he always believed in me. He said, 'We're gonna do it.' And it all made total sense 'cause we were young and naive and gung-ho. We had great fun. Definitely more fun than now, in terms of having freedom and dreams.

"Now you're forced to make gigantic decisions that affect hundreds of people's lives. It's so weird. You say something offhand, and it becomes law to people around you, and you start to weigh all you say."

"That's why I like tap dancing," Steve says. "It's like playing the banjo. You don't have to answer to anybody. It's up to you; it doesn't affect anybody else. It's just: how good can you get? It's the only goal. How good can you get?" —*Parade,* **November 9, 1980**

Steve Martin may have made it as a comedian who could also dance, juggle, play banjo, and do magic tricks, but he was also an accomplished writer. As noted in the article, he had a bestselling book, *Cruel Shoes,* and was writing screenplays with Carl Reiner. (I believe that the script known as *The Three Faces of Steve* became *All of Me,* in which the soul of a millionairess, played by Lily Tomlin, enters the body of her lawyer, played by Martin.)

In more recent years, he has contributed regularly to *The New Yorker* and has written several successful plays.

I think Steve got his start as a writer by sending letters to *Rolling Stone*. In 1977, I profiled the singer Natalie Cole and opened the story by referring to Martin's routine about being born a "poor black child." One day, the character heard some Lawrence Welk music on the radio, felt that he had finally discovered real music, and decided to become white.

Soon after that piece ran, I received, and the magazine published, the following:

Dear Ben Fong-Torres:

Of course, your mention of my name in the Natalie Cole article is very flattering. However, as you know, I am not seeking every little blurb I can get. An artist has to live on his works, and not that Farrah just happened to call him late one night. You, as a sensationalist writer, probably don't understand that. You would prefer to write about my secret jaunt to Wisconsin on a private jet ($600 per hour) than my latest accomplishments in comedy. To prove my point, not one writer has yet to point out that the phrase "wild and crazy guy" is an anagram for the Egyptian "have a happy day." That's right—you, Fong-Torres; you, Felton—you gobble up comedy and spit out the most important part: the seed! So please, do not use my name, Steve Martin (I think it would be okay to use my real name, Pigeye Jackson), in any of your stories, other than to talk about comedy . . . per se?

—Steve Martin

THE ROLLING STONES

Mick Jagger and Keith Richards

Through 1981, *Parade* magazine kept me busy. I did profiles of Linda Ronstadt, baseball manager Billy Martin, Donna Summer, and James Taylor. I also did a piece on three up-and-coming women musicians who, unfortunately, up and went nowhere.

In June, I got a call from Paul Wasserman, publicist for the Rolling Stones. The Stones were one of the few bands that engaged a publicist for the purpose of keeping the press away. This attitude—or pose—is pretty common these days, but back in the '70s and '80s, it was almost unheard of. But the band didn't need publicity, and, in the aftermath of drug busts, deaths, personnel changes, and a wedding or two, its core members preferred not to bother with being bothered.

So I'm not sure why "Wasso," as he was called, was calling, except that I'd covered the Stones a couple of times while at *Rolling Stone*. Although I thought, and soon confirmed, that *Parade* was not the right home for a piece on this group of latter-day punks, I wound up doing the article for a magazine that was right in my hometown.

Hal Silverman, the editor of *California Living*, part of the big *San Francisco Chronicle/Examiner* package, had been after me to write for him. As a freelancer,

I was still doing mostly national stories. With the Stones tour set to hit the Bay Area (as their tours invariably did), Silverman said he wanted the story. I joined the band for their first date, in late September, at JFK Stadium in Philadelphia, where they played in front of 90,000 fans. Three weeks later, they were in San Francisco, where more than 140,000 people were jammed into the old Candlestick Park. (The Beatles had drawn 25,000 there for what turned out to be their last live concert in August of 1966.) The Stones were only ten or so dates into a 50-concert tour, but Jagger had already—can you imagine this?—stopped talking to the press. Fortunately, we'd had a sit-down in Philadelphia.

Years ago, smug in his richness and his youth, Mick Jagger swore he wouldn't be "leaping about, singing 'Satisfaction' at age 42."

Now, here he is, on the road again, leaping about and singing "Satisfaction" to bigger crowds than ever, for more money than ever. What a difference a payday makes. And so the Rolling Stones, their lead singer now 38, just keep rolling on.

They started 18 years ago, in 1963, playing R&B clubs around London. They broke through the next year, and right away they were the dark, flip side of the Beatles. The Fab Four were cute, precocious, and seemingly innocent. The Stones were ugly, malicious, and clearly dangerous.

And they have survived. They weathered the '60s, which ended for them with the free and ultimately deadly concert in Altamont. They got through the '70s, which started with their unofficial crowning as "the greatest rock 'n' roll band in the world" and the death of original lead guitarist Brian Jones, and ended with lots of questions. Their music seemed to wallow in mid-decade and yet, every three years, they'd go on tour and rev up a storm of interest. Mick got married (in 1971) and seemed to revel in the jet set he used to despise but, onstage, he somehow maintained that nasty-little-boy image.

The Stones survived a serious drug conviction against guitarist Keith Richard and the loss of Brian Jones' replacement, Mick Taylor, and they persevered in the face of New Wave music and attacks by punk rockers that they, the original punks, had become rock 'n' roll dinosaurs. Still, just over a year ago, bass player Bill Wyman began talking about retirement.

So the question was: how long could they go on?

At this moment, the logical answer is: forever. Their recent tour sold out faster than any rock tour before it, even though half the dates were in large football and baseball stadiums with capacities of between 65,000 and 90,000. Additional shows had to be added in several cities. With admissions averaging about $15, the Stones figured to pull in a gross of some $30 million, $10 million more than the business they did three years ago.

And while the Stones have retained many of their original fans, they have also drawn teenagers, kids who weren't even born when the band started up, young fans who were turned on to the Stones by their own parents.

But the fans—their numbers and their age range—tell only part of the story. Newspapers, magazines, radio, and TV took to the Stones as never before. Wherever they went, the papers responded with front-page stories and ran whole series on them—their history, their future, the gossip about where they were staying, eating, and partying.

"The feeling among the media," said Paul Wasserman, the Stones' press agent, "was 'We gotta do something; we can't just ignore it.' There's a gut instinctive feeling that they're the big news."

Why? "Because they're the last survivors of the Golden Era," he said. "They're the last of the big three: Dylan, the Beatles, and the Stones—the three mythical characters of the '60s."

But the Stones were more than myth. The reality is that they helped shape and define and explain many of the social changes of the '60s. They also reflected the decadence, the self-love, the political frustrations and ennui, and the chi-chi rituals that prevailed in the '70s. And in the '80s, they've become legitimate news to the people who now decide what goes into the newspapers and onto the airwaves, people in their thirties, men and women who were raised on rock—and the Stones.

This, of course, is personal theorizing. For the Word, one must go to the source, the head Stone.

Jagger is not only the lead singer of the Rolling Stones; he's their manager as well. It's Mick who set up this tour, decided where to play, and how much to charge. The bad boy of old has become, of all things, respectable. In Philadelphia, he accepted a Liberty Bell on behalf of the band. In Boston, the mayor invited them to play a free concert downtown (the Stones declined). And in San Francisco, a properly suited Jagger rode a cable car with Mayor Dianne Feinstein and plugged her fund drive to save the city's moving landmarks.

Wherever he went, Jagger was a diplomat. For each performance, he wore an outfit to identify with the area he was visiting. In Philadelphia, he wore a Flyers jersey; in San Francisco, he paid tribute to the just-vanquished A's by wearing the Oakland team's uniform, with "Jagger" stitched on the back. It was Jagger the rock star/pro jock, the aging Brit as all-American kid, fantasies in full display.

When the Stones were in San Francisco for the Candlestick Park shows and a week of R & R, Jagger did not talk to the press. In fact, he had an altercation with a radio reporter who walked up to him in a restaurant with tape recorder rolling. But in Philadelphia, after the first concert of the tour, he sat for an interview in his suite at the Barclay Hotel. Scattered about his room were a few items—a running outfit, a racquetball racquet, and a memo from an aide reminding Jagger of things to do, including "exercise—outdoors if possible." Jagger was obviously following orders. He looked ridiculously healthy and as skinny as ever.

What are you, part Chinese? How do you keep looking so young?

Well, I think it's what you're born with. I was raised to be healthy. I bucked against it a lot in my teens and in my early twenties—but then you come back to it.

The last time around, in 1978, the press seemed interested in three subjects: Keith Richards' bust, your reaction to punk rock, and—

You can see how different this tour is; they're not interested in any of that.

This time, the hook seems to be, "Are the Stones too old to rock? Is this the last time around?"

That's an old perennial. I think it's we're so heavy on it last time, and then we do another one, so obviously they can't make such fools of themselves, just to keep hopping on it. It's a dead dog.

The tour is going to gross about $30 million. Has this passed . . .

Yeah, everyone's wildest dreams! We didn't expect to do this kind of business.

Part of that is because you're doing so many outdoor shows this time, which helps meet the demand for tickets and makes you more money, but you've said before that you didn't like doing the stadium shows.

I have no misconceptions that I can play to a stadium in the same way we can play to an arena. I think we're running on 15 percent efficiency in the stadium. I don't think we're pleasing the people enough.

Of course, for a lot of people, it's not so much the concert as the experience of being there, in the same place as the Stones.

With their friends, in their town or the surrounding areas, but yes, to be in the same place, and I think the music's incidental a lot. It could be us or several others.

Maybe . . .

It helps to be us. But c'mon, we're only an excuse; you might as well use us as anybody for them to have a good time. 'Cause they can't see from the back. I do the same thing. Those afternoons are quite like going to see a football game.

From today's show it is clear you are having as much fun onstage as ever.

Yeah. You can fool around and no one minds. And on an outdoor show in the afternoon with the sun shining, no one wants to hear about your problems. In other words, they don't want to hear you do a serious song too much.

In today's show, you played quite a few oldies.

Outdoor shows are different. You've got a pretty large cross section of people that like the Rolling Stones because they've been around for a long time, and you don't want to pander to them; you want to be able to play new stuff at least half of the show. But yes, it's basically hits, uptempos and a few ballads, whereas indoors you can stretch yourself a bit more and play nearly all new stuff.

A lot of younger Stones fans say they first heard you through their parents. Which is quite a distance from the '60s, when a lot of the appeal of the Stones was from how you outraged parents.

I can't see how they can be outraged about the Rolling Stones. No parent in the mid-thirties age group is outraged. Maybe we *should* outrage them.

But, as you yourself have said, there's nothing new any more in rock 'n' roll, it's all "recycled past."

The thing about rock 'n' roll . . . the influence of rock 'n' roll is all-pervasive in all other forms of music, as the other forms of music are in rock 'n' roll. You've got these intertwinings, but the real rock 'n' roll and excitement—if you have a new artist with a "new sound," it tends to be what the old sound was. What people like is purity. Rock 'n' roll is a traditional form now.

But if the music's just going around in circles, where does your own continuing interest in it come from? Is it just what you do, or is there still something that the music does?

Well, I think that I still live in hope that rock 'n' roll will turn a corner and doesn't just keep reverting. I think it will eventually. Hope I'll be around when it does.

You sound like a serious musician, which kind of contradicts the image that you have in the gossip columns.

But I certainly don't invite it. I don't do talk shows. I don't do *People* magazine. I don't try and get on the gossip circuit.

But you're still on it . . .

Well, you know, that's how it goes. It started in England when I was very young, when I was 20. It took me one year to get to that elevated level without actually wanting it. And it took me 20 years to do it in America! But. . . I guess after a tour it tends to disappear.

Even as we were talking, though, there were knots of people ten floors below, waiting for him or another Stone—but preferably him—to show his face.

When he finally left the hotel for a late dinner, he was rushed by fans, some of whom got past security guards and grabbed at his hair, at his scarf, at any possible souvenir. When he returned, at three in the morning, they were still there. Mick says the fans don't bother him. "I don't think they want a piece of me." And the fans, at the stadiums and at the hotels, served to remind him that, in his nineteenth year with the company, business is still very good.

—*California Living,* January 10, 1982

In 1981, when Jagger and company were heading towards rock 'n' roll retirement age, Britney Spears was born. So was Justin Timberlake, along with Beyonce Knowles and Kelly Rowland of Destiny's Child. Today, they are established music stars. Not rock stars, since—at least according to the media, including almighty radio—rock is dead. Still, the Stones roll on, doing the occasional tour, enduring jokes about their age from headline writers and late-night TV comics, and pulling in ever more money for a retirement that will never come.

In late 2005 and 2006, with Jagger having reached age 62, they were still at it, setting off on the "Bigger Bang Tour" and rocking through auditoriums and ballparks in 32 cities. And that was just the 2005 segment of the tour. Once again—the jokes, the onstage spectacles, the sellout crowds, and the rousing sing-alongs to "Brown Sugar" and "Satisfaction."

What's changed?

In 1981, it cost a hefty $15 to get into the ballpark. In 2006, in Boston and New York, tickets ranged from $75 to $475.

But, hey, when the guys do their "This Could Be the Last Time Tour" in 2020, $475 will be a stone *bargain.*

PAUL MCCARTNEY

"WHAT I MEANT WAS . . ."

While the Stones had no particular use for press, Paul McCartney was a master media manipulator. As I said in *Not Fade Away*, introducing my on-tour-with-Wings piece: "I came to see him as a good deal more than the artist formerly known as 'the cute Beatle.' He was also, quite possibly, the smartest, most savvy of the Fab Four—at least when it came to marketing himself. He was not only unfailingly agreeable and cooperative in interviews, but he also knew how to switch gears, depending on who his visitor was and which publication he or she was representing."

"And," I wrote in notes to myself before writing the article, "even with only an hour per interview, he seems to give it his all, making one think he's the only thing on his mind. He's a charmer from way back. It's the Beatles press-conference mastery all grown up."

None other than John Lennon, talking with Jann Wenner about how McCartney beat him to the punch announcing the dissolution of the Beatles, noted: "He's a good PR man, that's all. He's about the best in the world, probably. He really does a job."

McCartney's smoothness was exactly why I was inspired to take a specific angle for this piece for *Parade* magazine. *Parade* isn't interested in typical profiles of celebrities. Its editors wanted some kind of angle that would jus-tify their carrying a story most likely being published in any number of other newspapers and magazines.

My angle was simple. Paul McCartney, this savvy puppeteer of the press, had screwed up. Big time. And he might just want to right himself. Where bet-ter than in the largest circulation magazine in America?

One never forgets the loss of a loved one. But when Paul McCartney thinks about John Lennon, shot down in New York City on December 8, 1980, there's more than the pain of his death and of the way he died. McCartney also carries the memory of the way he himself came across on television after hearing the news. Standing outside a recording studio in London, he chewed gum and muttered to a reporter, "It's a drag, innit?"

Later, off camera, he'd issue a formal statement about how John would be remembered "for his unique contribution to art, music, and world peace." But most television producers chose to run only McCartney's gum-chewing shrug of a eulogy: "It's a drag, innit?"

For more than a year afterward, McCartney chose to avoid public state-ments and work on his album for Columbia Records, *Tug of War*. When it came out, it included a sad, touching song, "Here Today," clearly sung to Lennon.

In Los Angeles this spring to work on some recordings with Michael Jackson, Paul took time out for an interview.

I recalled a film clip of the Beatles. The camera pans from one to the next. Third in line is John, who suddenly breaks out in a spasmodic array of funny faces. Then the camera moves to Paul and captures him perfectly: the good boy, slightly embarrassed by his clown of an older brother. And he just smiles his shy, hope-you-like-me smile.

At 41, McCartney himself is finally beginning to look like an older brother. The famous mop top is flecked with gray, and age has drawn a few lines around his eyes. But he's much like his younger self, as eager to please as ever.

"In truth," he said, "all I was doing was saying whatever came to my head. If I'd have had a good answer, then I would've been faking it. That wasn't a day to have a good answer.

"A lot of people have said," McCartney went on, sounding somewhat put off, 'Well, that's some comment, isn't it? Is that all you've got to say?' They're sitting at home in front of the telly, saying, 'Why didn't he have something better to say?' Or, 'Why wasn't he more emotional? If he'd just broken down and cried, it would've been great. We would've loved it. But here he is. Cynical beast.'" McCartney bit off the last word.

"There are some people that're just gifted in being able to say all the right things at all the right times," he added. "I'm no good on that kind of stuff. People expect, because you're a star, that you not have normal reactions, that you know 'the game.' But if I'd had that down that day, I wouldn't like me.

"I would've loved to be able to put it into words. I couldn't. I was trying to get out of the studio . . . big crowd. It wasn't enough that John's thing had happened. This was all happening as well, and I just felt incapable. And what I meant was, 'Isn't it one unholy goddamned endless drag?'

"I used to think of myself as a writer. Never wrote anything but used to smoke a pipe, top of the bus, and think I was Dylan Thomas. See someone: 'The old man, with his ragged coat.' Boring, but it was fun. My imagination works like that. I get plenty out of nothing."

And, in fact, he's getting a movie out of idle thoughts he's had while commuting. "I wrote a film script," he announced, "like everybody else in the world. It's basically a day in my life, and there's this sort of light drama thing going on. I just wrote it longhand in the car coming to and from the studio each day. It's very light. I wouldn't put it up with Shakespeare quite yet."

The movie is now in production in London under the title *Give My Regards to Broad Street*. It stars Paul, Linda McCartney, Ringo Starr, and actress Barbara Bach (Mrs. Starr).

Paul has stayed close to Ringo since the Beatles; he said he has rarely seen George Harrison. He recalled how, after the group disbanded, he took a "dip." "I never thought I was gonna feel it," he said. "But there was this huge kind of vacuum. The Beatles were a security blanket, all those mates of mine--even though it was tough sometimes. But it came back to the fact that, when we got back in the studio, you were with the Beatles, and that was a very secure feeling. If I wanted someone to comment on a song, I could run it past John Lennon, who to me was the best."

Paul swears he was writing just another song that day a few weeks after Lennon's death. "I was just sitting with the guitar. I didn't really have it in my mind to write a song about John, but I found myself thinking about him. And it flowed easily. And it was moving for me, because I was allowing myself to think about it, talk out loud about it."

"Have you gotten over it yet?" I asked.

Paul wrapped his arms around himself. "No. I can't believe it, still. It's a weird one. Still feels as though he's here, you know. But he sort of is, in a way."

—*Parade*, June 26, 1983

MICHAEL NESMITH

SHAKES THE MONKEE FROM HIS BACK

I**have no idea** how many articles I've written. I suppose I could go through files, boxes of old magazines, and tax returns and come up with an estimate. The only time I kept any kind of list was at *Rolling Stone,* and even that accounting is unreliable, since we often wrote stories without bylines—the better to avoid the impression that only a couple of us were writing the entire music or news section. At the end of my 11-year run there, I'd published about 400 pieces. Add articles from 20 years of writing for magazines and newspapers here, there, and everywhere, and a total of 1,000 articles is likely a conservative guess.

All of which is to say that I've screwed up assignments a few times. Since they're such painful, guilt-ridden experiences—at least for me—I can count them on one hand. Well, maybe three. Let's see: the Staples Singers. I loved them; visited them; never wrote the story for *Rolling Stone.* Simply a matter of other assignments getting in the way, and topicality vanishing. Ditto Dusty Springfield, although more about that in a future chapter. In post-*Rolling Stone* years, I had an assignment about superstar chefs—this would be for *GQ,* I believe—and did a ton of research, but never delivered. One chef was killed; another one or two had their restaurants closed; I could never keep up. And then there was the assignment from *Esquire* for a profile of Michael Nesmith.

I went to Carmel for an interview that seemed never to end. Nesmith was fascinating on levels far beyond his stint with the Monkees. He knew it and wanted to make sure I knew it. One interview led to another; one trip led to another. There was always another story, another detail, another person I ought to talk with about him. The story grew to gargantuan proportions and, ultimately, missed the *Esquire* deadline. I shelved it for a few months, until I began writing a music column for *GQ*. Suddenly, it had a new home—that is, if I could pare it down from somewhere in the 10,000-word range to a tidy 2,500 or so.

I'm not sure how tidy this is, and I'm glad "the Nez," as he was known, wasn't around to suffer every cut. But *GQ* was happy to get a column with all expenses paid by *Esquire,* and I was happy to get Nesmith's amazing story—or a decent slice of it, anyway—into print.

───────

Mike's the quiet Monkee with the drawly, groovy voice. He's cool without trying to be. And yet, at a minute's notice, he'll do the most insane things you've ever heard of . . . like putting tinfoil on the ceiling of his dressing room.

Mike enjoys being with people who make sense, because he makes sense. There's a way-out side to Mike, too. . . . Above all, being around Mike Nesmith is an experience you'll never forget as long as you live.

—Tiger Beat's Official Monkee Spectacular #1, 1967

The beard is just a little too neat. Otherwise, Michael Nesmith, standing at Sunset and Vine in his newspaper hawker's cap, loud tie over an equally vocal plaid shirt, and shiny old slacks, makes a pretty convincing derelict/street musician. His holey shoes are wrapped in rags, and through the open fingers of his gloves he attempts, with no apparent finesse, to play a song on his recorder.

Nesmith is filming a TV skit for NBC in front of the West Coast headquarters of its parent company, RCA. You'll excuse the irony of the location. After all, for the past decade he's been trying to escape the shadow of that building, the spot where the Monkees did much of their recording.

The skit is part of *Michael Nesmith in Television Parts* and is an offshoot of *Michael Nesmith in Elephant Parts,* an hour-long mix of comedy and pop videos that won him a Grammy in 1982 and a phone call from Brandon Tartikoff, president of NBC Entertainment. *Television Parts* will attempt, through short video clips, to do for comedians what MTV has done for rock groups. Eight episodes are scheduled to run on NBC this fall, beginning in mid-season.

Tartikoff's call should have been no surprise, for these days the 41-year-old Nesmith is known primarily as a video guru, a pioneer of the MTV generation. He runs his own home video distribution company, Pacific Arts Corp., near his home in Carmel, California, and he also recently produced two movies.

But if the turnaround is now complete, it wasn't easy. For years after the end of the TV series, the Monkees tag was a curse. Davy, Micky, Mike, and Peter—oh yeah, those zany guys who played instruments that weren't plugged in. Life, post-Monkees, began for Nesmith in 1977, when he made a short film illustrating his song "Rio." Suddenly, music videos took a giant leap. Nesmith mixed surrealism, comedy, acting, and flights of fancy with rock 'n' roll. In the "Rio" video, he sang, danced, and flew into the heavens with three women on his back.

After a few more videos, Nesmith did a series of clips for Warner Amex's cable TV service for kids, Nickelodeon. Called *Popclips,* it mixed esoteric clips from all over and was hosted by adventurous, unknown comics. It wasn't long before *Popclips,* watered down, was reborn as MTV.

If he is an innovator, a visionary, he certainly doesn't act the part. With steady brown eyes and a soft voice that carries an undercurrent of his Texas roots, he comes off serious, shy, even a little distant. He may best be introduced with a random batch of facts: He hates parties, and has told his kids that he doesn't celebrate birthdays. He knows he strikes people as arrogant. His acceptance speech at the recent American Video Awards, where he was named to their Hall of Fame, raised some hackles when he began by calling the program "a thin disguise for a television show."

He is a rich man, and on a whim has grabbed some friends, hopped into his Learjet, and had dinner in New Orleans. But even when he was broke, as he was ten years ago, he could—and did—spend his last three hundred dollars on a trip from Los Angeles to San Francisco for dinner at Ernie's.

"He's the truest artist I've met," says his wife of ten years, Kathryn. "He has a strong sense of what art is, and he's true to that. So he seems standoffish and cold. He's not interested in the bullshit."

Details of Nesmith's past are pried, word by word, out of him. His parents split when he was a kid, and he had a "poor, miserable" childhood with a mother he remembers as "a tortured woman." His escape was music: rock 'n' roll, R&B country, folk. He was amazed by the idea of live performance. While in the Air Force, he watched Hoyt Axton onstage. "He sat up there with a guitar and all of those people were nourished by it, and he was, too," Nesmith remembers. "It was a very high experience. I remember coming away absolutely convinced I was going to get a guitar."

Those who knew him at San Antonio College remember him as the shy guy who carried his guitar around campus. It was at San Antonio that he met his first wife, Phyllis Barbour, and his first singing partner, John Kuehne, a bass player. With vague notions of cracking the music biz, they all moved to Los Angeles, where they did odd jobs, cut a few singles, and hung out at the Troubadour, doing hootenannies. Then Nesmith spotted an ad in *Variety:*

MADNESS!!
Auditions
Folk & Roll Musicians-Singers
for acting roles in new TV series.
Running parts for 4 insane boys, age 17-21.
Want spirited Ben Franks types.

Nesmith and Kuehne weren't actors, they'd both seen the last of age 21 a few years before, and they were more given to folkie blazers than the mock Carnaby Street threads worn by the kids who hung out at Ben Franks on Sunset Strip.

So Nesmith tried harder. "He was always an immaculate dresser," Kuehne remembers, "but on the day of the audition he had on a blue-jean jacket and carried a harmonica rack. On the way, he ran into a store and grabbed a wool hat. At the office, we were filling out a questionnaire, and I looked over at his, and where you put down your experience, he had written 'LIFE' and drawn a diagonal line through the rest of the sheet. I said, 'You can't do that.' But the producers took a look and said, 'This is the guy for us.'"

The Monkees were an immediate smash. They spawned fan clubs, magazines, books, and the usual assortment of teen memorabilia. They sold millions of records and caused riots. And yet they were never perceived as the real thing: if the Beatles were the Fab Four, the Monkees were the fabricated four.

The group, after all, sang songs written by pop composers and played by session musicians. Nesmith—by then famous for his wool hat—was said to be the only real musician among the Monkees. The acclaim was hardly consolation.

"It bothered him very deeply that he couldn't express himself musically," says former Monkees drummer Micky Dolenz, now a TV, film, and theatrical director in London. "Peter [Tork] and I were happy to be actors, but there was an ongoing battle with the producers to let us do our own music. It was probably one of the main reasons we broke up."

Nesmith never thought of the Monkees as a group. "*The Monkees,*" he says firmly, "was a TV series that was hoped would mirror the times. The four of us were hired as actors. And the show fell right onto the horns of a dilemma. It was perceived not as a TV show but as a rock 'n' roll group that had landed a series. We weren't a rock 'n' roll band, but as the thing began to twist around, it became, 'Here are these guys who're nothing but a TV show coming on like they're a group.'

"The fact that the press expected us to make serious music was strange. It was like condemning a Chevrolet station wagon for not performing well at the Indianapolis 500."

After the group disbanded in 1969 (a year after Tork's departure), Davy Jones and Dolenz tried a couple of times to rekindle the spark, but neither a tour of the US in 1975 (with Tommy Boyce and Bobby Hart in place of Tork and Nesmith) nor a tour of the Far East a couple of years ago brought back Monkeemania.

Dolenz, 39, the lead vocalist on many of the Monkees' hits, says he's lost the desire to perform.

"I used to hear from David every couple of years about a reunion of the whole band, but it's never gone beyond that." In London, where he has lived since 1977, Dolenz has directed children's shows for TV and staged a theatrical adaptation of *Bugsy Malone*.

Davy Jones, the little one, has returned to his pre-Monkee love: jockeying. He's training for the 1985 Grand National on his farm in Sussex. Now 37, he has a wife and daughter and works on stage and television in England. But his memories die hard, and he is at work on a book, *They Made a Monkee Out of Me*. It won't be bitter, he has said. "When little kids ask me, 'You weren't in the Monkees, were you?' you can't say, 'Piss off, I don't want to talk about the Monkees.'"

Peter Tork, 39, has had the toughest time of the former Monkees. For him the '70s were ridden with problems—drugs, alcohol, and an arrest for hashish possession. For a time, he had to find work as a singing waiter. He says he quit drinking in mid-1980, quit drugs the next year. Now living in Venice, California, he leads a band, the Peter Tork Project, that features the occasional oldie. "People come because I used to be a Monkee," he recently told *BAM* magazine.

After the Monkees, Nesmith went back to country music. In a series of albums on RCA, he made some of the finest music never heard. He was among the first to explore what would become "country rock," and even had a Top 30 song, 1970's "Joanne." (Linda Ronstadt, an old friend whose first hit was the Nesmith-penned "Different Drum," remembers predicting, long before "Joanne," "If you ever do a song where you crack into falsetto, you'll have a hit.")

For a long time, though, the Monkees stigma stuck. Rock critics refused to take him seriously. Onstage those days in the early '70s, Nesmith was a combination of racked nerves and defensive pomposity. Then, through lavish spending and poor tax planning, he lost most of the million dollars he'd made with the Monkees. At about the same time, his first marriage broke up after ten years.

In late 1976 Nesmith came out with a conventional pop album; when his label in Europe called and asked for a promo to go along with "Rio," Nesmith produced one and, in the process, found a new career. Ever since he first saw the Pong video game in 1972, Nesmith had been thinking of new applications for TV. "That game," he says, "represented a fundamental change of thinking in the way people viewed television sets." He knew about the developing technology that would ultimately place videocassettes and discs in millions of homes. With an earlier concept album, *The Prison,* he had experimented mixing printed visuals with music.

By 1980 he was in such demand as a video producer that he closed down the record company he had set up. Brashly predicting that vinyl audio-only records would be obsolete by the early '90s, he turned his attention fully to video and sank most of his money into *Elephant Parts.* "It wasn't a very good risk, but it was just a love of the form and a trust in the inevitability of good."

Then his mother died and made him a millionaire again. In 1951, after toiling for years as a secretary, Bette Nesmith Graham came up with one of those ideas: something she called first Mistake Out, then Liquid Paper. In 1979, two years before she died, she sold her company to Gillette for more than $47 million.

Nesmith inherited about $25 million; he earns a royalty on every bottle of Liquid Paper sold. He is low-key about his fortune, still questions checks and budgets. But he's also no Scrooge. He owns several pieces of property in Carmel, including a house on woodsy Jack's Peak with Reggie Jackson as a neighbor, and has invested heavily in a $42-million luxury condo in the Gulf of Texas. He also expresses his lifelong love of cars with a Porsche, two Mercedes, and a few toys, such as a BMW R 100 RT motorcycle and the Class 8 off-road race truck in which he occasionally roars through Baja California.

One evening in Carmel, Nesmith is test-driving a Mercedes 500 SEL. He races up the hills overlooking Seaside. "I like the fact that it's bad," he says. "Bad spelled with three a's."

The salesman offers to let him have the car for the night, and he drives to nearby Monterey for dinner.

"My life," Nesmith says, "is no different than it was before I had money. Sure, the usual response is, 'Oh, come on, man, you've got a Learjet, you're out there looking at this $53,000 car, don't tell me your life hasn't changed.' But all that is the same as going out and being thrilled at getting a set of new towels, and having someone swing by and take you to work instead of having to ride the bus. I have the same balance of payments that I had, except now there's six more zeroes on the end of the numbers. That's all that's happened."

Oh, come on, man . . .

Nesmith pushes on: "You might be able to go and satisfy some temporary desires, but you get no peace of mind. There's no permanent satisfaction or joy anywhere in it. You can't buy class; you can't buy appreciation of beauty; you can't buy a closeness to God or your fellow man. It's not for sale. There is no wisdom shop."

Later, at home, Nesmith sits with his feet up on an ottoman. He sips tea and continues on the subject of getting rich quick. "One thing I was frightened of was that somehow, something would come over me and I would just sit and not do anything. I could sit back and relax, race cars and fly airplanes . . . and that worried me. I felt that would be a type of death. I'd no longer be contributing."

Nesmith has used his wealth to buy freedom. He can make his own movies, as he did with a 1983 action feature called *Timerider* and last spring's *Repo Man.* Or he can choose to step back into something he's avoided since the Monkees: prime-time TV.

"I think Brandon Tartikoff is willing to explore some new types of programming," says Nesmith of the NBC wunderkind. "I think prime-time television is ready to really rethink itself."

Television Parts is a series of comedy clips, some of which Nesmith performs in. The show features Martin Mull, Gary Shandling, Jim Stafford, and the Funny Boys. "It could be the new *Laugh-In,*" Tartikoff said recently. "Every teenager in America will watch it. Nesmith is so good. It's great to be in the presence of people to whom you say, 'How do you do that?' as opposed to most people, to whom you say, 'Here's how you should have done it.' "

Next, Nesmith says, he wants to do what he calls "special-event cinema," a motion picture taken one step further—something like his long-gestating *Video Ranch.* Nesmith puts on a tape of a few new songs that he envisions in *Video Ranch.* There is a funny one, driven by a pulsing beat and campy native chanting, à la King Kong movies, that is about a Tahitian condo; and there is a lilting number, "I'll Remember You," a thank you to Fred and Ginger and to John, Paul, George, and Ringo.

To the obvious question, he responds: "I wrote that before John died. It was a way of communicating with John across the country. I just wanted to say 'Hello, how are you, I'm out here, things are great.'

"I'd spent four or five days with him in London when he was doing *Sgt. Pepper's,* and there was an odd camaraderie between us. He really understood that ours was a television show, that we weren't a group. But we were caught up in the same sort of foment. In his case it was a serious respect. In my case it was just media hype, yet there wasn't any difference."

In the hush of late-night Carmel, he is thinking about inspirations.

Like Walt Disney. Someday, he says, "we're gonna realize what an extraordinary individual this guy was and what an incredible contribution he made. His politics were from some other planet. But what he developed, the enchanted land, was an incredible gift to us. His ability to paint these wonderful worlds very much formulated some of my objectives as an artist—which is to provide a place for people to go. A window into another world.

"If I could do it like Disney, then I would begin to feel very good."

Did you know that Mike . . .
says his motto is, "If there's no wind, row!"
　　　　—Tiger Beat's Monkee Spectacular

—GQ, August 1984

GROUPIES OF THE '80S

STILL GRABBIN' FOR THE STARS

The G.T.O.s, Girls Together Outrageously

few years into freelancing, I began writing for the *San Francisco Chronicle* on a regular basis, contributing mostly feature articles on a wide range of subjects. Understandably, I got a number of assignments that took advantage of my time at *Rolling Stone.*

Here's a piece about groupies, a subject *Rolling Stone* first took on in 1969. Here in 1984, had that much changed? Of course not; not even with the advent of the AIDS crisis. The article makes use of interviews with current musicians and fans. But there was no way I couldn't make use of a trove of letters I'd received a few years before from Cynthia Bowman, who'd been my assistant at *Rolling Stone* before she left to become a publicist for Jefferson Starship.

For no reason that either she or I can remember, she gave me a sack of letters one day, letters that Spencer Dryden, the drummer with Jefferson Airplane in its peak years, had received from women he'd, er, known from his tours with the band. Perhaps Dryden had married and given Bowman the letters to hide; perhaps Bowman gave me the letters for a possible book about the Airplane, about Dryden, or about groupies. All I do know is that when Dryden agreed to be interviewed, I returned the letters to him, and, with him looking them over, they helped to frame the story.

Sweet Spencer,

So many feelings I have experienced with you that you have become a part of me. The other day, from out of a heavy, lifeless mood, I discovered a great new feeling—experience . . . I love you. There is a simple need to stand by you and feel the wind from the stars.   *Always, Judi*

P.S. Burn this letter.

They are in shoeboxes, paper sacks, and accordion files. Some of them are scattered among other papers in a cardboard box in the laundry room. They are memories, on paper, of the groupies in the long, lustful life of Spencer Dryden, drummer with Jefferson Airplane, the New Riders of the Purple Sage and, now, the Dinosaurs.

"These letters," he says, spreading a short stack over the kitchen table at his house in Marin County, "are from groupies I had affairs with all over the country."

Jefferson Airplane in its '60s heyday enjoyed not only spectacular commercial success, but a vast array of willing young women backstage at every concert and in the lobby at every hotel.

"Most of my real wild days," says Dryden, "were with the New Riders. In the Airplane, I was mostly with Grace [Slick], and there were things going on, but with New Riders there was even more 'cause I was the guy from the Airplane. 'He's different, so let's get him.' And I'd be interested. I had about ten years of groupies. Just too many opportunities presented themselves."

Ah, groupies. They rose as such a phenomenon in the late '60s that they warranted their own book and documentary album. Various of them became famous—the Plaster Casters, who as their name implies, made plaster molds of the genitalia of rock stars; the G.T.O.s, or "Girls Together Outrageously," sponsored by Frank Zappa as a fledgling performance unit.

"It's the spotlight," Dryden says, "like the moth attracted to the flame." As Sandy Einstein at Journey's management company puts it, "As long as there are performers and people that enjoy them, there'll be groupies. Women's liberation? I don't see it at Journey shows. You still see the girls."

"We have a chauvinistic, crotch-rock attitude toward women," says Nikki Sixx of Motley Crue. "We have nothing against women's rights. It's just a male-dominated world and we are dominant males."

Sorry, liberated women: liberated and mostly young, female rock fans willing to give their all for a moment of glory are as much a part of the scene as they were in the days of Jimi Hendrix and a younger Mick Jagger.

If anything, says Sheila Rene, longtime Bay Area rock writer, "the economy is bringing out more groupies than ever. Ticket prices are so high, a girl's got to work awfully hard to buy tickets. One way to get in free is to meet someone in the road crew. Roadies check out the girls for the groups. There's a backstage pass many groups give out that's just for the groupies. And the economy has made it so that bands can't travel so much with women. So there's groupies in every town, more than ever.

"Groupies never died down," she concludes. "The press just stopped writing about it."

And most musicians would just as soon groupies never go away. After all, what is rock 'n' roll if not electric, sexual energy? There are artists who are sincere when they say the music comes first. But there are plenty with other priorities. "I'm definitely attracted to the business for the ladies and parties," Eddie Money declares. "The money comes last."

Eddie Murphy started doing comedy at age 16, but before that, he says, "I had a band. I couldn't sing, but you didn't get no girls by telling jokes."

Frank Zappa, founding father of the Mothers of Invention, says groupies helped his band's music. "It's only when they weren't there that you had guys grumbling. It's that little present at the end of the night that has made rock 'n' roll the greatest art form that America has to offer."

Women rockers also draw groupies, but female musicians generally seem to have less interest in casual sex than their male counterparts.

"When I've experienced a guy who wants to f—," says Debora Iyall, lead singer with the New Wave band Romeo Void, "it's like he's trying to have a claim to fame. That turns me off."

"I see a lot of women go after guys at shows," says Sandy Sledge, drummer with the all-women heavy-metal band Rude Girl, "but that's the guys' aim, to get a girl. Our aim is to say things with our music."

"I don't pay attention to groupies," Rude Girl's lead singer "Leather" declares. "I don't let people mooch off me. Groupies who want to f—, or be seen with me, they don't have anything to offer me."

Women rockers often intimidate male groupies. "We're pretty scary-looking," says Susan Kuchinskas of Boy Trouble, an all-women rock band of primarily lesbians. "We're heavy and mean. And we're probably not that receptive to groupies. We're not into cheap, casual sex. And the fact is that women tend to be more serious about sex, love, and intimacy." Iyall says her groupies aren't even interested in sex. "They usually want to talk to me about their lives. They bring stuff they wrote. With punks, it's like a beatnik-type thing. 'Let's buy a bottle of wine, run around the streets, and talk.'" What about the guys in the band? Iyall laughs. The answer is as old-wave as can be: "Oh, yeah," she says. "Lots of girls like to hang around, and on the road, usually at the beginning, when people are feeling their oats. Like, we share rooms on the road, and I've wound up sleeping on the floor."

"People, men and women, are going after the same thing," says Linda Donahoo, Boy Trouble's guitarist. They have different ways of going after it, though. Women don't ask you right off. More men come out with, 'Hey, let's go party.' With women, there's usually a little conversation. Nine out of ten of the offensive ones would be men."

Men, she says, "are real interested in women who play music. They're interested in that fact, and in sex."

As for her response to come-ons: "I don't want quick sex with a groupie," she says, then notes with a laugh: "It depends how drunk I am."

Donahoo says there are two couples within the band, "but we do what we want. I'm primarily gay, but when I'm drunk . . ."

And what happens when a male pursuer learns she's primarily gay? "Most of them are cool," she says. "In San Francisco they're used to it."

Despite the large gay population in this area, there aren't many openly gay male musicians in mainstream bands. "Every band's got their queen," says Bill Spooner, guitarist with the Tubes. He won't name names, but says he knows of "at least two bisexuals" in his own band.

But most of Spooner's memories, dating to the beginnings of the Tubes in 1972, are of heterosexual romps. "Oh, we were perverted and decadent," he says with a lilt in his voice. Not that those days are in the past.

"Today's groupies are a lot more sophisticated," he says. "They're into the music. And we've always drawn more artistic and intellectual groupies."

But the bottom line is the same: "We take them to their houses and we debauch. It brings back your spirit of youth."

BECOMING ALMOST FAMOUS

Dear Spencer,

Fuzzy is writing this for me, becuz I've got a very bad case of poison ivy on my right hand.

You don't have to worry about telling Billy that I'm carrying his child. I miscarried. It's for the best I know, but you'll never know how much I wanted that baby. I truly do love Billy and that baby would have been a part of him that I could have cherished for eternity. Now I have nothing but memories.

Well, how's life treatin' you?

Take good care of all your ('Portland Women') girls. (Smile.)

Love & Peace,
Paula

Spencer Dryden's girlfriend is 33, with the quaint but real name of Layla. She prides herself on being, as she says, Dryden's first non-groupie mate.

With Dryden momentarily out of earshot, Layla Sarakalo expresses concern about what an overdose of groupies can do to a person. "The psychology of it—it's devastating. I wonder how long it'll be before this person can be human again.

"You're wanted just 'cause you're a body up there. It's so twisted. And he had hundreds of women. They have no equation of love and pleasure. It's sex equals god knows what. And he cannot relate on the level of love. It freaked me out for a while."

Spencer, back in the room, says he doesn't feel guilty about his past life. "The early '70s brought the 'Me' philosophy to the fore: 'Let it all hang out,' 'Anything goes,' which became a savior to anybody who was burning the candle at both ends," he says. "I read it in a book: 'Don't feel guilty.'"

He looks at the stack of groupie setters. One of them, from a woman in Marin County, includes a jagged shard of mirror that she picked off the street because it reminded her of Dryden. "A month ago I couldn't even spell vegetable," she writes. "Now I are one."

"Sometimes," Spencer is saying, "I read those letters. Some of them are from people who got hurt, and I start thinking . . ." He cuts himself short, but not before admitting: "If I did that I might as well call it quits. If I thought about everybody I'd tromped on . . ." He looks a little pleading. "I wanted to be gentle."

Among the letters Dryden reveals is a bitter farewell from one of his three former wives. She wrote it shortly after discovering Dryden's "black book." She began by copying down some 22 names, addresses, and phone numbers of groupies.

Then she wrote: "There's really nothing left for us. Memories, but mostly a lot of emptiness . . . from too much loneliness and lying and spending nights wondering if you'd come home at all even if you were in town." Her sign-off: "Here's to your booze, your broads, and may you do it till your d— drops off."

Dryden sighs. "There were about 175 names in my black book when she found it." The action died down, he says, after he switched from drummer to manager of the New Riders. But now that he's playing again with the Dinosaurs, a band comprised of alumni of various '60s San Francisco groups, he's seeing those backstage scenes again. "There are four girls who come around, and they're pretty—constant."

But, at age 46, he says he's no longer interested in groupies. "I've had some of these 17-, 18-year-old girls, and I feel like a father figure. I'm just not attracted. I'm just amazed that it still goes on."

Indeed it does. The latest from his house is that he's departed the premises. He was kicked out by Layla after she returned from out of town to discover that he'd made his acquaintance with a young woman who had been a fixture at Dinosaurs concerts.

"It's so pathetic that at this age he's doing this," says Layla. "He says he's just on a tangent, that he needs to do this.

"She doesn't care about him. She even told me, 'I'm only here for as long as it lasts.' But she does everything for him. She makes him feel like a rock star again."

It is the moth and the flame. An old flame, yes, and an uncertain one, to be sure. But it beats the darkness.

—*San Francisco Chronicle*, **September 30, 1984**

Spencer Dryden died on January 10, 2005, at age 66, three months after he'd been diagnosed with colon cancer while preparing for heart surgery.

Sally Mann Romano, who was prominently featured in *Rolling Stone's* special issue on groupies in 1969, and who married Dryden in 1970, spoke with me for the obituary I wrote for *Rolling Stone.* She said they were married only three years. "Spencer had dalliances on the road," she said, "and that led to our breakup. But once the rancor disappeared, there was never a cross word between us. He was great with Jes (their son), and he was my best friend."

Grace Slick, who lived with Dryden before he married Sally, helped raise money for Spencer when he fell on hard times. "It's like Janis sang: 'Take another piece of my heart,'" she said. "That's how it feels to me."

WHY LINDA RONSTADT

SPENT VALENTINE'S DAY ALONE

Ben and Linda Ronstadt

So, here's how I got to write a column in *GQ*.

As a kid, I was always daydreaming about one day writing for a big newspaper and, preferably, being a columnist, like Bill Fiset, who wrote a man-about-town column in the *Oakland Tribune*. Or, even better, like Herb Caen, the *San Francisco Chronicle*'s star columnist. I did a faux Caen column for my paper at SF State, but along came *Rolling Stone,* and there went my dreams of becoming a latter-day Walter Winchell.

But after leaving *Rolling Stone,* I got an assignment from *GQ*—to hang out with the upstart star, Darryl Hannah in L.A. —and that piece led to an invitation to write the magazine's music column.

It didn't take long for me to appreciate my brethren in the columning business. Whether you have a daily, weekly, or monthly deadline, you're vulnerable to sitting there in front of your typewriter or computer (the PC was just coming into play—and work—in the early '80s).

A year into my stint at *GQ,* I had my moment. A couple of ideas hadn't worked out; a couple of interviews had been postponed, and I was facing a 1,000-word void.

Fortunately, my editor—Paul Scanlon, with whom I'd worked at *Rolling Stone,* and who I'd known from back in our days together at the *Daily Gater* at SF State—had asked about my doing a column introducing myself. So what if it turned out I took a year to get to it?

Later, as I published books and did more readings and talks, the column came in handy for those inevitable questions about favorite pieces, favorite subjects, worst interviews and, always, what is Hunter S. Thompson really like?

I offer you my crib sheet-as-column.

Here it is: my first anniversary writing this column. Time flies when you're on deadline.

It occurs to me that we haven't been properly (or in any other way) introduced. The editors probably didn't think it was necessary. Just keep saying he used to work at *Rolling Stone;* that's all people need to know.

In a way, they're right. Eleven years with a notorious magazine, 11 years of a strange, hyphenated byline, and you're forever tagged. As Jann Wenner himself told me on one recent occasion, "You're always gonna be *Rolling Stone.*"

Which I suppose is better than, say, "You're always gonna be *Us Weekly.*" In any case, wherever I go—especially if it's to a public appearance of some sort—I've got that tag with me: I am always the guy who toured with various Beatles and Stones, with Crosby, Stills, Nash & Young and Elton John, who's hung out with Linda Ronstadt and Marvin Gaye, Bob Dylan and Dick Clark, and even Rodney Dangerfield.

People want to know what it was like covering those stars, those times. So step right up and pop your questions:

What's been your most frightening experience with a Beatle?

I wasn't in the business early enough to get stomped by rioting Beatlemaniacs. The only time I saw them live was in August 1966 at Candlestick Park, which turned out to be their last concert. I observed that George Harrison was wearing white socks—which was only mildly frightening.

Eight years later, I sat face-to-face with Harrison; he was on tour, with Ravi Shankar as the opening act. He wore out his voice before the tour even began, and in city after city, critics raked him over for not doing enough Beatles' songs, for mangling what familiar songs he did deign to perform, and for letting Shankar and his ensemble take up too much of the show.

When I asked George about all this, he got a little annoyed. He said God was in control of everything, even the rehearsal schedule that destroyed his voice. He said the audience's nostalgia for him was their problem. "Gandhi says create and preserve the image of your choice. The image of my choice is not Beatle George. If they want to do that, they can go and see Wings . . .

"Fuck it," he said, hiding his anger behind a forced smile. "My life belongs to me. It actually doesn't. It belongs to the Lord Krishna"—he fingered a medallion he had on a necklace—"and there's me dog collar to prove it. I'm just a dog, and I'm led around by me collar by Krishna . . . I'm the servant of the servant of the servant of the servant of the servant of Krishna. I'm just a groveling lumberjack lucky to be a grain of dirt in creation. Never been so humble in all my life, and I feel great."

Besides George Harrison, have you ever pissed off an interview subject?

Yes. That's how you know you're asking the right questions. On the Wings tour in 1976, I met Linda McCartney at a sound check and, first things first, mentioned how the critics were attacking her first solo vocal on a song called "Cook of the House," a celebration of a woman's place. She swiveled quickly on her piano bench. "My answer," she said, "is always 'Fuck off!'" And when I met Ray Charles—a dream assignment come true— I couldn't help mentioning Joe Cocker to him. In 1972, Ray was nowhere to be found on the pop charts while this British guy got hit after hit, with a voice and a style of phrasing that seemed a soulful mirror of Charles'.

Now, the Genius is a proud sonofabitch. During our sessions, he'd punctuate a point by suddenly standing and shouting "HEL-lo!" When I told him Cocker was getting the young white record buyers with his sound, Ray quickly stood up.

"Listen, I'll tell you somethin'. Back maybe 13 to 14 years ago, they had ads in the paper where they were tryin' to find anybody to sing like me. You think about that for a minute . . . I guarantee Joe Cocker ain't never appealed more to the young people who raised me up. He appeals to the young white because he's white. Shit, man. That ain't a mad statement, that's just the truth. . . .

"I say two things. First of all, in order for that guy to copy me, he gotta wait till I do it first. Now the second thing I feel, well, if you take this guy over me and he's just an imitation of me, then that says to me that I must be pretty damn good. Because I don't know nobody that you wanna copy that ain't worth a damn. All right, HEL-lo!"

Which star awed you the most?

Jagger has never failed to awe me. There's something about the guy. Even when he doesn't mean to test you, he puts on a look, half teasing, half menacing, that can stop you in your tracks. Sitting with the central figure in the greatest pure rock 'n' roll band of all time unnerved me in a way that sitting with Jim Morrison, Keith Moon, Stevie Wonder, Paul McCartney, or Joni Mitchell never did.

What's Bob Dylan like to talk with?

He was doing the tour with The Band in 1974, which I followed through a couple of cities before running into him in a hotel hallway in Toronto. He put me through a little audition, a chat in the midst of a post-show party, before allowing a full session. Then at the beginning of our actual interview, he pulled a surprise: he asked that I not use my tape recorder. He was having some problems with bootleggers, with people turning his every word, and even the garbage from his apartment, into fodder for public amusement.

So now, on top of being nervous, I had to scribble furiously while he talked. He was in good form, as when I asked if he still felt the need for "message songs." "There's still a message," he said. "The same electric spark that went off back then could still go off again—the spark that led to nothing. Our kids will probably protest, too. Protest is an old thing. Sometimes protest is deeper or different—the Haymarket Square or the Russian Revolution. There's always a need for protest songs. You just gotta tap it."

What's Bruce Springsteen really like?

I haven't interviewed him yet, but Dianne, my wife, exchanged looks with him once. She was at Macy's, in the lingerie department, when she saw him, waiting around for his girlfriend to finish up a purchase. This was a few years ago, after *Born to Run* but before Bruce was a household face. Anyway, Dianne gave him a look, as if to say, "Is that you?" And he gave her a look, as if to say, "Yeah, but don't tell nobody." Of course she did, and has, and will again.

And what about Hunter S. Thompson?

Hunter is a low-key, unassuming kind of party animal. Actually, I think of him as an innocent. It's just that he does things in a way that surprises you.

One enduring image of him is when we were in Palm Springs, attending an editorial conference on a Fourth of July weekend. The meeting wound up with all of us raving on a psilocybin high—all except Hunter, who'd handed out the little tablets. It was evening, and some of us were freaking over some movie, while others were in the Jacuzzi, and here was Hunter deciding it was time to set off the fireworks. Out by the pool, he was carrying this box of Roman candles, but he couldn't make out the instructions in the dark. So with the explosives in one hand, he lit a match with the other. That's about when those of us who hadn't yet passed out, passed out.

What was it like on the road? Was it really "sex, drugs, and rock 'n' roll?"

Yes. And don't forget the big bucks.

Don't dodge the question.

I wish you wouldn't question my dodge. Boring as it will seem, on the road I've had mostly rock 'n' roll. Drugs, of course, were part of the scene. On the job, I preferred to take notes than anything else, but I didn't always say no, sometimes thinking I was being social, other times knowing I was being stupid. I never went beyond grass, despite plenty of chances. I recall one night watching a very well-known musician methodically sifting cocaine from one Tupperware bowl into another. I never mentioned that scene, but as things turned out, I didn't have to. The artist's career took a nosedive, and today, after several comeback attempts, he's on probation from a coke bust.

What's the biggest rock 'n' roll entourage you've ever seen?

First, let's define the term. An entourage is a coterie of people who accompany a rock star, usually on tour. Its members range from business associates, roadies, guards, and flacks to drinking buddies and groupies. As an indication of a star's status, an entourage is every bit as important as limos, private jets, and total creative control of T-shirt designs.

The biggest entourage I've seen is Cyndi Lauper's wrestler friend, if you're talking the one-man variety. Otherwise, it's Sly Stone. Wherever he was, and at whatever hour of the night or day, he kept a legion of aides and advisers around him, all dressed either to kill or to hit the stage themselves.

Have you ever been thrown out of a concert by Bill Graham?

You haven't really lived till you've been given the heave-ho by "Mistuh Graham." Actually, he's never tossed me, but once, in 1969, after *Rolling Stone* published one of numerous articles that rubbed him wrong, he spotted me at the old Fillmore West doing an interview with Ian Anderson of Jethro Tull, and he pronounced: "I do not want to see you ever again on my property." After all these years, he hasn't forgiven me for having had the poor judgment to continue to work for *Rolling Stone*. But he's always been as professional in interviews as he's been in producing concerts.

Have you ever become more than friends with a rock star?

Friends, yes. More than friends . . . yes. It was one hot night in Manhattan, a year after I'd written a story on her. P.S.: She is not any of the women named in this column. Next question, hurry.

What's the best opening line you've heard?

I was waiting to interview Marvin Gaye at his home in Detroit. As he strode into the living room, he said: "Can I offer you something? Scotch? Grass? Gimlet?"

How about the best quote?

I'd say it came from Linda Ronstadt, who said about Led Zeppelin: "Their stuff is like insect music to me. I can't listen for a long time without getting a headache. What's [Robert] Plant look like? That's such a great name for someone who sings like that."

What moments do you remember most?

First, Gary Busey. He'd just finished starring in *The Buddy Holly Story,* and I watched him rip up a surfer bar in Redondo Beach, with a table-hopping, beer-spilling set of no-prisoners rock 'n' roll. Women hopped around the room like kangaroos; men pounded on tabletops, screaming the name of Busey's character from *Big Wednesday: "Mas-o-chist . . . Mas-o-chist . . . Mas-o-chist!"*

Also captivating, in their own way, were Crosby, Stills & Nash in three-part harmony—not at any coliseum, but in a living room in Los Angeles, doing an impromptu run-through of "You Don't Have to Cry."

Another quiet moment: Marvin Gaye, in mid-interview in his living room, putting on a backing tape of some songs he'd composed with Sammy Davis, Jr. in mind. Then Marvin was singing about lonely summer days and salty kisses by the ocean. Strange music to be hearing from the man who'd just given us *What's Going On* and Gaye knew it. "On me, now, this is no good," he said before singing. For that moment, though, I was happy to be in his very private cocktail lounge.

In 1981 I saw early appearances by Huey Lewis & the News at Uncle Charlie's, a club in a shopping center in Marin County, and I saw Prince at the Stone, a 700-seat club in San Francisco's North Beach. I remember Springsteen in 1975 stunning the audience at the Oakland Paramount with his wanton energy. I remember Bette Midler at the Boarding House in 1973, spending herself in front of 500 people (with arranger Barry Manilow at the piano), then sitting, all alone, in the tiny dressing room.

Away from the stage, I remember wanting to hug Linda Ronstadt one Valentine's night. She was riding high on *Heart Like a Wheel*. She was on tour, in Honolulu, and her boyfriend was in Los Angeles. After the concert, I escorted her to her hotel. While waiting for the elevator, she saw a couple holding hands. "Oh, I don't have anybody to kiss me," she said with a pout. And it just didn't seem fair.

—*GQ*, June 1985

HANK BALLARD'S

FISTFUL

OF HITS

Ben with Hank Ballard

I **first met** Hank Ballard in late 1985, when he came to San Francisco for a nightclub engagement. Interviewing him for the *Chronicle,* I found him . . . well, engaging. Here was one of the most influential writers and performers in the early history of rock 'n' roll, who broke into the R&B charts in the '50s with "dirty" songs like "Work with Me Annie," who wrote "The Twist" (only to see another artist, Chubby Checker, get a hit with it), and who hadn't worked steadily since the mid-'60s. But he had this wonderful, positive attitude, even if its foundation went right by me. Here's how he put it: "I never got into that star complex. That ego is nothing but destruction in disguise. My theory is, how can you think you're God when *Billboard*'s got a thing called the Hot 100? There can't be a hundred gods."

Right. So, anyway, when he came back to town the following spring, I grabbed him for an update, reworked what I'd written for the *Chronicle,* and, just like that, Hank Ballard got what he so richly deserved: a bit of national press.

They didn't check their egos at the door of the Rock and Roll Hall of Fame.

I was talking with a friend of mine the other day who was involved in the banquet held earlier this year in New York City. The induction of the first ten famers was nothing if not a supreme video opportunity. What a crowd! Ray Charles. James Brown. Chuck Berry. Little Richard. Jerry Lee Lewis. Fats Domino. The Everly Brothers. The memories of Elvis, Buddy, and, bringing it on home, Sam Cooke. And, of course, the jammers at the induction dinner, among them Keith Richards, John Fogerty, Steve Winwood, Neil Young, and Chubby Checker. On paper and tape, a rockin' good time was had by all.

But when I told my friend that I'd just interviewed James Brown, he let out a big sigh. He couldn't resist passing on a bit of backstage gossip. The Godfather of Soul, he said, was why the induction dinner at the Waldorf-Astoria had started late. Mr. Dynamite had to have his hair done just so before he could make his entrance. Soul Brother Number One insisted on assurances that he wouldn't have to sit next to, or pose for photos with, Chuck Berry.

And, a couple of weeks later when I asked Brown about being in the Rock Hall, he said, "I didn't deserve to be in there. I came with soul music. I feel my career has spanned much broader than any entertainer that ever lived."

Kinda moving, isn't it?

Meeting Brown—and now hearing about his behavior at the Hall of Fame—reminded me of another musical pioneer I'd just met.

His name—Hank Ballard—doesn't ignite a string of song titles the way Brown's does. But Ballard's got a fistful of credits. He wrote and recorded "The Twist," though it was Chubby Checker who turned it into the biggest dance-fad record ever.

With the early R&B group the Royals, Ballard wrote the classic "dirty" song "Work with Me Annie," but the Royals got confused with another group, "5" Royales, and had to change their name to the Midnighters.

He and the group did have some other hits; in fact, in 1960 they were the first act ever to have three singles in the *Billboard* Hot 100 simultaneously—"Finger Poppin' Time," "Let's Go, Let's Go, Let's Go," and "The Twist." (That record would be broken four years later by the Beatles.) But it's been almost a quarter of a century since he's been near the *Billboard* charts as anything but a reader.

So when it came time for the first inductions into the Rock and Roll Hall of Fame, Hank Ballard learned that his time had not yet come. He got onto the list of the 41 to be considered, but, given a projected rate of three new inductees a year, Hank Ballard may wind up as the Phil Rizzuto or Billy Williams of rock 'n' roll. No matter how many hits, dazzling plays or homers, they'll be left at the door year after year.

But Ballard is as bitter as James Brown is humble. In fact, he talked as if he'd been inducted. "I feel very joyed," he said about being nominated. "It gave my sense of importance a big lift."

He is in San Francisco for a one-nighter at a dance club, and he is staying in a funky flat with a couple of the local musicians who'll be backing him.

Ballard, a fit and youthful 49, has been on the comeback trail longer than most singers have had careers. Attempts at recording—including a trip to the recording studio a few years ago with James Brown as producer—have gone nowhere. But he's not angry. "You're gonna have your highs and lows," he says. "I never got into that star complex. How can you think you're God when *Billboard*'s got a thing called the Hot 100? There can't be a hundred gods."

That's about as serious as Ballard gets. Most of the time he's laughing. Recalling the sweeter moments of his past, he fills the air with cascading whoops of laughter. Talking about how one member of the Midnighters stopped a college concert by climbing a pole and dropping his trousers, "showing his black butt," he doubles up on the couch and almost loses control.

It's hard to tell if Hank Ballard laughs to keep from crying, but my guess is that he counts rewards in ways that have nothing to do with record royalties and chart positions. He's pleased about the Hall of Fame nomination, but no less pleased about a record collectors' magazine, *Goldmine*, naming a British re-release of his "What You Get When the Gettin' Gets Good" as last year's "Best '50s Artist Reissue" in R&B.

Thirty years ago, Ballard was one of the phenoms in the gospel-to-popular-R&B transition, a kid from Detroit with a high, searching voice and a knack for putting what he heard on the streets into song. That's all he was doing when he came up with "Work with Me Annie."

"Annie," with lines like "Annie please don't cheat/Give me all your meat," was banned from the radio. That naturally sent the record through the roof, to the top of the R&B charts in May and June 1954. "Annie" inspired a long string of answer songs, among them Etta James' "Roll with Me Henry" (which became a big pop hit in a cleansed version, "Dance with Me Henry," sung by Georgia Gibbs) and Ballard's "Annie Had a Baby." Annie, he sang, "can't work no more . . . that's what happens when the gettin' gets good."

"Work with Me Annie" started out as "Sock It to Me Annie." "But they [King Records] were afraid of that title," says Ballard. "Then we went to 'Roll with Me Annie,' and that was too suggestive. Well, in the ghetto in Detroit, there was a slang for 'sex'—it was 'work.' 'Say, man, you was out last night. Did you get into work?'" Ballard was inspired to write what he himself calls "raunchy, suggestive" songs by the success of the Dominoes' 1951 record *Sixty Minute Man.* "So I wrote 'Get It.'" Ballard sings, "Get it, get it, get it; You know I wanna see you with it," and laughs. "They bought about 250,000, and I said, 'There's a market out there!'" Judging by the campaign against explicit rock lyrics, there still is. And, surprisingly, Ballard is on the parents' side.

"I have kids; I have grandchildren. And if I had to do it all over again, I wouldn't record a thing like ["Annie"] now. I was a teenager then, I was just having fun making things rhyme. If I'd known that lyrics would come off as a bad image for kids, I would never have recorded those songs. I wouldn't dare write the things I hear today . . . like 'Relax when you wanna come.' That's just too direct. At least mine had double meanings. Give me some room for curiosity."

But, Ballard adds, "I'm not gonna knock them. Let them have their day; I had mine."

In the Midnighters' days, the group did substantial business at colleges. "We had a white audience," he says, "'cause they loved those dirty records. The college crowd wanted you to get down. We'd be singing 'Finger Poppin' Time' and they'd be singing something else!" Ballard starts roaring again. "You can imagine. It wasn't finger-*poppin'* time. They were drinking that 90-proof grain alcohol!"

The Midnighters were a match for the audience any night. Besides Henry Booth, who occasionally misplaced his trousers, there was Lawson

Smith, who "had a gimmick with women's panties he would do on 'Annie Had a Baby.' I used to laugh so hard I couldn't get to the next song."

Ironically, the Midnighters were doing good business because of Chubby Checker's success with "The Twist," a Ballard song based on the Midnighters' moves onstage.

"I'll tell you how I feel about 'The Twist,'" says Ballard. "Dick Clark and Chubby Checker did me a favor. I knew the song could be a monster, but King Records hated it. They said, '"The Twist" is nuthin'.' [King put "The Twist" out as a flip side.] But kids saw us doing it, and this DJ, Buddy Deane out of Baltimore, called Dick Clark and said, 'The kids are going crazy over this record.' Dick said, 'I don't wanna hear it; they cut all those dirty songs.'"

When Freddy Cannon's manager, a friend of Clark's, also praised the record, Clark, who had business interests in various record labels and artists, found Ernest Evans through auditions and gave him his idea of a rock 'n' roll name: Chubby Checker. (Fats Domino. Get it?)

"Chubby came closest to my sound," says Ballard. "Dick took him into the studio and did a clone of my 'Twist.' "Ballard recalls being in Miami for an engagement when he first heard the record. "I was in a pool, and I heard it on a pop [that is, white-dominated Top 40] station, and I said, 'Wow, I'm getting pop play now.' I thought it was me!" Ballard lapses into laughter, and it goes on so long that he breaks to catch his breath. "Oh, man!"

One reason Ballard can look back without anger is that he earned composer's royalties on "The Twist." Also, he believes that as consolation for blocking the Midnighters' "Twist," Clark gave plentiful exposure to "Finger Poppin' Time," which hit the Top 10 and stayed on the charts for half of 1960.

A few lucrative years later, the group broke up over spiritual differences. The Midnighters became Muslims, Ballard didn't.

"They got so into Islam," Ballard says of the other members, "that they lost all their stage presence." And they refused "to sign white autographs or play white dates." Ballard continued to work, using other singers, but the steam was gone. "I really missed them. That's why I dropped out of sight."

For the past ten years, he says, he's been trying to regain his songwriting touch; he's dabbled in rock, country, ballads, and some "hard-core blues."

His voice, he says, "is far better now than it was 20 years ago. Far better. I haven't abused myself; I didn't get messed up in drugs and all that crap.

"You can come back if you get the right song," says Ballard. "That was proven by Tina Turner." And by James Brown and Little Richard. And, if there's any justice in the land of radio and records, by Hank Ballard, someday soon. There are signs. Last year he appeared on CBS's *West 57th* and one of his blues tunes was used in a scene. Liz Claiborne, the fashion magnate, was tuned in, got in touch, and has since invested $100,000 in Ballard and his new Midnighters: three backup singers and an eight-piece band including Alex Schultz, son of Liz Claiborne, on bass.

Other help is at hand.

James Brown, who credits Ballard with assisting him early in his career, still wants to produce some tracks with him. "We've got to bring a lot of these people back," Brown says. "Look at Tina. She was always there; she just didn't get the breaks. So give Hank the breaks." That, however, may just be talk. Action has come in the form of a duet with Manhattan Transfer's Tim Hauser, who's made a solo album of '50s material. Another supporter is the Reverend Richard Penniman.

"Little Richard's trying to get me a record deal," says Ballard. "He's hot as a firecracker all over again. And I'm next. I've got to be next!"

He lets out another healthy roar. Rock history hasn't been all that kind to Hank Ballard, but he's happy to have been a rousing part of it. And whatever happens—or doesn't happen—he'll have the last laugh.

—*GQ*, June 1986

Hank Ballard was inducted into the Rock and Roll Hall of Fame in 1990. He died in March 2003 in Los Angeles. The cause of death was throat cancer.

LOU REED

THE PRINCE
OF DARKNESS
LIGHTENS UP

One day I was visiting Carmen McRae for *The Chronicle*; the next, I was on to another subject, another column for *GQ*. Lou Reed was in town for a benefit concert for Amnesty International. Reed is someone whose music was largely unfamiliar to me. Call me West Coast-centric if you must; I did leave too many New York acts off my radar. And when an artist has built up a discography and reputation as formidable as Velvet Underground's—and as Reed did on his own—an initial meeting can be intimidating, and uneasy, and unproductive. Since *GQ* welcomed a personal perspective in its columns, I chose to include my nervousness in my report.

I never saw the Velvet Underground during their five-year lurch through the New York music scene. From 1965 to 1970 I was on the Left Coast, soaking up good, good, good, good vibrations. And though the Velvets were considered a psychedelic band, they never belonged in that cozy cluster.

Lou Reed and company (John Cale, Doug Yule, Maureen Tucker, Sterling Morrison, and, for a while, the unforgettable Nico) played a bit of folk-rock and a lot of acid rock. But their acid had little to do with lysergic acid diethylamide. Theirs was aimed at exposing the dark side of the underground, where desperadoes roamed Harlem looking for a fix, where girls lost their identities in an S&M world. The Velvets' music was by turns sparse and pretty, then thick, fuzz-guitared, and heavy-metal. The lyrics—by Lou Reed—were stark and direct, journalistic and novelistic, painful and poetic.

But when the band visited San Francisco as part of Andy Warhol's multimedia Exploding Plastic Inevitable road show, the hippies weren't impressed. And critics heard little more than the sound of posing. New York. Heroin. Decadence. Oh, far out.

Still, the Velvets were like none before them. After them came Bowie and Eno, Roxy Music and the Psychedelic Furs, Patti Smith and Talking Heads, Joy Division, Tom Verlaine, the Cars and the Modern Lovers, and garages full of others—all indebted.

But the Velvets never sold records in great numbers; neither has Reed, who's been issuing his own albums since 1972. Maybe it's because, of all the artists influenced by the Velvets, he has been the most deeply affected. He has never wavered from his roots: gritty New York and rock 'n' roll. From that basis, he's given us some great moments, "Rock 'n' Roll" and "Walk on the Wild Side" among them. But he's also confused and maddened both fans and critics with his dark, nihilistic parables of sex and violence.

After making an album with David Bowie in 1972, Reed took to wearing heavy eye makeup and purple nail polish; in 1976, he lived with a boyfriend named Rachel. In the studio, he was erratic. His excesses (listen, if you can, to *Metal Machine Music,* from 1975) got critics begging him to quit the business.

In recent years, Reed has gone through a remarkable transformation. He got married in 1980, beat the bottle in 1983, and issued albums that got critics raving. *Growing Up in Public, The Blue Mask, Legendary Hearts,* and *New Sensations* had to be hits, they said. A 1984 single, "I Love You, Suzanne," got a decent ride on FM radio, but Reed has never sold more than 200,000 copies of an album.

Although his eminently danceable "Rock 'n' Roll" dates back to his nights with the Velvets, current observers have detected an increased interest in a dance groove. Others note the mellowing of Lou Reed. Along with acerbic commentaries on social-political ailments and backward looks on the wild sides of mankind, there are flat-out love songs, odes to domestic tranquility and the simple things in life. It'll never be California dreamin', but it is the reality of the '80s dance tunes, videos, Honda commercials, and all.

But on the eve of my meeting with Lou Reed, I wasn't sure which Reed—the '60s rebel, the '80s survivor, or that maddening mix of the '70s—I was going to meet. Actually, I wasn't sure I wanted to meet any of them. After all, if I upset him with a wrong question, he might tear my face off, just as he did to himself in the video of "No Money Down." He might walk out or, even worse, pull a McKenna. I was thinking of a 1984 face-off he had with Kristine McKenna in *L.A. Weekly,* in which Reed turned an interview into an ice capade:

What's the most significant change you've observed in yourself in recent years?
I hope somebody told you I don't like to answer personal questions. I consider that a personal question.

Uh . . . okay. What do you consider to be your chief strength as an artist?
I never thought about it, and that's not a question I could answer glibly off the top of my head.

In 1977, you made the comment, "I came through because I have a demented sense of humor." Is that still your most valuable survival tool?
I don't comment on past quotes, which are secondary information at best. . . .

Have the culture's social and sexual taboos changed since you began making music 18 years ago?
I'm a rock 'n' roll person and I'm not interested in answering questions like that. . . ."

And I wanted to talk to this guy?

Reed was in San Francisco for the first Amnesty International benefit concert, along with Sting, U2, Jackson Browne, Bryan Adams, Peter Gabriel, Joan Baez, and the Neville Brothers. I was told beforehand that he probably wouldn't find time to talk. "He doesn't respect the press," said Paula Batson, a publicist at RCA Records, "because it hasn't helped. He thinks it's radio that may take him to the next level." (Of record sales, of course.) When he does interviews, she assured me, he can be talkative.

Just to say hello I dropped by KFOG-FM, where Reed and Gabriel were scheduled to do a satellite-broadcast show to promote the concerts. In a desultory-looking conference room, laden with untouched cheese and bottles of white wine, I shook hands with Reed and his wife, Sylvia. A shy man, Reed seemed particularly withdrawn. I learned later that he was upset because Gabriel hadn't shown up, leaving him as the only "star." On the air, Reed meant to be friendly, but with his detached monotone and his economy with words you couldn't be sure.

The next afternoon, at a jammed press conference at the Cow Palace, Reed had all the company he could want, and he seemed content to sit mute while Sting, Bono (U2's lead singer), and Baez, along with Jack Healey, the US executive director of Amnesty International, carried on.

When, an hour into the conference, Reed got a question about why rock stars are now considered "responsible members of the community instead of a rebel who walks on the wild side," he was genuinely surprised, and his eyes did a little bug-out.

"Wow," he drawled. "You had to get to me, right?" He equated rock with freedom and, thus, with Amnesty International. Then, staring at the gathered media, he added, "I don't know why—and I mean this seriously— why rock 'n' roll should not be thought of as respectfully as journalism."

The reporters tittered. Reed mumbled, "Thank you," and looked down. There was no follow-up question.

So when word came that I could have maybe 30 minutes with Reed, I was surprised as well as nervous. But hey, guess what? Lou Reed is a pussycat.

Maybe I happened upon him at a good time; a successful sound check can do wonders for a musician's spirits. Whatever it was, he was more charming than an author on a talk show.

I began with a safe opening question about the uselessness of the print medium. He clicked right in. "I've had the best reviews in the world and the worst ones," he said. "I've had reviews that say, 'Why don't you just die?'—and it hasn't seemed to make a difference." He finds fan letters more provocative. "A lot of times, what they say is illuminating to me 'cause they take something in a way I literally wasn't aware of. I'm not the expert on my own work. I'm not being cute when I say I don't really know what the album's about. Give me two, three years' distance on it. Then I'll start figuring out just what's in those lyrics."

Reed, who's issued 18 albums, said songs come to him in two ways: either the Muse drops by, and he's not much more than a medium, or he sits and sweats it out, "hitting my head against the wall. Then I have to wait for the other thing to take over, and it'll write the whole thing from beginning to end." One of the wildest songs on his new album, *Mistrial,* a rap called "The Original Wrapper," came the hard way. Addressing sexually transmitted diseases, Reed advises, "Better check that sausage before you put it in the waffle."

Now, just a minute. Sausage and waffle? Is he trying to sneak something past concerned parents? Reed smiled. "You're the only person who's known that," he said. "That's really funny. To me it seems so obvious. I was worried that I made it a little heavy-handed. But apparently not."

The song, he said, was designed "to be the all-time rap lyric. I read it to my friend [*Basketball Diaries* author] Jim Carroll, and he said, 'You already did that with "Street Hassle" [1978].' I said, 'Oh—that's true.'"

To some ears, Reed does repeat himself. But *Mistrial* is a clear step away from his past, a celebration of his undiminishing power to communicate through rock 'n' roll. When I asked what compels him to stay in music, he replied unabashedly, "I really love it. I kept thinking about writing the great American novel. I think my novel is all these things lined up and played in order."

The latest chapter, it appears, has the old rebel going commercial on us. But even in the old days, said Reed, he wanted to sell records. "The Velvet Underground would've loved to have been popular. It's very easy to see that the person who wrote the Velvet Underground stuff wrote this [new] album. It's not all that different; it's just a little older."

His understated pitch for Honda scooters, he said, has drawn overwhelmingly positive reaction from his fans. "Who else," he asked rhetorically, "could make a scooter hip?" He added, "If you really think about it, what does selling out mean? If you think of rock 'n' roll as this antiestablishment, rebellious-type thing, well, you wouldn't make a record. Look who's recording you—the same people who manufacture missiles. You could really start tearing it apart."

Reed said he did the commercial—and would do others—for two reasons: "For money and to try to sell my records. The main thing is to get people to listen to the records, 'cause I really like them and really think people would like them. Plus, if you get into one of my records, there's like 17 or 18 records sitting back there. I'm not a bad thing to get addicted to."

Reed's manager signaled the need to wrap things up, and I felt awful. No matter how friendly he'd been, I couldn't just start asking this man I'd known for 30 minutes, this man who does not like to answer personal questions, about both his musical glorification and his denunciation of smack and booze, about his glam rock days with Bowie and Rachel.

I took the roundabout (chicken's) way in. "Have your various images worked for or against you?" I asked. He didn't rip off my face. "It can do both," he said after a moment of pondering. "I can use it to keep people away from me. If I see someone I don't like, I can be 'that' Lou Reed—the bad one." But he wishes people wouldn't confuse the characters he portrays on record with himself. "I understand why people are interested; I'm performing these things. But what I see myself as, is a writer. Whether I'm a nice guy, whether I'm a liar, whether I'm immoral, should have nothing to do with it."

At the Amnesty concert, Reed was dressed in his customary black leather, but it was his nice-guy persona that dominated. He kicked off with "I Love You, Suzanne."

The positivism continued through "New Sensations" and the warm "Tell It to Your Heart." Reed barely has a performing style: he plants his feet, stands up straight behind his guitar, and sings. He looked as if he were reading a book report in front of a class, his eyes bugged out like a rock 'n' roll Judge Reinhold's. Still, he was singing a ballad, and some of the kids, raised on Bryan Adams, shrieked. Reed sang his near-hit "No Money Down," then announced, "In case you don't know this next song, it's the Honda commercial." A high-pitched sonic wave of recognition greeted "Walk on the Wild Side," which Reed updated in a rolling, rumbling style. He wrapped up with "Video Violence" and strode off to a sustained cheer. Lou Reed, age 43, was a hit. As he passed the front of the stage, he extended his arms and waved his hands, managing, in one smooth move, both a good-bye and a signal to please keep your distance, thank you.

—GQ, September 1986

A MIND-BLOWING
ARRAY OF MUSIC

THE SUMMER
OF LOVE

Sometimes you can be assigned a story and you just keep a straight face while you're smiling smugly inside. Such was the case when, in 1987, the *Chronicle,* succumbing—as all media do—to anniversaries, decided to do a to-do on what it decided was the 20th anniversary of the Summer of Love. Whatever that was. And whenever it was. According to *I Want to Take You Higher,* a book issued by the Rock and Roll Hall of Fame and Museum, "popular myth holds that 1967 was the Summer of Love in London and San Francisco. The truth of the matter is that 1966 was the real Summer of Love in both cities and that 1967 was the beginning of the end."

Yeah, but that's when the media caught on to what was happening. And so it was that, when the hordes invaded Carnaby and Haight Streets in London and San Francisco, 1967 became widely considered as THE year.

What-*ev.* I'd already done the anniversary thing, way back when it was the 10th anniversary and I was at *Rolling Stone,* writing up the music angle and interviewing all the usual suspects. Those interviews became part of a syndicated radio special that *Rolling Stone* produced, and that I wrote and narrated.

So when the *Chronicle* asked about a piece reflecting on that summer, I could only smile. And I only had to go to my tape recorder, play back the special, and start writing.

Sure, I was using a shortcut. But why not? The quotes were good ones; they were accurate (after all, they were on tape) and they were extracted while the speakers' minds and memories were still reasonably intact.

"I never felt that the music coming out of San Francisco was so revolutionary," says record producer David Rubinson, "but I think it was a revolutionary attitude of the bands and of the audience that swept the country."

In the mid-'60s, the San Francisco Bay Area delivered unto the world a mind-blowing array of popular bands, among them Jefferson Airplane, Big Brother & the Holding Company (with Janis Joplin), the Grateful Dead, Country Joe & the Fish, Quicksilver Messenger Service, Sons of Champlin, Moby Grape, Blue Cheer, It's a Beautiful Day, Great Society, and the Charlatans.

Before the Summer of Love was over, however long it actually lasted, many of the bands had been signed by big record companies, new recording studios sprang up in San Francisco, in Marin, and on the Peninsula, the Airplane was on the cover of *Life* magazine, and "acid rock" and "the San Francisco Sound" had joined the trend-watcher's vocabulary.

The music—first played at parties, then on the streets and in the parks, then in clubs and concert halls, and finally on radio and records—was the constant backdrop for the times. "Rock 'n' roll," says promoter Bill Graham, "was one of the means of expression for people who were looking at life differently."

The music, says Paul Kantner, now with the Kantner-Balin-Casady Band, "was a good clarion call to action." It was, says Country Joe McDonald, "a very important part of solidifying the community. It was a morale booster; it'd make everybody feel good, and they'd go home being more convinced than ever."

But, as some of the musicians will admit, there never was an actual "San Francisco Sound." There was a volume level: way up. Before there was such a thing as a "lifestyle," there was a style and an attitude—a combination of laissez-faire and too-stoned-to-care.

And then there was the music.

Steve Miller, a young graduate of the blues scene in Chicago, visited the Fillmore on arrival in San Francisco and couldn't believe his ears. "I went, 'What is this?' I couldn't understand how the Airplane and the Dead and Quicksilver were playing to people; at that time they weren't very good bands. The Airplane were like giving flowers to the first girl singer (Signe Anderson) 'cause she was leaving. It was a social trip . . . it was not really a musical trip."

Yeah, man. But that was the idea—or at least one of the essential ingredients in the San Francisco mix. Though many of the musicians were serious, just as many of them weren't. Bands got together on whims, because the Beatles made it look like fun, or because Dylan had expanded the sound and vocabulary of folk music, from which so many of the college-educated hipsters came.

One of the first bands on the scene, the Charlatans, was put together by a designer, George Hunter, who was far more interested in image and style than in music. Drummer Dan Hicks explains the band's reputation for looking better than they played: "It had a little to do with the fact that the leader didn't play any instruments. And at rehearsals, he'd say things like, 'When we get to this place here, we'll get . . . far out.'" Grace Slick remembers why she and her filmmaker husband, Jerry Slick, formed Great Society: "'Cause we went to see Jefferson Airplane. And we said, 'Well, that was better than what we're doing now, which isn't anything.' He was going to school and I was modeling, which, if you're five foot seven and 104 pounds, is meager."

The Grateful Dead began as the Warlocks and had played fraternity parties and topless bars. Jerry Garcia remembers: "We said, 'This is awful; this eats it.'" But the Dead, as popular as they became, never expected to be commercial: "We never had that glamour flash that the Airplane or Moby Dick—or Grape, whatever it was—had, that was sellable." Instead, the Dead immersed themselves in Ken Kesey and his Merry Pranksters' various "acid tests" and "trips festivals," events that helped set, however blurrily, some of the standards of the scene:

• The long, meandering, improvisational "jams" identified with jazz and Latino music. "Sometimes," says Garcia, "we'd play for five minutes and freak out: 'I can't play any more; it's too weird!' When you're high, sometimes you want to play for hours, sometimes you want to stick your head in a bucket of water, or have some Jell-O."

- In the ballrooms, early concerts became multimedia "happenings," where the lines between stage and audience were dismantled. "There was a move to bridge the gap," says Paul Kantner, "to make the audience more performers, and the band more a part of the audience." "What was going on," Joe McDonald learned, "was a hell of a lot bigger than we were. It was light shows, stage production, the audience, and the musicians."

- The light shows—swirling, bubbling liquids projected onto walls, mixed with slides and loopy films—became a regular part of the dance concert scene. Along with the surrealistic posters that advertised the concerts, they spread quickly around the country.

- The music had no singular sound. Bands might be based on folk-rock, R&B, blues, or country-swing. As time went on, some dabbled in Indian ragas, jazz, and experimental, electronic sounds. "That was an issue of the times," says Kantner, "to expand, to enter forbidden zones."

- The dance-concerts produced by Chet Helms at the Avalon Ballroom and Bill Graham at the Fillmore encompassed much more than rock 'n' roll. Graham booked jazz, blues, Motown acts, and the occasional poet. "My background wasn't rock 'n' roll," says Graham. "The musicians here and the visiting artists told me where their roots lay. [Michael] Bloomfield came in with [Paul] Butterfield, who told me about Cream and Chuck Berry and Otis Rush—and one thing led to another."

- Much of the music of the day was based on drugs. Jerry Garcia switched from banjo to guitar after taking acid. "LSD," he once explained, "made me want to hear longer sounds."

- Beginning with the Berkeley-based Country Joe & the Fish and hitting a peak in 1968 with the Airplane's "We Can Be Together" (with its incendiary line, "Up against the wall, mother—,"), the music could be political. "That was scary," says McDonald, "'cause we had grown up in a period of real conservatism and conformity." The Fish came to precede their antiwar song, "I-Feel-Like-I'm-Fixin'-to-Die Rag," with a spell-it-out "Fish Cheer." When the band began encouraging the lusty spelling out of a word other than "fish," they were banned from numerous concert halls and kicked off *The Ed Sullivan Show*.

- Early on, local bands seemed willing to play anywhere for free. But once they were being courted by record companies from Los Angeles and New York, they used their power well: in 1966, the Airplane scored a then-unprecedented advance of $25,000 from RCA; Steve Miller, the savvy guitarist from Texas and Chicago, received more than $50,000 from Capitol and forged the way for other bands to make similar deals.

- Finally, it was in San Francisco that KMPX, the first FM "underground" rock station, took to the air, 21 years and a day ago. Tom Donahue, an exile of Top 40 radio, turned the station into a phenomenon and changed the face of FM radio.

These days, sex, drugs, and politics rarely make the charts, there's no identifiable new wave of San Francisco bands, the barriers are back up between bands and fans, radio is formatted as tight as Prince's pants, and the Beatles' "Revolution" is being used to sell Nike shoes. And, oh yes, the Airplane's "White Rabbit," having been used in the Academy Award-winning movie *Platoon,* is out again, complete with a video on MTV.

Did anything really change?

"No," says Grace Slick. "I thought that, with an incredible amount of media blitzing and books and knowledge, you could change people. But you can't. The only person I can change is me."

Maybe, says McDonald, who now sings and works for Vietnam vets and against ongoing wars, and whose office at Fantasy Records in Berkeley features a God's Eye on one wall. "Life is more interesting now, and more amusing and entertaining."

But as he thinks back 20 years, he grows wistful. "We really thought we were going to convince the whole world to love each other by getting them to listen to rock 'n' roll music and taking a drug called LSD. Our generation had a lot of casualties; we paid a heavy price. And when you look back at the beginning of the end of the Summer of Love, to the battle going on in America, you realize that the Establishment did not voluntarily relinquish its control over the government and the culture. And that we survived that, is unbelievable."

—*San Francisco Chronicle,* **April 9, 1987**

LAND OF
THE DEAD

_____

SAN FRANCISCO,
WHERE IT
ALL BEGAN

Whenever a rock musician of note passes away, my phone begins to do whatever it is phones do these days when someone calls. And the calls are from radio and television stations, newspapers and magazines, online and off, looking for comments and sound bites.

Sometimes, they're looking for instant articles as well. That was the case when Jerry Garcia died on August 9, 1995. The next day, a top editor at *People* called. The magazine was putting together a special issue on Garcia, and wanted me to handle Garcia's life story. I would have one week to complete it. Later that day, *Rolling Stone* called, asking for a 1,000-word report from San Francisco, telling of Garcia and the Grateful Dead's special connections to the city and how they defined what came to be known as the San Francisco Scene of the '60s. Could I submit it in five days?

I checked with *People* to be sure they were agreeable to my writing for another magazine—albeit not just another magazine. They were fine, and, within a week, both magazines had their articles. For *Rolling Stone,* I submitted the following reflections, not only on Jerry Garcia and the Dead, but also on the San Francisco they—and many of us—had left behind a long time ago.

When in the mid-'60s San Francisco came to represent nothing left to lose, there was a handful of identifiable pioneers that changed the face, the sound, and the style of pop culture. The changers included the concert promoters Bill Graham and Chet Helms, poster and light show artists, hosts and alchemists like Ken Kesey and Augustus Owsley Stanley, radio pioneer Tom Donahue, jazz critic Ralph J. Gleason and—yes—*Rolling Stone.*

At the epicenter, of course, were the musicians. Early on, the Grateful Dead, along with a few others, played free concerts as often as paying gigs. Extending their songs into jazz-like improvisatory jams, they broke down the lines between artist and audience.

Back then we—*Rolling Stone* and the Grateful Dead—were brothers in arms. The Dead did it onstage; we watched and listened, reported, ranted, and raved.

For our very first issue—published in November 1967—we lucked, journalistically speaking, into a story for the ages: the Grateful Dead getting busted at their Haight-Ashbury digs. The police had had it up to their badges with freaks flaunting various laws. Inviting local media along for the roust, they barged into the house at 710 Ashbury Street, where most of the Dead and their old ladies lived, and arrested two band members and nine associates and friends on dope charges (Jerry Garcia wasn't one of them; he was out at the time).

Baron Wolman, *Rolling Stone's* first photographer, snapped shots of Bob Weir walking down the front steps cuffed to Phil Lesh's girlfriend, and Ron "Pigpen" McKernan and Phil Lesh outside their bail bondsman's office across from the Hall of Justice. The next day, after a festive press conference at the house, Wolman shot photographs of a band of unrepentant freaks— now joined by Garcia, posing in front of 710, with Pigpen brandishing a rifle. The photos took up most of a two-page spread.

The lead, by an uncredited Jann S. Wenner, was textbook hook 'em news writing: "'That's what ya get for dealing the killer weed,' laughed state narcotics agent Jerry Van Ramm at the 11 members of the Grateful Dead household he and his agents had rounded up into the Dead's kitchen."

The band and the magazine always had a special relationship, despite the occasional negative album review or report on an unpleasant incident or *Rolling Stone's* move to New York in 1977. Our common roots transcended trivia; our love of great music kept us bonded.

One day in early 1970 we got an impromptu visit from the management and various members of the Dead. The band had just wrapped up recording *Workingman's Dead*. They knew the album was something special, and they wanted to share it right away. Magazine staffers gathered in the only sizable office (Jann's, of course) and listened in awe to pedal steel licks and tight, pretty country harmonies—from the Dead!—on "Uncle John's Band," "Dire Wolf," and "Casey Jones." Our minds, as someone would later say, were young and blown.

In later years I had occasion to interview Garcia and profile the Dead. Every five years it seemed there would be an anniversary of some sort, and the Dead were always there. And Garcia was always there—was always present—for you. Even his most offhand remarks rang true, like the best of Robert Hunter's lyrics.

It was a Saturday afternoon in late November 1975, and we were preparing for a special issue on the 10th anniversary of the San Francisco Scene. Garcia greeted some scruffy press at His Master's Wheels, a studio in an alley off Market Street in San Francisco, and I asked him about the warping of time.

"It seems like hundreds of years," Garcia said, "and it also seems like not too much time at all. I don't know. Time, you know. Some things haven't changed at all, really. And the world has changed." Perhaps not enough, but in his own quiet, unassuming, different-beat way, Jerry Garcia did his best to change it—or at least to loosen it up a little.

In his successes, in his failures, and in the way he addressed them both, with candor, humility, and beatific good humor, he was quintessentially San Franciscan. We were his, and he was ours.

Along with names forgotten by all but the most avid poster collectors—those of the Marbles, the Mystery Trend, Frumious Bandersnatch, Chocolate Watch Band—the Grateful Dead were at the vanguard of what became known as the San Francisco Scene, the Summer of Love, the '60s. But of all the bands—including Jefferson Airplane, Big Brother & the Holding Company, Country Joe & the Fish, Quicksilver Messenger Service, the Charlatans, Moby Grape, the Steve Miller Blues Band—it was the Dead that remained intact (more than less) and carried the San Francisco banner for three decades.

Sure, the Dead moved out of their Haight-Ashbury digs shortly after that bust in the fall of 1967, fanning out to Marin County to the north.

But they were forever tied to San Francisco and the '60s, and they never resisted or disavowed those bonds. It wasn't just that the Dead were born in the city. It was that the city was reborn with the Dead. San Francisco, as Ralph Gleason put it, was suddenly "the Liverpool of the West."

And in the spirit of a restless town in restless times, the Dead rolled on, breaking and making up rules as they went, eschewing recordings as stepping-stones to riches and relying on concerts instead. But as far from home as the road took them, they returned to punctuate their tour schedule with New Year's Eve concerts in Oakland or San Francisco, year-end runs that took Bay Area Deadheads to Mardi Gras, Halloween, Chinese New Year, and Acid Test all at once.

"Jerry was a true San Franciscan," says Deborah Koons Garcia, his wife of a year and a half, by way of explaining why any memorial event, any celebration of Jerry Garcia's life, would have to be in San Francisco. And so it was, in the Polo Field of Golden Gate Park, where the Dead had played the Human Be-In in 1967 and, most recently, the memorial concert for Bill Graham in 1991. But this time, the Dead's music was on tape, and the band members were there to address the crowd.

Bob Weir, his arms raised to the heavens, said that Garcia "filled this world full of clouds of joy. Just take a little bit of that and reflect it back up to him." And they did—50,000 arms lifted to the sky, holding imaginary mirrors and sending a bit of San Francisco to wherever he might be.

—*Rolling Stone*, **September 21, 1995**

I DON'T WANNA HEAR YOUR BODY TALK!

Olivia Newton-John

I n 1991, I published Hickory Wind, my biography of Gram Parsons (which the *New York Times*, writing about Parsons in 2002, referred to as "the definitive biography" of the pioneer country-rocker). I then wrote my memoir, The Rice Room, which would be published in 1994. . By then, in order to write those books, I'd left the *San Francisco Chronicle* and joined *Gavin*, a locally based radio and recording industry magazine, as managing editor. There, I also wrote a casual column (the only kind I know, actually), commenting on anything I might want to in the worlds of radio and records.

The following piece was a response to the publication of a book about bad songs. Needless to say, it was a good book. But any time there's a list of songs—best songs, worst songs, best summer songs, worst disco songs—you know, the whole *Entertainment Weekly* thing, there's bound to be arguments and calls for additions and deletions. I simply put mine into a column.

Just because you're in the music business doesn't mean you like all the music you hear. In fact, you're probably in the industry because you have some talent for distinguishing between good and bad, whether to sign and market for a record label, or to play and praise on the radio.

Today, we talk about the bad.

That's because Dave Barry, the columnist whose occasional "Bad Song Surveys" have invariably drawn the most, and most fervid, responses, has compiled the bad and baddest into *Dave Barry's Book of Bad Songs*.

For $12.95, you get nothing short of a laff riot, as they used to say, and lots of fodder for heated debates, whether around the office or on the air.

I love this book. That's mainly because I agree with every one of the "bad songs" Barry has collected. And so, while good music may inspire you to sing along, this book will have you nodding along in agreement, as Barry cites lines from Neil Diamond ("I am, I said to no one there, and no one heard at all, not even the chair"), reveals the all-time worst song ("MacArthur Park"), or reprints comments from readers ("Whenever I hear the Four Seasons' 'Walk Like a Man' I want to scream, 'Frankie, SING like a man!'" or, in response to Olivia Newton-John's "Physical," "I don't want to hear anybody's body talk").

At 88 pages, *Bad Songs* is barely longer than several tunes considered not only lame but too long, among them "In-A-Gadda-Da-Vida," "American Pie," "Taxi," and "Hey Jude."

"I know these are great rock classics," says Barry. "I'm just saying that after a while they get to be great boring rock classics whose primary musical value seems to be that they give radio DJs time to go to the bathroom."

Barry scored big points with me for pointing out two of the songs I revile most: "Honey," as performed by the great Bobby Goldsboro, with that mind-bending heck/neck rhyme. You remember. C'mon, nod along:

She wrecked the car and she was sad
And so afraid that I'd be mad
But what the heck
Tho' I pretended hard to be,
Guess you could say she saw through me
And hugged my neck . . .

The second song that gets me humming music from the new Jack Kervorkian CD is in Barry's "Weenie Music" chapter. No, not "Feelings," which kicks off the chapter with . . . feeling. But Dan Hill's "Sometimes

When We Touch," because of these lyrics, which are, as Ed Grimley, Jr., would put it, "sadder than sad, I must say":

I want to hold you till I die
Till we both break down and cry . . .

Barry didn't include every song ever mentioned to him. Maybe that's why I didn't read about the Staple Singers' "Respect Yourself," which advises how to fight air pollution:

Put your hand on your mouth when you cough
That will help the solution

Or Bobby Vee's "Stayin' In," featuring one of the all-time great rhymes:

He was saying things that weren't true about her
So I let him have it, in the cafeteria

Or the grammar lesson from Little Caesar and the Romeos:

Those oldies but goodies reminds me of you . . .

Or . . . well, I could write a book. Fortunately, thanks to Dave Barry, the best such book has already been published.

And don't worry. There's no accompanying CD.

—*Gavin*, July 11, 1997

SINATRA

NIGHT

AND DAY

In late 1996** *People* magazine, which had engaged me to help on its Jerry Garcia tribute issue the year before, contacted me again. They were preparing a special issue on Frank Sinatra, who was ailing and didn't appear to have long to live. Could I recommend writers for a bio of the Chairman? I sent off a couple of names, adding that I was also quite familiar with Sinatra's music and story, and that I had in my library not only a good number of Sinatra recordings but also books, from gossipy tomes to Will Friedwald's splendid *Sinatra! The Song Is You.*

I got the assignment and found myself, once more, enmeshed in the fabled Time Life editorial machinery. I remember hearing, many years before, about it. Reporters for *Time* and its various sisters—*Life, Sports Illustrated, People,* and others—never actually wrote articles, it was said. They simply submitted files, which, after fact-checking, would disappear into a Time Life maw and be spit out, in a matter of days, as a part of the latest issue. It was hard to believe, but it seemed true enough when I got an assignment from *People* in 1983 for a piece on Ali McGraw, who was in a miniseries on television, *Winds of War.* I was asked to interview her and submit an article. But I was told that my submission would be used as the basis for an article that might or might not resemble what I sent in. What was published went through more than the winds of editing. It was not my article at all, and I was shocked to see the credits at the end: "Written by Chet Flippo, reported by Ben Fong-Torres." Chet, of course, was a fellow alumnus of *Rolling Stone;* he'd wound up as a staff writer at *People* before returning to his true love: writing about country music, which he does to this day.

As the years went by, policies changed, and my Jerry Garcia bio piece got into print pretty much intact, except for some trimming for space.

But *People* and its various siblings didn't get to the top of the charts by improvising. For the Sinatra assignment, I got specific directions from the editor, Cutler Durkee: start with about 100 lines (whatever those were) telling readers who Sinatra was and "why we cared," then start telling the life story. My piece, he said, would be the one that would tell the whole Sinatra story, so he advised taking it step by step. Which is exactly what I did. You can even see that in the first paragraphs. But I took too many steps and wrote about 10,000 words, when Durkee had requested between 3,500 and 4,000. But, hey, the research team at *People* had sent me printouts of more than 100 articles about Sinatra, just in case my library of Sinatra books, CDs, albums, and videos wasn't sufficient.

Given only eight days to produce the biography, I'd taken a few days off from *Gavin* to write it, then spent an entire Sunday slashing it down, to about 5,300, and let the pros at *People* do the rest. They found another 2,000 words that didn't need to be there, and we met the deadline.

Only a year and a half before Sinatra died on May 14, 1998.

Scene: 1944. Thirty thousand teenage girls, unable to get seats at Manhattan's Paramount Theatre, riot in Times Square, stopping cars and breaking shop windows. The object of their adoration? A 28-year-old big-eared beanpole named Frank Sinatra.

Scene: 1947. Upset with a newspaper columnist who wrote about his socializing with Mafia chieftains, Sinatra spots the journalist at a New York City nightclub, belts him, and is arrested for assault.

Scene: 1953. With his record sales dropping and his movie career in a tailspin, Sinatra reinvents himself with an Oscar-winning performance in *From Here to Eternity.*

Scene: 1961. Frank Sinatra, pop singer and power broker, produces the inaugural celebration for his friend President John F. Kennedy and escorts Jackie to the gala.

Scene: 1963. Sinatra delivers $240,000 to a deserted Los Angeles gas station for the safe return of his kidnapped son, Frank Jr.

Scene: 1973. At a pre-inaugural party for Richard Nixon, an out-of-control Sinatra lashes out at *Washington Post* columnist Maxine Cheshire, calling her a $2 whore and stuffing $2 into her glass.

Scene: 1995. For Sinatra's eightieth birthday, a multigenerational Who's Who of showbiz gathers at the Shrine Auditorium in Los Angeles. They range from Tony Bennett to Ray Charles to Bruce Springsteen, Bob Dylan, Bono, and Salt-N-Pepa—a trio of young women who strut, hip-hop, and coo slightly revised lyrics from one of their songs: "Whatta man, whatta man, whatta man, whatta mighty good man, Ol' Blue Eyes."

In a career encompassing some 2,000 recorded songs, almost 300 albums, 60-some films, and countless TV shows and concerts, Frank Sinatra worked alongside both Bing Crosby, who preceded him, and Elvis Presley, who followed him as a teen idol. He walked with Presidents and visited with Nikita Khrushchev and Queen Elizabeth. He squired a Who's Hot of Hollywood stars, among them Ava Gardner, Marilyn Monroe, Lauren Bacall, Grace Kelly, Kim Novak, and Mia Farrow.

At the eightieth birthday tribute, jokes are told about Sinatra's penchant for fisticuffs, and a video montage includes headlines about his numerous amours, dustups, and friends in low places. Sinatra smiles through it all. For every little dig, there are heartfelt salutes. "What Toscanini was to classical music," says Bennett, "Frank Sinatra is to American popular songs." As the stars convene for the finale, "New York, New York," Sinatra shakes off Bennett, who offers an arm to help him to the stage, and takes the microphone. The Voice, frayed at the edges like a musical Old Glory, roars out the final words—NEWWWW . . . YORRRORRRRRK!—holding the last note for an impressive 12 seconds.

Whatta man, indeed. When Frank Sinatra died of a heart attack on May 14, the accolades began again, this time from around the world. Radio and television stations played Sinatra tributes all weekend. Los Angeles' landmark circular Capitol Records building was draped in black. Presidents spoke—when remembering Frank, said Bill Clinton, "I think every American would have to smile and say he really did it his way"—and so, as the song goes, did puppets, paupers, pirates, poets, pawns, and a King (Alan, who said, "In a hundred years, when people get together to study pop music, Sinatra will be taught—for his phrasing, his musicianship, his style."). After 82 years, it seemed almost everyone knew—and had an opinion about—the skinny kid from Hoboken.

According to family lore, Francis Albert Sinatra entered the world fighting for his life. Born on December 12, 1915, he weighed a hefty 13½ pounds but wasn't breathing. Legend had it that he took his first gasps of air only after his grandmother held him under a cold faucet. During the difficult delivery, the doctor tore the boy's left earlobe and cheek. Sinatra would carry the scars for the rest of his life.

An only child, Frank grew up in the Little Italy section of Hoboken, New Jersey, a former resort town just across the Hudson River from Manhattan. "My mother was very modern in a sense and fairly ambitious," Sinatra said. "She went to nursing school and became a midwife. And she was a troubleshooter." Natalie Catherine "Dolly" Sinatra was, in fact, a fixer: Frank's father, Martin, a soft-spoken former boxer, owed his later career as a fireman to her connections. A woman of prodigious political skills, she became a prominent Democratic party district leader who could go to city hall and extract favors for family, friends, and neighbors. In the Prohibition era she opened a tavern. Extending her work beyond midwifery, she also performed abortions.

At 15, Sinatra was expelled from A.J. Demarest High School for what he later characterized as "general rowdiness." He worked on the waterfront and at a local paper, but his heart was in having a singing career like his idol, Bing Crosby. Dolly bought him a $65 sound system that gave him an edge over the competition. Later, when she heard that a local group, the Three Flashes, was to appear on a popular radio show, *Major Bowes and His Original Amateur Hour,* Dolly leaned on the boys to bring her son onboard. Appearing on *Bowes* as the Hoboken Four, they were such a hit that Bowes booked them for a national caravan tour.

Performing one-nighters from Chicago to Seattle, Sinatra learned his craft. He also learned about jealousy: when women in the audience showed a distinct preference for Frank, other members of the Hoboken Four took to beating him up after the shows. He left the tour early.

His next break came while he was working as a singing waiter and emcee at the Rustic Cabin near Alpine, New Jersey. The pay wasn't much—$15 a week—but Sinatra knew the club's shows were broadcast on radio and recognized the value of publicity. One evening trumpeter Harry James, who was starting his own band, came by to hear the singing waiter from Hoboken—and signed him for $75 per week. Neither Frank nor his new wife, former childhood sweetheart Nancy Barbato, could believe their luck.

Still, Sinatra was thinking bigger. Soon he heard that Tommy Dorsey, one of the most popular bandleaders of the day, was looking for a new singer. James, ever the gentleman, tore up Sinatra's contract and let him go. At his first performance with Dorsey, in Indianapolis in February 1940, Sinatra "broke it up completely," Jack Egan, a Dorsey friend, recalled. "When Frank started slurring down on those notes . . . the kids started screaming."

And so it began. By the end of that year, Sinatra had his first No. 1 hit, "I'll Never Smile Again," and in 1941 he was named top male vocalist by *Billboard*. In later years, Sinatra always said that he learned to breathe properly and hold notes for exceptionally long stretches by watching how Dorsey played the trombone. "Instead of singing only two bars or four bars of music at a time—like most of the other guys around—I was able to sing six bars, and in some songs eight bars, without taking a visible or audible breath." That flowing quality of his singing became a Sinatra signature.

After an acrimonious split from Dorsey—who tried to hold Sinatra to an extortionate ten-year contract—Sinatra went solo and was booked as an "extra added attraction" with King of Swing Benny Goodman for the New Year's show at New York City's Paramount Theatre. The moment Sinatra stepped onstage, he later recalled, "the sound that greeted me was absolutely deafening, a tremendous roar . . . I was scared stiff. . . . Benny froze too. He turned around, looked at the audience and said, 'What the hell is that?' I burst out laughing." Sinatra's press agent George Evans later admitted he had paid a gaggle of teenage girls to scream Frankie's name and faint on cue. From that small spark did a wildfire ensue: soon thousands of bobby-soxers were swooning for real, starting fan clubs like Slaves of Sinatra and the Hotra Sinatra Club, and buying records by the truckload. The singer, unfit for military service because of a punctured eardrum incurred at birth, thought wartime emotions played a role in his popularity. "It was the war years, and there was a great loneliness. I was the boy in every corner drugstore, the boy who'd gone off to war."

The spotlight Sinatra had sought so hungrily was his. It brought attention from the press, which he came to despise. Of Hollywood reporters in particular he once said, "All day long they lie in the sun, and when the sun goes down, they lie some more." Still, much of the trouble was his own making. In 1947 he traveled to Havana and fraternized with gang lord Lucky Luciano. A journalist, Lee Mortimer, berated the singer in his column for meeting with mobsters. When Sinatra later spotted Mortimer in a bar, he punched him. Sinatra also drew attention to himself with a string of affairs, including a protracted and very public courtship of Ava Gardner. The Sinatras, who by 1950 had three children—Nancy, nine, Frank Jr., six, and Tina, nearly two—separated that year and would soon divorce.

By then Sinatra's career was in trouble. He had displayed his versatility in several movies and earned a special Oscar for *The House I Live In,* a short film about tolerance. But more recent movies, like *The Kissing Bandit,* had flopped, his record sales were falling, and one night at the Copacabana his voice gave out completely. (Doctors later determined that a vocal cord had hemorrhaged.) His personal life was also a mess: in 1950, on the outs with Gardner, who would become his second wife, he phoned her from a hotel room and told her, "I can't stand it any longer, I'm going to kill myself—now!" and fired two shots into a mattress, leaving her to think he had taken his life. (Alerted by Gardner, friends found the inebriated singer and cleared up any evidence of trouble before police arrived.)

Written off as yesterday's teen fad, Sinatra battled tenaciously to come back. A gritty movie role as a tough, good-hearted soldier from Brooklyn in *From Here to Eternity* brought him a 1953 Oscar and the respect he craved. Almost simultaneously, his new bosses at Capitol Records, where he had signed a one-year contract, paired him with arranger Nelson Riddle. With Riddle's encouragement, Sinatra, a longtime jazz fan, began to swing a little, toying with phrasing and lyrics.

"I don't know what other singers feel when they articulate lyrics," he once told *Playboy* magazine, by way of explaining his ability to connect with listeners. "But being an 18-carat manic-depressive and having lived a life of violent emotional contradiction, I have an over-acute capacity for sadness as well as elation." By 1954 he was on the charts with "Young at Heart," and began to strut again.

As always, he made news—good and bad. When pal Sammy Davis, Jr. lost an eye in an automobile accident, Sinatra rushed to the hospital to offer comfort. He gave lavishly to charity and performed at benefits. But there were other headlines too. In a 1954 scandal that became known as the "wrong door raid," persons unknown kicked down the front door of a Hollywood apartment. Evidence mounted that Sinatra and his friend Joe DiMaggio were behind the raid and had been looking for DiMaggio's estranged wife, Marilyn Monroe. During hearings a potential witness told the police he had been beaten up by men he believed were sent by Sinatra. No indictments were ever issued.

Predictably, Sinatra was unhappy with his portrayal in the press. A six-part series by syndicated columnist Dorothy Kilgallen so riled him that he sent her a tombstone engraved with her name. For years afterward, he would insult her during his shows, calling her "the chinless wonder." (Later, hearing of her death, Sinatra remarked, "Guess I got to change my whole act.") Public vilification of perceived enemies would become a trademark.

There was no controversy, however, about the quality of his singing. In 1958, *Come Fly with Me* topped the charts, *Frank Sinatra Sings for Only the Lonely* was a moper's masterpiece, and *Come Dance with Me!* earned two 1959 Grammys, for album of the year and best vocal performance, male. Sinatra also commanded the world stage, emceeing a film premiere attended by Queen Elizabeth and hosting a luncheon honoring Soviet Premier Nikita Khrushchev.

Sinatra had recently met John F. Kennedy, the young Massachusetts senator whose sister was married to actor Peter Lawford, a Sinatra pal. A lifelong Democrat, Sinatra was excited to be enlisted for the Kennedy campaign. He re-recorded his hit "High Hopes" with special, pro-JFK lyrics and in late 1959 entertained Kennedy at his Palm Springs compound. Later, Sinatra put a brass plaque that read "John F. Kennedy Slept Here" on a guest bedroom door.

When Kennedy won the election, Sinatra was exultant. Asked to oversee the inaugural, he commandeered performers—including Nat King Cole and Jimmy Durante—and attended to every detail. Jacqueline Kennedy arrived at the gala on Frank's arm. Sinatra was in his glory.

And then the roof fell in.

After the election, Robert Kennedy, the newly appointed attorney general, studied FBI files on Sinatra and, citing the singer's alleged mob affiliations, suggested that his brother cool the relationship. Sinatra, in anticipation of a long-scheduled presidential visit, had added on to his

Palm Springs house and even built a helipad. At the last minute, President Kennedy canceled the Sinatra visit and stayed nearby with Bing Crosby instead. Humiliated and angry, Sinatra reportedly smashed the helipad with a sledgehammer.

Professionally, Sinatra was going gangbusters in 1963. One report estimated he was earning $20 million a year from records, movies, and ownership or interest in film companies, radio stations, a record company, and real estate, including a casino, the Cal-Neva Lodge. His associations once again made headlines when the Nevada Gaming Commission accused him of knowingly playing host to Sam Giancana, a notorious mobster, at Cal-Neva. When Commissioner Edward Olsen launched an investigation, Sinatra, he said, phoned him and "called me every name in the book. I had never heard some of the things he called me." Just before a formal hearing was to take place, Sinatra sold his interest in Cal-Neva.

The assassination of President Kennedy that November devastated Sinatra. "For three days . . . my father grieved alone, locked away in his bedroom," his daughter Nancy later wrote. But there was little time to mourn. Sixteen days after Kennedy's death, thugs broke into a Lake Tahoe lodge and kidnapped Frank Sinatra, Jr., then 19, who had embarked on a singing career. After two tense days, Sinatra paid a $240,000 ransom, Frank Jr. was released, and the three kidnappers were quickly apprehended. At the trial, their lawyer claimed that the entire episode had been set up by Frank Jr. to get publicity. Scoffed Sinatra Sr.: "This family needs publicity like it needs peritonitis." The jury didn't buy the argument either. Two of the kidnappers were sentenced to life in prison, the third to 75 years.

Sinatra turned 50 in 1965 and—after a brief engagement to Juliet Prowse and relationships with actress Jill St. John and others—announced that he didn't want to marry anyone in show business. Then, promptly, he contradicted himself in spectacular style: following a whirlwind public courtship, he married actress Mia Farrow, 21, in 1966. Sixteen months later they separated. Farrow confessed that, despite their love, she could never fit in with his life of gambling, bar brawls, and carousing.

His career only improved. "Strangers in the Night," with its throwaway "doobie-doobie do," gave him his first No. 1 single in more than a decade. "That's Life" again pumped him into the Top 10. Finally, in 1967, he scored a multimillion-selling single, "Somethin' Stupid," by teaming up with daughter Nancy. It was cotton candy on vinyl, but it clicked.

The dark side of Frank, as always, continued to make news. A dinner party at the Polo Lounge to celebrate Dean Martin's birthday erupted in an argument between Sinatra and a businessman at a nearby booth. The businessman ended up at a hospital with a skull fracture. No one was ever charged.

In Las Vegas, at the Sands casino—home turf of the Rat Pack, Sinatra's hard-partying band of showbiz pals—Sinatra allegedly went on a rampage when the house cut off his credit line after he ran up some $50,000 in gambling debts. He confronted a Sands executive, Carl Cohen, and tried to hurl a table at him. Cohen responded by punching Sinatra in the mouth. (A similar incident, again sparked by gambling debts, occurred at Caesars Palace three years later. That one ended only after Sanford Waterman, the casino's manager, drew a pistol on Sinatra.) Sinatra wrapped up 1968 by recording his almost belligerent manifesto, "My Way."

In March 1971, at age 55, Sinatra did the utterly unexpected: he announced his retirement. "It has been a fruitful, busy, uptight, loose, sometimes boisterous, occasionally sad but always exciting three decades," he said. Now, he wanted time "for reflection, reading, self-examination." He denied that he was ill or that he feared becoming stale: "I just quit, that's all. I don't want to put any more makeup on. I don't want to perform anymore. I'm not going to stop living. Maybe I'm going to start living." For his final number at his farewell concert in Los Angeles, he sang an old saloon song, "Angel Eyes." After the last line, "Excuse me while I disappear," he walked slowly offstage.

Sinatra stayed retired—for all of 16 months. Feeling spurned by the Democrats, he supported Richard Nixon in 1972 and became good buddies with Spiro Agnew. In 1973 he performed at the White House and, warmed by the reception, began thinking seriously about a return to the public stage.

The comeback came in the form of a TV special and an album, both titled *Ol' Blue Eyes Is Back*. The inevitable headlines followed close behind. On a tour of Australia, members of his entourage got physical when a reporter approached to ask for an interview. Sinatra didn't help the situation when he publicly called local reporters "parasites, hookers, and pimps." Australian unions showed their outrage by refusing to move stage props, deliver room service, or even fuel Sinatra's plane until he apologized. He did, grudgingly.

The late '70s and '80s saw the emergence of Sinatra as the tuxedoed gray eminence of pop. He settled, at last, into a marriage that worked: fourth wife Barbara Marx was a former showgirl and an ex-wife of Marx Brother Zeppo Marx. She understood his world and was willing, as two previous Mrs. Sinatras had not been, to play the role of supportive wife.

Professionally he showed no hint of retiring. He organized Ronald Reagan's inaugural galas in 1981 and 1985 and served as unofficial entertainment coordinator at White House functions. He gathered awards, including the Kennedy Center Honor for Lifetime Achievement in 1983 and an honorary doctorate from the Stevens Institute of Technology in Hoboken, where as a youth he had hoped to study bridge building. "I wanted to be an engineer," Sinatra recalled. "It was my great desire until I got mixed up in vocalizing."

He hit the road with Sammy and Dean in 1988 (an ailing Martin would soon be replaced by Liza Minnelli) and, for good measure, released the best-selling album of his entire career, *Duets,* in 1993. More than 50 years after he began singing professionally, Frank Sinatra gave his last full concert, in Japan, on December 20, 1994.

By the time he turned 80, Sinatra had well earned the party at the Shrine. The last performer that night was the first to break form, to not do a Sinatra song or a number customized for the honoree. But Bob Dylan, in singing his 1964 ballad "Restless Farewell," chose wisely. The song concluded:

> *Oh a false clock tries to tick out my time*
> *To disgrace, distract, and bother me.*
> *And the dirt of gossip blows into my face,*
> *And the dust of rumors covers me.*
> *But if the arrow is straight and the point is slick,*
> *It can pierce through dust no matter how thick.*
> *So I'll make my stand*
> *And remain as I am*
> *And bid farewell and not give a damn.*

Sinatra, who most likely did not have a Dylan album in his collection, beamed. **—*People*, May 1998**

DUSTY SPRINGFIELD

"THAT NOISE IS THE JOY"

I **mentioned in** my introduction to the Michael Nesmith piece various artists who I interviewed, but whose articles never materialized, for one reason or another. I went on guilt trips about Dusty Springfield, the Staple Singers, and Bill Graham, who I interviewed at length in the mid-'70s for an official *Rolling Stone* Interview that, due to his schedule and ever-shifting priorities, never got completed.

Fortunately, I was able to revive one of these stories when, in 1999, I heard from the editors of a new music Web site, allmusic.com. They were looking for "content" for their online magazine and hoped I'd write a regular column. Although the *All Music Guide* series of books was well established, the site was a start-up; it needed to build up as many articles, old and new, as possible, so the editor offered plentiful latitude in what I could write about. As long as my articles could link to other sites, so that readers could quickly find CDs, memorabilia, or additional information about the subjects, allmusic.com would be happy.

So I pitched Dusty Springfield, who had just been inducted into the Rock and Roll Hall of Fame. I had my notes from our interview in L.A. back in 1973, and as I reviewed them, I was reminded of the many characteristics she displayed during our visit—tough, sad, vulnerable, self-critical, and, most of all, candid.

It was just one of those things. I interviewed Dusty Springfield for two hours in Beverly Hills one afternoon in May 1973, for *Rolling Stone*. She was feeling down in the dumps, unhappy with her latest album and uncertain about her musical direction, but we had a good time, talking in her apartment, in a car, and at a Mexican restaurant.

I never wrote the story. I'm not sure why. It may have been the press of other articles, or it may have been her album, *Cameo*. It was doing a quick fade by the time we got together, and, although critics were kind to her, Dusty declared herself "embarrassed" by the album. She would have her day in *Rolling Stone*, but under someone else's byline.

Dusty, born in London in 1939, died this year on March 2 after a long battle against breast cancer. She died on the eve of her induction into the Rock and Roll Hall of Fame.

As I searched for my tapes of our interview, her music came readily to mind. And what a range she covered, from the rip-roaring "I Only Want to Be with You" in 1964 (Dusty was the first British female to hit the charts during the British Invasion) to dramatic ballads ("You Don't Have to Say You Love Me") and pop tunes by turns silly and sultry ("Wishin' and Hopin'", "The Look of Love"). She infused soul into all her work, and her 1968 album, *Dusty in Memphis,* which contained the hit, "Son of a Preacher Man," is still considered her masterpiece.

She was successful, influential, and beloved. The Pet Shop Boys called on her to co-star in their 1987 recording of "What Have I Done to Deserve This?", she received the Order of the British Empire award in January, and Elton John did the honors at her posthumous Hall of Fame induction in mid-March. But, despite the praise, she was deeply insecure and self-critical to the extreme.

On the day we met, she was charming, joking about her "mishmash" of an outfit, from a floppy London hat to clattering Moroccan necklaces to what she called "apologetic platforms." Born Mary Catherine Isabel Bernadette O'Brien, she said she was known as "Pudge" as a kid. She spoke with intensity about her battles to make music on her own terms. But she also broke up, laughing, when she got to recalling food fights in the good old days. Here are some excerpts from our day together.

Dusty on *Dusty in Memphis*

I hated it for a long time, and then I liked it. I don't like all of it.

Why did you hate it?

I just didn't like the mix. The songs, I liked. I had lots to do with choosing them. I don't know what went wrong. They just couldn't find more material for me; they didn't know what to do with me.

I didn't like "Son of a Preacher Man." I knew it was a hit song, but I didn't like the record; I liked the other side ["Just a Little Lovin'"].

What was the overall experience of recording in Memphis?

That really threw me. I wasn't used to working with just a rhythm section—with sweetening afterwards, and I was very unhappy. I'm the kind of singer that wants to bounce off the whole . . . setup.

You mean you want the string section, the whole orchestra, there?

Yeah, I want to hear them coming through those [headphones]. I just want one date, you go in there, and you hear all these gorgeous sounds in your ears. One day someone's going to invent a system where a singer can just stand in the middle of the studio and have that noise. That noise is the joy, and the joy gets rid of the inhibition, and makes me sing the best way I can sing.

After Memphis, you did A Brand New Me *in Philadelphia with two great producers, Gamble and Huff—Kenny and Leon. What did you think of the album?*

I was disappointed. While I was making it, I was entranced, because I loved the musicians and the way they played. But the end result wasn't really exciting. I was trying things that really weren't in me. For example, there's a song called 'Let's Get Together' or something. It needed a much more loose singer. When Kenny sang it, teaching it to me, he sounded terrific, natural. I had to think about it a lot, and it sounded like it.

I loved them very much, but the kind of music they like takes a lot of improvisation, and I'm not that kind of singer. Basically I'm a melodic singer; it's hard for me to ad lib.

On Songwriters

Do you have any favorite composers?

I like to listen to Randy Newman. Valerie Simpson writes great. Holland-Dozier-Holland. I think "Ain't No Mountain High Enough" is a great song. There must be other people that I like. Name me some people.

Carole King . . .

I love Carole King! I used to collect Carole King demos, from the beginning. I think she's fantastic, just fantastic. "Might as Well Rain (Until September)." Loved that song. There was a song, "Goin' Back," that she wanted me to do, that she didn't want anyone else to do. I did "Goin' Back" in England, and it's got fantastic orchestration, and I was proud of it. Another one of hers is "Some of Your Lovin'." I was so happy with that, with Doris Troy and Madeline Bell in the background, and it was a hit. She was happy with it too. She really loved it.

On Her First Music

As a child, I heard classical and some New Orleans, Jelly Roll Morton. I picked up what my brother played. Tom's a songwriter. He wrote "Georgy Girl."

When did you start to sing?

When I was very small. I was very interested in film musicals—especially 20th Century Fox. My brother and I would set up a broadcast system, neighbors would come in and sit in one room, we'd sing and play piano in the other room.

You sang with another group, even did a little television work, before Tom formed the Springfields in 1961.

The Springfields happened at the right time. We were an extraordinary mixture of pseudo-country, folk . . . indescribable, I would put it. There were two guitars and me in the middle trying to find room to move my arms. I felt like I was directing traffic.

The Springfields hit with "Silver Threads and Golden Needles," and then you went solo and got a reputation for sounding black.

When I first started, I copied every black singer. One week I was Baby Washington, next week I was the lead singer of the Shirelles. You know, I had no style at all.

I never pretended to be black, and I didn't really sound black. People put that label on me. It was only an influence. There were just certain things in it; an empathy, whatever you like.

I listened to Motown—early Motown. The Contours, Mary Wells. In London, I was a host of a show called *The Motown Revue,* an hour special. I was the only white artist on it, with the Miracles, the Temptations, the Supremes, Stevie Wonder, the Vandellas. Also, I played the Brooklyn Fox for a Murray the K show with literally a Motown revue.

Your first Top Ten hit in the United States was "Wishin' and Hopin'," which, in retrospect, was pretty sexist.

Yeah, but I don't see that at all. Nothing. I have a blank spot. That people can see that [sexism] is absolutely amazing. Because I don't think in those terms.

That was the follow-up to "I Only Want to Be with You."

I just knew it was a hit, and did it. I didn't think about the lyrics at all. But my god, I did think about the lyrics of "You Don't Have to Say You Love Me." I heard that song a year beforehand, in Italian, in San Remo, and cried. When that happens to me, I know it's going to work.

"The Look of Love" certainly worked both in the movie Casino Royale *and on the radio.*

Musicians tell me they liked "The Look of Love," but I hit so many flat notes on it! I did it at ten o'clock in the morning.

On Being Demanding

During the Springfields era, I found that to speak my mind was the best thing. When I did my first sessions for Philips Records, I had a kind of recording manager who allowed me to take over. All the hit records I had in England were found, produced, almost promoted by me. I never took any credit. It wasn't fashionable for women to have credit. Now it's very fashionable. But I did the whole bloody lot myself! If you knew how hard it was to work for Philips . . . Every damn thing was against you. Changing promotion men, each one was worse than the other.

How'd you rise above it?

My strength can transcend that kind of shit. I really can do that.

What's your favorite part about performing?

Well, I'm not good at stage patter. I'm very aloof. I want to make them smile. Nothing makes me happier than seeing somebody that, maybe it's a big night out for them, and just to see a smile of enjoyment. And yet, it's funny, I communicate mostly with audiences with sad songs.

People seem to find they can relate to . . . there is a sadness there in my voice, I don't know why, it didn't grow on me. I was born with it. Sort of melancholy. Comes with being Irish-Scottish. Automatically melancholy and mad at the same time.

On Her Reputation

Speaking of "mad," how do you feel about the tabloids in England and all the talk about your personal life?

I've given up on this business about "gay reputation." I had a reputation before I did anything. I was once accused of raping a 13-year-old black boy in the corridors of *Ready Steady Go,* so I really don't know where I'm at!

On this whole gay thing, I've been misquoted so on it, that I really— my god . . . I really think, settling back on an old cliché, that it's no one's business, and it really has no bearing on anything.

It does have a bearing if decisions are made based on reasons people might have for liking or disliking you. And one of those reasons could be a prejudice towards gay people.

That is, IF I am . . . or if they think I am . . . yes. One of the reasons I'm very insecure is that I have many reputations, and many things that are totally unfounded. Being unreliable. Not turning up for a show. Never finishing an engagement. Doing the craziest things.

In the early days I was pretty wild. I came in on the wave of Beatlemania, and they somehow associated me with the Beatles. [At the Brooklyn Fox] I only had to stick my head out in the street—and [screams, high-pitched] *AGGGGH!!!*

It was amazing, when I first started singing on my own. There were crazy scenes, because it was sort of asexual. They didn't mind that you were a boy or a girl. They would come up sort of onstage. The minute I appeared onstage, girls would scream. Purely because they were so hyped up on the whole atmosphere of a rock 'n' roll show.

The whole troupe thought I was crazy. My brother and I had a habit of throwing things, particularly dishes. It saved washing them. I got a reputation in England because I'd start throwing food at people. My brother was the instigator. I threw two parties that completely disintegrated. People you'd least expect. Martha and the Vandellas—all their hatred, all those suppressed feelings came out with long French loaves that they were belting each other over the heads. Kim Weston was cowering behind a lounge chair in her mink coat. Gene Pitney was sliding around. Everyone was coated in flour. Nobody hit anybody; people just laughed and laughed. I remember aiming a sardine across the room at one of the Shangri-Las, straight down the front of her dress!

It started with a slice of salami. There was an agent's wife with a low-back dress, so we snuck the salami down her back, and gradually the whole thing took off.

And to think that, as a teenager, you were a clerk in a department store . . .
You've been reading old Philips bios.

Let's see: "'My favorite actor is Daffy Duck,' bubbles Dusty Springfield . . ."
Well, I still like Daffy Duck. Can't think of anyone I like better. Actually, that's who I'm having an affair with. Difficult, but rewarding!

—*allmusic.com,* **September 1999**

GEORGE HARRISON:

A LOVE-HAIGHT RELATIONSHIP

Soon after George Harrison died on November 29, 2001, the phone started ringing—it was those damned media outlets again—before I had time to sort out my thoughts about him. I'd covered a tour of his for a *Rolling Stone* cover story in 1974. That may have explained the volume of calls. But when one of the callers turned out to be the *San Francisco Chronicle* looking for a set of recollections, I had to untangle my various feelings about "Beatle George," from admiration for his musical accomplishments—especially in the shadow of John and Paul—to a lingering uneasiness about the article I'd written way back when. That piece, along with a report on the furious reactions to it from some Harrison fans, is in *Not Fade Away*. I was witness to the beginning of that tour, and it was a rough start. I reported what I saw and heard, and still stand by my article, which included an interview with a defensive, defiant Harrison.

But now, with Harrison gone at age 58, and knowing that he'd had a difficult last few years—including the diagnosis of throat cancer in 1998 and a horrific knife attack by an crazed intruder at his home the following year—I wanted to offer an appreciation. A balanced one, but an appreciation nonetheless.

It would be a stretch to say that George Harrison ever left his heart in San Francisco.

But the last time he was in the Bay Area, on a 1974 tour I covered for *Rolling Stone* magazine, he left a lot of much-needed money and single-handedly kept a major part of the Haight-Ashbury Free Clinic afloat.

Harrison played in the Bay Area three times as a Beatle and once by himself. When the Beatles first performed in the city (or just across the southern border, in Daly City, at the Cow Palace) in August 1964, their appearance marked the first of the Fab Four's first full tour of the United States and Canada.

A year later, again in August, again at the Cow Palace, they performed the last show of a brief, two-week tour that started just after the release of their second film, *Help!*

And then, on August 29, 1966, they played Candlestick Park in San Francisco proper, not knowing that they were performing their last paid concert. (Their 1969 rooftop romp at Abbey Road Studios in London was a freebie, filmed for the documentary that would be titled *Let It Be.*)

Although I was a certifiable Beatlemaniac and had every song on *Rubber Soul* memorized, I didn't see the band live until that summer evening in 1966 at Candlestick Park. I vividly remember George Harrison as the man in white. Socks, that is. I remember the sonic blur of their music—they played, as Paul McCartney once told me, at double-speed and couldn't hear themselves above the teenaged din—and I recall telephoning a college buddy (the *Chronicle*'s Pat Sullivan) at home, so that he could at least hear some of the din. But most of all, I remember George's white socks. He may have been the "quiet Beatle," but he knew how to stand out.

As shy and reclusive as he was said to be, George stood out again when he came back to San Francisco on August 8, 1967, and visited the Haight. He and Patti had traveled from England to Los Angeles the week before, renting a house on Blue Jay Way, which gave Harrison an idea for a tune. He'd helped promote and had attended a concert by Ravi Shankar, the Indian composer and sitar player, in Hollywood.

He told reporters that he was simply curious about the San Francisco hippie phenomenon. George, then 24, Patti, and press agent Derek Taylor drove into the area in the early evening and strolled, unnoticed, along Haight Street. They reached the sector of Golden Gate Park then known as

"Hippie Hill," where they found a young man performing before a gathering of about 20 long-haired youths. After a few minutes, Harrison asked to borrow the musician's guitar, and proceeded to play. A few more minutes later, one young woman finally recognized him.

"Hey," *she shouted.* "That's George Harrison. That's George Harrison!"

David Swanston, a *Chronicle* reporter on the scene, noted what happened next:

> As the cry echoed through the park, hippies clambered down hills, dropped from trees, and sprang from behind bushes. A sizable crowd formed.
>
> Harrison played for about ten more minutes and then shouted, "Let's go for a walk."
>
> "Yeah," shouted the hippies, "let's go."
>
> And off they went. Harrison strumming the guitar, the hippies following along. As the crowd left the park and moved down Haight, it grew. And grew.
>
> As Harrison strolled and strummed, hippies bubbled up beside him and posed questions:
>
> "How does it feel to have the family all together?" one asked.
>
> "It's gettin' better all the time," Harrison responded.
>
> "What do ya think of the Haight-Ashbury?" another queried.
>
> "Wow, if it's all like this it's all too much," Harrison answered.

That's not what he told others, though. In *Dark Horse,* a Harrison biography, author Geoffrey Giuliano quotes him saying that he'd thought the Haight "would be something like King's Road (in London), only more. Somehow I expected them to all own their own little shops. I expected them to be nice and clean and happy."

Instead, he said, he found the hippies "hideous, spotty little teenagers."

But Harrison didn't forget the Haight.

Riding high on his triumphant 1971 solo debut, *All Things Must Pass,* and his trend-setting, all-star "Concert for Bangladesh"—a fund-raiser for that country's starving children—Harrison decided to turn several stops on his 1974 tour into benefits. And he had heard about the plight of San Francisco's Haight-Ashbury Free Medical Clinic.

The clinic opened in 1967, the year of Harrison's first visit, and had survived the district's post-Summer-of-Love speed/rip-off/deterioration phase. The clinic had grown, but had suffered some financial setbacks and was getting ready to shut down the medical sector, which had spent $67,500 the previous year to treat 10,000 patients. Harrison donated net profits from his first Bay Area concert to the clinic—a total of $66,000.

The day after that first concert, Harrison, his future wife, Olivia Arias, who was at that time working for his record label, Dark Horse, and several others visited the clinic. This time, he was no pied piper leading an adoring mass. Patients at the clinic recognized him. But, as founder Dr. David E. Smith said, "Nobody gaped; nobody mobbed him or kissed his ass."

Harrison toured the facilities and chatted with several staff members. "He said he hoped to start a ripple with other musicians doing the same kind of things," writer Amie Hill, a clinic volunteer, reported. "The doctors gave him a plaque, and someone told me he said, 'Don't thank me; it's not me, it's something else over us that acts through people like me. I'm just an instrument.'"

And as he spoke, he broke into one of his songs, "The Lord Loves the One."

Which brings us to the matter of the mixed reviews. On his tour, which began in Vancouver and Seattle, then headed into San Francisco and Oakland, Harrison pointedly disavowed his Beatle past at the risk of upsetting his fans. Now a devotee of Indian music and Eastern spiritualism, he wanted his fans to listen to Ravi Shankar's music, and gave a large portion of the concert over to Shankar's Indian orchestra. When Harrison deigned to perform Beatles songs or hits of his own, he changed lyrics, so that it was "In my life, I love *God* more," and the guitar no longer gently wept, but smiled. He sang those lyrics in a voice strained by overuse during rehearsals. As it turned out, the protests came not only from newspaper critics, but from his inner circle, and from some fans as well.

I covered the beginning of the tour for *Rolling Stone* magazine. After the Bay Area shows, we met between concerts at the Forum in Los Angeles, where, backed by Olivia and several others, he stoutly and stubbornly held his ground. I asked what he had to say to those fans who'd paid $9.50— then a top price for concert tickets—and wanted at least a taste of "Beatle George."

Harrison leaned forward: "Well, why do they want to see if there is a Beatle George? I don't say I'm Beatle George."

"Well, one of the things you don't control . . ."

"I *do* control . . ."

" . . . is how the audience feels about you. The conceptions . . ."

"Okay, but I certainly am going to control my own concept of me. Gandhi says create and preserve the image of your choice. The image of my choice is not Beatle George. If they want to do that they can go and see Wings, then."

At a pre-tour press conference, Harrison had opened with an odd statement: "I really didn't want to do this for a living. I've always wanted to be a lumberjack." When I asked what he meant by that, I got a dose of the humor that, like his musicianship, was noted all too little.

"What I mean," he said, "is like Billy Preston says, 'I ain't tryin' to be your hero.' But I'm just a lumberjack." Softly, Harrison began to sing Monty Python and the Flying Circus' ludicrous and lusty anthem about the joys of being a lumberjack. But as the laughter in the room subsided, it was clear that Harrison had a serious point to make.

"I'd rather try and uphold something that I believe in than destroy something I don't believe in. Because it's a waste of time."

In the end, he said, "My life belongs to me." He quickly corrected himself. "It actually doesn't. It belongs to Him. My life belongs to the Lord Krishna and there's me dog collar to prove it. I'm just a dog and I'm led around by me collar by Krishna . . . I'm the servant of the servant of the servant of the servant of the servant of Krishna. I'm just a groveling lumberjack lucky to be a grain of dirt in creation. That's how I feel. Never been so humble in all my life, and I feel great."

I believe that he truly did. No matter how he sounded, and no matter the poor reception he had received. And no matter that the article I wrote drew the most negative mail in my dozen years at the magazine. He was a happy grain of dirt, and I was happy for his happiness.

We had both come a long way since I saw him at Candlestick and found myself so taken by his white socks.

—*San Francisco Chronicle,* **December 2, 2001**

SHERYL CROW

"I'M WHERE
I'M SUPPOSED
TO BE"

So, how do you get an assignment from *Parade*? You just drop into the office every 15 years or so.

Somewhere in the mid-'80s I'd stopped writing for the magazine. There was no particular reason, and I stayed busy with the *Chronicle,* with other magazines, and with book projects. In 2001, I was vice president of content at a company that created e-magazines, largely comprised of articles from various print publications. I called *Parade* and found an editor, Lamar Graham, who'd logged time at Wenner Media, home of *Rolling Stone, Men's Journal,* and *US Weekly.* We had something else in common: a love of the latest high-tech gadgets. Soon, we were enjoying easy conversations on the phone.

On a visit to New York, I arranged to meet Lamar for lunch, and popped into *Parade's* offices. Taking a quick tour, I ran into a couple of the editors I'd worked with in the '80s, and the question arose: Why don't you do a piece for us? Just as it was back then, *Parade* was looking to keep its readership as young as possible, and pop culture articles were crucial to its editorial mix. Soon enough, I'd dispatched a memo with a few ideas. Top of the list: Sheryl Crow.

We visited when she came to San Francisco for a concert and, just like that, I was back in the saddle. But my article did require some work. Over the years,

I'd noticed that *Parade* interviews generally began with a quote. Try as I might, I couldn't find one that worked—that summarized the story, or could grab the reader's attention. So the opening of my first draft went like this:

"Sheryl Crow is looking frazzled as we meet, an hour past our appointed time, in the lobby of the stylish Mocambo Hotel in downtown San Francisco. Even frazzled, the 40-year-old rock star looks ab fab. Her hair is still perfect from a photo session, her skin is aglow from several recent outdoor concerts, and her dress is an I'm-so-sheer, low-cut summer frock.

"A lousy hour late? No problem.

"She apologizes profusely—her voice raised, her Southern accent is more evident than usual—but, moments after being seated in a banquette in the adjoining Grand Café, she orders up a beer, a pesto pasta with rock shrimp, and all is well."

Well. That was just too long to go without a quote. I submitted the article with apologies and some trepidation. But my editor went to work and soon found a comment of Crow's that I had near the end of the article, moved it up to the top, and, as a bonus, found another quote to go with her cover photo: "This Life Is Right and Perfect."

Sometimes, it is.

━━━━━

"Even though it's a real happy, upbeat record, it was a constant battle with mourning things I had let go of, particularly in my personal life," Sheryl Crow says about her latest hit album, *C'mon, C'mon.* In the process of recording it, she tells me over lunch in San Francisco, she had just ended a relationship (with actor Owen Wilson) and was facing turning 40. "I felt like I had given up having kids and a family because of this particular record, and I had to go in and make it when I should just walk away and find a husband and get married. I was hanging onto my music and my career like it was a lifebuoy and felt like if I let it go, I wouldn't have anything. I felt like I was in a state of mourning while I was making the record."

And yet, the result was an upbeat album featuring one of the big hits of the summer, "Soak Up the Sun." It's the latest in a nine-year string of hits for Sheryl, including "All I Wanna Do," "Leaving Las Vegas," "Strong Enough," "If It Makes You Happy," and "Every Day Is a Winding Road."

Sheryl's road began in tiny Kennett, Missouri, where she was born to Bernice and Wendell Crow, who were musicians. Sheryl was writing songs

*Ben and
Sheryl Crow*

and playing keyboards in cover bands while attending the University of Missouri. She earned a degree in classical piano and a teaching credential.

Teaching, she says, was simply "the right thing to do. Both my parents, particularly my dad, had this really strong puritan work ethic. My dad is 70, he's a lawyer, and he still hasn't retired. He goes to work every day, tries cases. He raised us with this strong concept of giving back to the community." And teaching, she thought, "was a good usage for what I knew how to do best."

After graduation, she went to St. Louis, where she taught choral lessons from kindergarten through sixth grade, continued to perform with a band, and got engaged. "That was the course I was on," she said, "and I *loved* teaching. I think I was good at it. Because I'd been in bands, I was able to bring things into the classroom that a lot of kids wouldn't have been able to see.

"It's interesting with music," she says. "You're just basically helping kids try to define their personalities, more than anything else. You're teaching them discipline, appreciation, and how to define themselves creatively."

In turn, Sheryl says, the children taught her a few things: "Patience. A sense of fairness. Kids will just totally slay you with their honesty." She enjoyed teaching so much, she says, that she still dreams about it.

When Sheryl's fiancé, a churchgoing musician, told her that she should be singing "for the Lord" instead of for rock audiences, she left him and

St. Louis for Los Angeles, where she was determined to find larger audiences. In Hollywood, she knew next to nobody and survived on spunk. Hearing about a closed audition for backup singers for a Michael Jackson tour, she crashed it and got a job. But when the tour ended, Sheryl was back in Los Angeles, writing songs, waiting on tables, and falling into a funk.

"I felt like I had taken a crash course in the music industry," she says, "and I didn't realize that everything doesn't work just because you work hard and you have good intentions. I got a glimpse into big management signing you to contracts where you don't own anything. I got introduced to sexual harassment. This particular person on the Michael Jackson tour was interested in taking me on as a client, and the next thing I knew, I was having to protect and defend myself. It all crashed around me. I couldn't figure out why I was there anymore. I didn't want to be a part of it."

Sheryl pauses and smiles. "It's really funny—I spent about seven months in bed. I've had this thing with depression since I was little. I wound up downwardly spiraling into a place that I couldn't see my way out of. I remember my mom calling and saying she was going to fly out to L.A. and drag me up, and that just seemed too mortifying!" She laughs at the thought. "I wound up dragging myself up and getting myself together."

These days, she says, she's aware of carrying "a strong sense of melancholy" with her. "Depression," she notes, "is nothing more than depressing something—whether it's anger, or sadness, or whatever it is. I think, to a certain extent, you come into the world with a certain disposition, and you work with that. I'm aware of it, and I live by the newest medical findings and stuff, so there are things I feel I can do to have a more even, balanced life."

It helps that Sheryl stays close to her parents and siblings: a brother and two sisters. She's written songs with sister Kathy, and she invited her father, who used to play saxophone in swing bands, to play on her debut album, *Tuesday Night Music Club,* on a song she wrote about him.

"It always stuns me how many people I deal with who don't like some of the members of their family," says Sheryl. "My life lesson is, you get born into a family of people, and you may not be that much alike, but if you're really lucky, you'll like them and you'll love them—and I'm really lucky, 'cause I enjoy my family. There's a lot you can learn from being a family member about empathy and forgiveness, and that's what it's really all about for me."

Over the years, Sheryl, who has dated several celebrities, including Eric Clapton, has learned a few lessons about love. They haven't always been easy. "I've had relationships with people who have a perverse way of looking at love, like love is something that you earn, or that you don't deserve love."

In "If It Makes You Happy," Sheryl sang, "I'm not the kind of girl you take home." Actually, she recently declared in a television interview, "I think I'm the *perfect* girl to take home!" Now, over lunch, she agrees that, given her celebrity, she poses a challenge for many potential suitors.

"It's actually sort of sad," she says, "because I feel like who I am is who I am all the time. When I walk out onstage, I don't feel like I'm taking on an alter ego, even though I think it'd be fun. But I haven't been that disciplined or even that interested." And so, she says, if men have thought that the playful, fun-loving, ready-to-rock persona that Sheryl presents is a pose, Sheryl has news. That's her.

But she has few regrets. "I have had really great relationships with famous people and not-famous people," she says. "At the end of the day, I've gotten to love and be loved, and isn't that what it's about? I don't feel like I've missed out on anything."

Sheryl, who, in a word, is beautiful, is aware that many people have been attracted to her because of her looks. "It used to feel like a nuisance," she says, "'cause I always felt like it would rob me of my ability to be credible." In fact, after her debut CD broke through, she affected goth-punk eye makeup and glowered out of her second album cover. "I was just completely militant about not wanting to look like the girl next door," she says.

But now, "I have a better sense of humor about it. I'm willing to play with it, knowing that it can't rob me of anything I have." She even posed in bikini wear for a men's magazine earlier this year. "I enjoyed it," she says. "I liked the playfulness of it, even though rock 'n' roll, for me, is based on sexual energy, not overt sexualness. But it was fun.

"I do feel really happy being 40," she says. "I don't feel like this is the end-all, that I gotta keep on making music." In fact, she adds, "to be honest, I think this will be my last foray into the pop domain." What? But, no, Sheryl's not hanging up her guitar. It's just that, as she puts it, "I'm not really interested in competing in the pop world." She's grateful that *C'mon, C'mon* has received radio exposure, given that most of what's on the air is boy bands, hip-hop, and dance beats.

Even if she leaves the "pop domain," Sheryl says, "that doesn't mean my best work isn't ahead of me. I'm inspired by people like Emmylou Harris. She's as sexy as she ever was, the last couple of records she's made are her best work ever, and I'm hoping my career will also take a graceful course."

At this moment, she does appear to be on the right path.

"I do believe that this life is right and perfect," she says, "and you do have choices to make. I don't believe luck is everything, and I'm not sure it even exists. I think that where I am now is a result of a lot of good choices and a lot of mistakes, but all of them perfect to lead me to where I am, and that's where I'm supposed to be."

—*Parade*, **November 10, 2002**

AL GREEN

SOUL
SAVIOR

Al Green and
Ben Fong-Torres

When my first compilation, *Not Fade Away,* came out, one of the strongest responses to the book—and especially to the on-tour-with pieces—was sheer amazement at the access I had to the stars. At *Rolling Stone* we pretty much decided what we wanted, called the record label, publicist, or manager, and got it done. If we needed to be with the artists for several days, we'd be given their itinerary, their hotel information, tickets to the shows—whatever we required. We could set up interviews or catch them on the run, talking with them and others on a bus, a plane (in Elton John's case, a private luxury jet), backstage, or in a hotel room. We could tell publicists to get lost while we did our job. And, while we might give the story prominence in the magazine, and time its publication for a concert tour or a new album release, we rarely promised a cover.

But that was then, and, back then, *Rolling Stone* was not only a music power-house, but just about the only powerhouse around. Mainstream media were still slow catching on to rock culture; there was no cable or satellite television, no music channels and entertainment news and gossip shows, and, of course, no Internet. We had it good—except for having to fend off so many inquiries from bands and publicists for whom there was no room at the powerhouse.

Today? If a publicist, or whoever's handling an artist's media, chooses your outlet to have the honor of an interview, the agent will often insist on a cover, and name preferred or acceptable writers. And photographers as well.

An interview may run anywhere between 15 and 45 minutes. And they watch the clock. An interview may or may not be in person. "Phoners" are often the only available option. If in person, a publicist or other guardian of what the star may or may not be asked, is often stationed in the room. Or a writer may be grouped with several others, reduced to taking part in a mini-press conference with the star.

There are, of course, variations, depending on who you are (or represent) and who the star is. For Sheryl Crow, I had a nice lunch with her, and only her. But a time limit applied. For Tim McGraw, for whom I traveled from San Francisco to Cincinnati, I still had only 30 minutes. (I begged for, and got, another 15, later. A phoner, of course.)

But when I visited the Eagles in New York in spring of 2005 for a short piece for *TV Guide,* it was a flashback; pure early *Rolling Stone.* I could roam the catacombs of Madison Square Garden and talk with whoever happened to be around. Management made all four Eagles accessible and let me observe a sound check, in case I needed more color. But that's because the Eagles are from the '70s, when freedom rang. And it didn't hurt that they knew me from the magazine with which they had a love-hate relationship (except for the "love" part).

As for Al Green: even though we'd met several times in those old days, and he'd attended an office party at *Rolling Stone,* and we'd done a television interview as well as two or three for print, and *even though* one of those pieces is now prominently displayed in the Al Green exhibit at the Stax Museum of American Soul Music in Memphis, when I began work on an interview with him in 2005, I was reminded—in no uncertain terms—that it was 2005.

Yes, it was for *Parade,* the largest circulation magazine in the known world. Yes, I'd be coming into Memphis to see the now Reverend Al Green and to watch him perform one of his sermons at his church. But I'd have 45 minutes. The label's publicist, J.R. Rich, would have to be there. (That was OK with me. She'd proven to be a delightful host before, taking us around town to all the Elvis and other historical landmarks Dianne and I might want to see.) And, she said, Green would prefer no personal questions.

Fun, hey? As things turned out, Rev. Green was battling a cold, and J.R. could tell that he was not in top form. And on Sunday, he was too wiped out to give a sermon. In light of the near total disaster, J.R. set up another visit, a month or so later, in a hotel in Los Angeles. And I got my story.

Meanwhile, I went through my transcript from Memphis and, in advance of a visit from Green to the Bay Area, put this piece together for the *San Francisco Chronicle.*

While the *Parade* article told his life story (and, yes, did quote a most willing Rev. Green about personal matters), this was a more musical article.

Memphis—When the Rev. Al Green returned to singing love songs, he did more than revive his pop music career. He may have saved a life.

Green had enjoyed a string of hits in the early '70s with smooth, sensuous songs such as "Let's Stay Together," "I'm Still in Love with You," and "You Ought to Be with Me." But by mid-decade, he'd been born again, switched to gospel music, become an ordained minister, and opened his own church in Memphis.

Then, early last year, he heard that Willie Mitchell, the veteran Memphis musician and producer who'd recorded and, in some cases, co-written many of Green's biggest hits, was in the hospital with diabetes.

"Willie was in bad shape," says Green, in his office behind his Full Gospel Tabernacle church. On a wintry spring afternoon in Memphis, he's nursing a cold, but looks dapper in a crisp black suit over a black V-neck shirt and vest. He wears shades and just a bit of bling—a gold chain, a gold watch, and a couple of bracelets.

Mitchell, he recounts, had been in the hospital for a week. "He was drinking—which is not good for his sugar diabetes—and not caring. Earlier this last year he'd lost his wife, and then his brother."

Green visited his musical mentor. "I said the first thing we should do is give him something to do, something that knocks his socks off. And what has he wanted to do all this time but cut an album with Al Green?" He flashes a broad smile. "*That's* it! Oh, man. He sits up. He said, 'When we gonna get started?' Well, that type of thing gives you the energi-o, the energy to perk up." "It was a nice boost," says Mitchell, still dapper at 77. He is in the control room of his funky Royal Recording Studios, a former movie house in a residential neighborhood. "I was really sick, and everybody said you can't even go into the studio. But we started cutting the album, and it brought some kind of life to me."

The result was the album *I Can't Stop,* which earned critical praise and a Grammy nomination. In May, Green issued another co-production with Mitchell, *Everything's OK.*

In his memoir, *Take Me to the River,* Green, who is 59, refers to Mitchell as a father figure. It was a role, he wrote, that was "vacant since that day I had marched out of the apartment and turned my back on my daddy's plans for my life."

That apartment was in Grand Rapids, Michigan, where Al, the sixth of ten children, and his parents had moved, looking for a better life than they'd had in Forrest City, Arkansas. There, Robert Greene (whose son later changed the spelling of his surname) was a sharecropper, and he'd formed a family gospel group. Al, however, also loved the music of Sam Cooke, Jackie Wilson, James Brown, and Elvis Presley.

Elvis? "I loved the music," he says. "The shake, rattle and roll, hip-swinging, hair-down-in-your-face—that was one of my little fantasies, and this guy filled it really well."

Al would sneak records into the apartment, and one day, his father, who'd forbidden the playing of secular music, caught him dancing to a Jackie Wilson record. Al, only 14, left home to move in with a friend who lived nearby.

He soon formed a singing group with some buddies. But, he says, he made certain to finish school. "I wanted to prove something to my dad. When someone tells you you're not gonna do something, then I made up my mind I was going to do it."

In 1969, Green was a struggling young singer with one modest hit record, "Back Up Train," when he met Mitchell, a saxophone player, bandleader, and record producer, at a nightclub in Midland, Texas. Mitchell liked Green's voice, and they were soon working together at Mitchell's studios. After a couple of duds, they clicked with a song Green wrote, "Tired of Being Alone." With "Let's Stay Together" hitting No. 1 in late 1971, Green became a star, and in 1972 and 1973, he sold 20 million records.

Now, Green has written six songs for another album. And Mitchell, he says, is raring to go again.

"He wants to 'finish the oil painting.' He doesn't refer to me as Al, but as an oil painting. 'Al,' he said, 'It's a masterpiece. You've got to finish it, and be proud of it and sign your name to the bottom of it.'" Another album or two, Green says, should complete the painting. Mitchell, who has said that he considers Green the greatest singer he's ever heard, told him that he needed to defend the turf he'd claimed back in the '70s.

"He said, 'You take a stand on that land and claim it and defend it,'" says Green. "'You can have the whole world if you want it; you just have to want it. And if you want it, take it. If you don't take it, somebody else will walk away with it.'" "You just stopped," Green says Mitchell told him, "because of religion and because you don't understand who you are and what you're doing and what God is doing for you!"

"And I didn't!" Green says. When he began contemplating a return to love songs, he says he had a consultation with God. "And God said, 'Al, I gave you the songs, they are wonderful songs, they are beautiful songs.'

"Nobody's shooting or killing or anything in here, these are what you call life songs, life experience songs."

And so, in concert these days, the Rev. Al Green sprinkles a couple of gospel favorites into a show that features hits from the '70s and his more recent recordings. He clearly favors, and savors, the early hits.

In fact, in his office in Memphis, he interrupts our interview to go to his desk, where he finds a recording of "I'm Still in Love with You" to play for me. It's not a remake, an alternative take, or a live version of that 1972 hit. He just wants to hear it.

"I'm talking about how fresh it is, with today's music," he says. "It still sounds new. I was listening to it the other day, and Willie started laughing with me!"

He plays it full blast. Soon, he is exulting in his own voice, punctuating his lines with whoops and shouts of "Right!" and "Yeah!" He scats, he dances a bit, and he laughs, out of sheer joy.

"*Woo!*" he shouts. He may have a cold, and the next day, a Sunday, he may not be able to preach to his flock. But right now, to the sound of his own timeless music, the Reverend is testifying.

—*San Francisco Chronicle,* June 11, 2005

RHYTHM 'N' WHITES

In **San Francisco,** it's easy to get wrapped up in the restaurant scene, what with great new ones popping up every few weeks. It's especially easy when one's spouse is an avid foodie, as mine is. And so, over the years, Dianne and I got to know chefs, maître d's, and owners at some of the city's best restaurants. And, given the nature of the business, we'd follow them from place to place, as they succeeded and expanded, or failed and moved, or left the city for the country—often, the Napa Valley wine country.

The chefs came to include members of the Back Burners Blues Band, comprised of four chefs who enjoyed making music just about as much as they liked creating dishes. Watching them jamming in the nightclub downstairs from one of their restaurants, I thought that the Burners might make a nice little newspaper or magazine article. Fortunately, Dianne was thinking bigger.

"Why not try *Gourmet* magazine?" she suggested. She read the magazine and knew that it made room for offbeat pieces that didn't necessarily focus on food and recipes, but on chefs and personalities.

I sent off a pitch and, soon enough, got an assignment—with the suggestion that this was a phenomenon that wasn't by any means limited to the Bay

Area. There were, an editor said, rockin' chefs in New York, Miami, and one in Dallas at the luxury hotel The Mansion on Turtle Creek.

And so it was that Dean Fearing, the chef at The Mansion, and his band, the Barbwires, would overtake an article that originally featured our friends, the Back Burners.

On a scorching July evening in Dallas, a hunka-hunka guy strides onto a stage in front of a magnificent stand of old oaks. He's dressed in a crisp white jacket, faded jeans, and a pair of custom Lucchese boots. Strumming his 1951 reissued Telecaster guitar, he eases into Hank Williams' "Lonesome Whistle." His voice is surprisingly worn, and you can't help but wonder what kind of trouble he'd gotten into the night before. He steps back and turns the microphone over to a tall, serious-looking fellow—Bryan Ferry meets Gregory Peck—who delivers a high and plaintive "Midnight Moonlight." He's followed by a heavyset guy whose gruff voice alternates with yet another fine singer on the classic "House of the Rising Sun." The crowd goes wild.

Who are these guys? Country rockers like Garth Brooks and Alan Jackson? Voices from out of *O Brother, Where Art Thou?* Actually, the performers in question on this sultry Texas evening are Dean Fearing, the chef here at The Mansion on Turtle Creek; Tim Keating, executive chef of Quattro at the Four Seasons in Houston; *Saveur* magazine editor Colman Andrews; and a Pittsburgh hotel consultant named Lynn Ferraro. Fearing's tore-down voice, it turns out, is the result of the nonstop schmoozing he's been doing here as host of his third annual BBQ Bash, a combination feast, auction, and concert to benefit the Texas Scottish Rite Hospital for Children.

To accommodate the 500 guests, everything from the circular driveway to the parking lot of the palatial Mansion has been co-opted by grills, dining tables, and gargantuan fans. Big-name chefs are everywhere, turning out endless variations on the Southern Barbecue theme. There's Miami's Norman Van Aken, spooning smoky plantain crema alongside tamarind-spiced barbecue duck. Nat Comisar and Bertrand Bouquin of Cincinnati's Maisonette are laboring over love-'em-tender, braised beef short ribs. New Orleans star Susan Spicer is plating honey-bourbon barbecue poussin with five bean salad, and Jonathan Waxman of New York City's Washington Park is doing the same with crispy quail and sweet corn salad.

While Fearing buzzes around, checking in with the various musicians, The Mansion's kitchen staff oversees his slow-cooked smoked leg of lamb gorditas and an array of side dishes. They're also handling Keating's citrus-glazed barbecue shrimp and scallops and Robert Del Grande's chile-crusted prime rib. Del Grande himself (of Houston's renowned Cafe Annie) is busy moonlighting as lead guitarist.

Juggling the roles of chef and musician is nothing new for the boys in this band. They've been performing together as the Barbwires since back in the early '80s, when Fearing and Del Grande met at a Texas Hill Country Wine & Food Festival and ended up in a hotel room, jamming into the night. "Parties started happening," says Del Grande, "and the Barbwires were born." (Boz Scaggs suggested that they change their name to the Texas Tournedos, but they have yet to take his sage advice.)

Start talking to chefs about their lives outside the kitchen, and you'll find that practically every one of them is involved in music. In San Francisco, there's the Back Burner Blues Band, comprising Keith Luce (drummer and chef at Merenda), Joey Altman (guitarist, chef, and host of local and national TV food shows), Scott Warner (guitarist and chef at Napa's Bistro Don Giovanni), and Gordon Drysdale (guitarist, mandolin player, and chef at San Jose's Pizza Antica). At a recent event at New York's Grand Central Station, restaurateur Drew Nieporent fronted the band Hiway 13 (featuring Noche's Michael Lomonaco on guitar) and poured himself into the Doors' "Roadhouse Blues" before rolling, baby, rolling into an exuberant reading of Dylan's "Rainy Day Women # 12 & 35."

Dante Boccucci, the chef at Manhattan's Aureole, was a founding member of the Back Burners and is now looking to form a band with Café Boulud's Andrew Carmellini, who plays electric guitar. (These last two have shared rock fantasies since rooming together at the Culinary Institute of America (CIA) in Hyde Park. "If I'm not cooking," says Boccucci, "I'm seeing bands or listening to music.")

Maisonnette's Comisar is a singer and guitarist, Rob Boone of Miami Beach's Metro Kitchen + Bar plays drums and guitar, and his neighbor Van Aken pulls out a harmonica whenever the mood strikes. Hell, even Emeril Lagasse has been known to join in with the bands that perform on his TV show. (He plays—what else?—drums. BAM!)

Although people like to say that chefs are the new rock stars, the statement is generally intended as metaphor. Sure, Wolfgang Puck works the dining room at Spago Beverly Hills as if it's one big stage. And Lagasse's audiences carry on like a bunch of rabid teenyboppers. (Emeril: "We're gonna add rice wine vinegar." Audience: "*Whooooo!*") Then there are the Rocco DiSpirito fans, who track that New York chef's actions the way people once did those of Jim Morrison. But even chefs at this level of fame will tell you that running a kitchen is a far cry from rocking out on an arena stage.

Still, there's no denying the parallel between the worlds of food and music. "The joy of music," says the Back Burners' Drysdale, "is absolutely akin to the joy of creating for the table."

"There's just a connection between cooking and creativity, and guitars and creativity," says Fearing, who as a CIA student in the mid-'70s was in a band known as Escoffier and the Sauciers. "Wherever there's chefs, there's music."

Scott Warner, who earned a master's degree in music at USC, says the two endeavors are "exactly the same"—just using different senses. "Rhythmically," he explains, "music does to the ears what food does to the taste sensations."

DiSpirito, who's been playing acoustic guitar since he was 11, also thinks of notes in terms of flavors. "I can articulate what I feel through flavors," he says, "but not with music." (Having hired a teacher to instruct him in rock, blues, and classical guitar, however, he hopes to change that soon.)

"With the craft of cooking, you have to build your chops," says Merenda's Luce, whose uncle is Steve Boone, bassist with the Lovin' Spoonful. As a teenager, he studied jazz at Manhattan's New School for Social Research. "You have to learn your scales, which are like basic techniques. Also, menu planning is very similar to putting together musical ideas. I think of a set list, almost."

"It's all the arts," shrugs Tim Keating. "It blends together."

Cooking and making music, concludes Carmellini, are "both visceral experiences. They affect people below the surface, immediately, and on a sensory and an emotional level."

Considering the high-pressure worlds that chefs inhabit, it's no wonder they feel the need to blow off some steam now and again. Miami's Boone, a major Pearl Jam fan, says he finds "pure escape" in strapping on his headphones and banging away on the drums.

For the Back Burner Blues Band, who joined forces in 1998, music is pure fun. Earlier this year, they played a fund-raiser at a private home in

Marin County while fellow chefs from the Bay Area whipped up small plates for the guests. Some of those guests didn't pay all that much attention to the Back Burners. No matter. "I just love playing," said Joey Altman, "so any opportunity to play with the band is just great, and if people are enjoying it and dancing, that's a bonus."

And people did enjoy them. After a solid-gone version of "Route 66," Piperade's Gerald Hirogoyen, who was serving up a warm sea scallop salad with piperade and parsley jus, showed his approval by banging a spatula against a sauté pan. "They're pretty good," he said. And, he added, a bit of marvel in his voice, "they've stuck together."

"One of the main reasons this band is still together," says Altman, "is that the restaurant industry is so stressful. There's so much pulling on us, from people working for us, to diners, to our bosses, to our investors. We have to satisfy so many people, and it's draining. Then, we come into the band and we're playing music. It's totally self-indulgent. We love it, it charges our batteries again, and it makes us feel like our life is not that bad."

Back at The Mansion in Dallas, everybody's batteries are charged. Richie Furay, formerly of Buffalo Springfield and Poco, has just delivered a show-stopping "Kind Woman," peaking with a gorgeous solo by Mickey Raphael, the harmonica wizard from Willie Nelson's band. And now the place is really coming alive, as singer-songwriter Rodney Crowell, a humming, strumming musical encyclopedia, takes the stage. With the first notes of "Brand New Heartache," the tanned, trim, boot-scootin' beauties in the audience begin dancing with a vengeance. And they show no sign of stopping. "Hey Baby," "Long Tall Texan," "Honky Tonk Women," "The Last Time" . . . the hits just keep on coming. Watching Fearing up there onstage, looking every bit the rock star as he trades licks with Del Grande and horns in on Crowell's mike to harmonize on the Stones' "It's All Over Now," it's hard to imagine him any happier wielding a wooden spoon. The crowd is blissfully singing along to "Twist and Shout" when fireworks suddenly come shooting up from a clearing behind the trees. People whoop with every *ka-boom*.

Ray Jacobi, a Mansion executive, leans over. "We were there the night The Mansion burned down," he jokes.

Nothing burned. But on this hot, hot Texas night, there sure was a lot of cooking.

—Gourmet, **October 2003**

After that visit to The Mansion, Fearing invited me back, along with Dianne. Chef Fearing had learned that I sing a little, so he wanted me to join the Barbwires for a song or two. And so, in 2004, I joined the gang, along with guest star Jim Messina, and did Ricky Nelson's "Stood Up" and Elvis' "Treat Me Nice." Messina was one among many who were shocked that I did a Presley impression. "Who died and made *you* Elvis?" he asked.

I wrote about that experience for *Paste,* a new music magazine out of Decatur, Georgia, and figured that was it. But no. In 2005 I made the trip again, this time strictly as a performer, doing three Elvis hits. Afterwards, guest star Wynonna Judd greeted me at our table. "Boy, you've got a lot of courage," she said.

I not only had some nerve, I had a case of nerves. I blew a line, and, as luck would have it, it was on "Don't Be Cruel," which the Judds have covered. But that was all right, mama. There were also some transcendent moments. The band, as it has for several years, included Tony Brown, the Nashville A&R wizard, producer, and record label head. He was also the last keyboard player on the road with Elvis Presley. And to have him kick off "Can't Help Falling in Love" was a thrill. Now, if only I can do my *Dean Martin. . . .*

THE NIGHT ROCK 'N' ROLL

WOKE

NOBODY

Ben at the controls at KSAN

The next few pieces cover one of my undying passions: radio. Growing up trapped in a Chinese restaurant family in the '50s and early '60s, I had radio as my lifeline to the outside world—to music, to baseball, and to other wonders. I got into radio in college, and that experience, along with a stint as an all-night announcer at a "beautiful music" station, can actually be credited with getting me in as a regular contributor to *Rolling Stone*. I'd only written a short item in March 1968 when the staff of KMPX, one of the first free-form FM rock stations in the country, went on strike. It was the first "hippie strike," as the papers put it. I offered to help cover the story, saying I had experience in FM radio. I was teamed with a staff writer, but after our first story, he left *Rolling Stone*. As the strike dragged on over several months, it became my beat, and when it finally ended, I moved on to other assignments.

On staff at the magazine, I continued to cover radio-related news, whether it was a fistfight at a Top 40 station or the FCC threatening to fine stations for airing songs containing lyrics about drugs.

At the *San Francisco Chronicle*, I wrote a radio column. That assignment may have come my way after I suggested the following, a first-person piece about that job at the "beautiful music" station.

After three years of mourning the death of the rock 'n' roll "jive 95" era of KSAN, where I spent nine years spinning records freely, I've found a new favorite radio station: KFOG. I love the way it came on, as low-profile as the "beautiful music" it used to play. Up to the second of the format change on September 18, 1982, there was no hint of anything afoot.

The same sonorous announcers, the same Muzak. But then at noon, one last reading of the slogan: "All music . . . all the time." And instead of a serge into Mantovani, it was THE STRAY CATS! "Rock This Town"! Then "Ticket to Ride"! Then a mistake, and we heard "Yesterday," the closest KFOG would get to the old sound again.

And it's been nonstop rock ever since, most of the latest stuff, blended with some of the best from the '60s, sometimes an LP side at a time tossed in, just like the old days of "free-form" radio, whenever the jocks had to visit the john. Features like "10 at 10" and "Psychedelic Supper" (programmed excuses for splurges of oldies).

Endorsements from rave comics such as Rodney Dangerfield and other goofy hirelings such as TV announcer Don Pardo. DJs with no discernible personalities, but all personable nonetheless.

But it may well be that I'm fond of KFOG for a whole 'nother reason. You see, I was the first DJ to play a rock song there, a bit before September 18, 1982. A good guess would be August 1967. That's when I was in the middle of six months there as the all-night announcer, my first break out of college. 1967. I know: the Summer of Love. Flowers in your hair. And there I was, playing Mancini and 101 Strings. But it was a radio job, in San Francisco, for pay ($400 a month for six nights a week, including typing program logs and writing commercial copy), and Kaiser Broadcasting, the owners back then, made me feel lucky.

I remember feeling pretty smug having to leave parties at 11:00 p.m. so that I could get to the station in time. And I remember feeling pretty nerdy when anyone asked *which* station. What a bummer. On top of that, my program was, in fact, someone else's, pre-taped and shipped to us by the sponsoring Holiday Inns. My job was to play the tapes and break in twice an hour for news and station IDs. All the other jocks at KFOG actually played records, and had their own rules: no vocals, and nothing even close to fast. Don't wanna wake the listeners, you know.

For someone who was regularly going to the Avalon and the Fillmore, who was building a record library ranging from Animals to Zombies with plenty of Kinks in between, who was getting high and watching the fireplace nearly every night with his roommates, KFOG was too weird. That's why, three months into the gig, in the middle of one of the numerous deep, dark nights I worked in that studio in Ghirardelli Square, I broke the rules.

I snuck in a couple of my own albums—not a particularly difficult feat, since there was no one else at the station except the announcer before me—and, at a point when I was feeling particularly revolutionary, dumped the Melachrino Strings and broadcast . . . yes, a VOCAL! And not just any vocal, but the Mamas & the Papas. And when no one called to fire me immediately, I went onto the ledge again, this time with the then-prince of psychedelia, Donovan. And, finally, totally gripped by the abandoned, wigged-out zeal of the Age of Aquarius (or maybe because it was the only other album I'd brought in), I played the group who'd quadruple-handedly begun the end of middle-of-the-road music, the kind of waste matter KFOG was airing. I played the Beatles.

I must admit here that it wasn't "Day Tripper," it was "Yesterday." And it wasn't "Universal Soldier," it was "Mellow Yellow." It wasn't "Straight Shooter," it was "California Dreamin'." In other words, I didn't disrupt the near-dead beat of the station. I didn't go all the way.

But it was far enough that I got some phone calls. Nobody upset, mind you, just a couple of my invalid regulars who needed the concept of "lyrics" explained to them. Plus a couple of my college pals who happened to be up at 3:00 a.m. (a common occurrence back then), tuned in to have a laugh on me, and got freaked out. One of them didn't even say anything. He just copied a trademark started by Russ "The Moose" Syracuse, then the all-night jock on the rock station KYA—a falsettoed, stretched out, questioning "WHAAAAT?"

And I felt just like The Moose. I felt like rock 'n' roll. It made my morning. It made me all the more appreciative of KMPX and KSAN, the pioneer "free-form" or "underground" stations; all the more sad when their time passed, all too soon, and all the more pleased that KFOG has come along. Again.

—*San Francisco Chronicle*, April 17, 1983

MY HOUR
IN THE
TOP 40
HOT SEAT

Ben at KSAN

Sometimes, an article is just plain fun—fun to report, research, and experience, as well as to write.

Since my early teens, I had been an avid fan of Top 40 radio, and although I knew that it was unrealistic for a Chinese-American kid in the late '50s and early '60s to aspire to be in radio, I did. But by the time I got in, it was *the* '60s, I was at *Rolling Stone,* and Top 40 was no longer the hippest thing on the air.

As I noted in my book on the history of Top 40 radio, *The Hits Just Keep On Coming:* "To our way of group thinking, what was groovy was on the emerging FM dial—the free-form stations sprouting in our hometown, as well as Los Angeles, New York, Boston, Detroit, and maybe a pirate operation off the coast of Britain. What was square? Top 40."

But I still loved Top 40 radio's energy, its unique rhythms, and even its corniness. By the mid-'80s FM had overtaken AM, and music stations of all formats had moved over to frequency modulation. But a few Top 40 stations remained on AM and, luckily for my *GQ* column-writing purposes, one of them was KFRC in San Francisco.

My purpose was to get to experience, if only once, the rush of executing the super-tight, high-energy format that I'd grown up loving, and that I feared was screaming its way to extinction. I wanted to give it one last hurrah; one last scream.

Peggy Stark, who was an associate justice of the student court, wrote in my high school yearbook, the *Oaken Bucket,* "Stay sharp and please be a DJ so I can hear your groovy jokes and lines." Judy Smith, treasurer for Oakland High's class of 1962, snarled, "I'll be listening for you on the radio—you better make it." It took a few years, Peg and Judy, but I made it. I got to be a Top 40 DJ.

In high school, everyone knew my fantasy. While others air-guitared or air-pitched, I pretended to be a DJ. I was the kid who never had a date but could be counted on to bring a stack of wax to any party. I set up turntables and blasted music through the cafeteria PA system at lunchtime. I planned and emceed the weekly assemblies primarily, I think, to try out jokes and sound effects. I remember my first radio being a toy, with an antenna wire I had to connect to our clothesline.

"As a kid I was fascinated with radio, and wanted to be on it. I constantly fantasized about being an announcer." Larry King wrote that in his autobiography. He could've been writing for thousands of us. The DJs were dashing local celebrities, playing the biggest hits, talking about the stars and emceeing big-name concerts. In Oakland, I heard voices on my radio that would go on to greater acclaim: Gary Owens, Casey Kasem, and "The Real" Don Steele. And I thought that if the world would ever be ready for a Chinese-American DJ, I'd be ready, too.

I did wind up, in the '70s, with a Sunday show on radio, but the station was progressive rock, on FM. There were no jingles, and there was no screaming, no "talking up" records (that is, talking over the beginning of a song until the exact microsecond before the vocals began), which I always considered true art. It was a dream job, but it wasn't my boyhood dream come true.

By that time, Top 40 was the flip side of freedom. In the mid-'60s, a shy, humorless DJ named Bill Drake had come onto a formula to refine and streamline rock radio: tight jingles, constant repetition of call letters, and DJs who kept talk to a minimum. The idea was More Music and Less Everything Else—especially personality. Drake masterminded things in Los Angeles, where he was said to have telephone connections to all the stations he consulted. At each station, a lieutenant kept a tight rein on the format and the jocks. With KFRC in San Francisco and KHJ in Los Angeles leading the way, "Boss Radio," as the Drake sound was called, swept the country.

The '70s brought us FM Top 40, and the Drake era was over. Today, AMs are littered across the radioscape. They're pinning what hopes they have on AM stereo. KFRC, "the Big 610," tried oldies and even—for a short, disastrous spell—game shows. Now it's brought back personality DJs, and it's going after the auto-bound audience (slogan: "The station worth saving a button for").

When I finally decide to feel some of the heat of that jingle-jangled format, I have only one station in mind. KFRC Program Director Dave Sholin, it turns out, understands all about boyhood fantasies. He sets up a guest DJ slot for me: Monday night from eleven to midnight, on Turi Ryder's show.

Through the years, I've heard about the pressures and the tolls on Top 40 announcers. To get some specifics, I call on Mike Phillips, one of the original jocks on KFRC, now program director of a light-rock station owned by the Mormons. Working for Drake, he says, "was like being in boot camp."

Surviving DJs talk about working in fear of the flashing big red lightbulb wired to "the Batphone." It meant Drake was listening—and not liking what he was hearing.

Phillips remembers one of the tougher program directors, Paul Drew. "The phone would ring at you at five-thirty in the morning. 'You realize what you did?' 'No.' 'You said "the Big 610" instead of KFRC.' They wanted it perfect."

The result, say Phillips and other Drake alumni, was predictable. "I was drinking every night," says Phillips, "partying till midnight or three. I'd take an amphetamine at five o'clock and be on the air at six."

Phillips, now 44, says he's stopped speeding. But he knows a lot of jocks who didn't. One former KFRC DJ committed suicide, another—"a heavy boozer"—died in a head-on collision. A third, who'd moved on to another station in town, left work one night on a stretcher, babbling like a madman on LSD—which he happened to be. And one of my favorites totaled a Jaguar XKE (a KFRC contest prize) and wound up working in Shreveport, Louisiana. "It seemed to be one big party," says Phillips. "Being a jock kinda gives you some license to be crazy because the public expects that, to some degree."

A couple of days before my appointed hour on the air, I sit in with Bobby Ocean (he was given that name by the Drake people), who's on his fourth tour of duty at KFRC. "I've been blown out a couple of times," he says. "Here at KFRC, drinking, I fell asleep on the air and had a half hour-plus of dead air."

Nowadays, Ocean limits his drinking to sugarless soda pop, operates a production company, and broadcasts on KFRC as much for fun as for the money. Commercial radio, however, is never just fun. Sitting under a track of lights that come on ten seconds before the end of a song, Ocean juggles dozens of tape cartridges (there is no turntable in sight) of songs, commercials, jingles, and sound effects. His show, which covers the commuting hours (3:00–7:00 p.m.), is studded with news and traffic reports. And each element has to hit at a specific time of the hour, as dictated by a "hot clock," in order to hold listeners long enough to ensure the accuracy of the ratings.

Ocean guides me through a "stop set"—a break for commercials—and explains how he keeps listeners tuned in. "I'm always billboarding," he says. "'Coming up'—something's always coming up. That's an old Drake-ism. The curtain's always rising."

Sunday afternoon: while my wife is out of the house, I try screaming "610 KFRC" and "the amazing AM." I listen to a playback. I decide I won't scream. I try talking up a record—Madonna's "Papa Don't Preach." I've got it down—after only a dozen attempts.

I write some "liners." Turi Ryder calls herself "the Lady of the Evening." I'm going to say she's charging me $100 for my hour there. Listeners will roar. The ratings will soar. I feel sick.

Sunday night: I drop in on my friend Russ "The Moose" Syracuse, a veteran DJ now working weekends at KFRC. To give me an idea of how it feels behind the controls, he lets me do a segue from one song into a quick jingle and into the next song. I manage that feat, but sitting there, waiting for the warning light, looking over the vast 22-input board, the nine cartridge slots, the music and program logs, and the myriad sheets of scripted public service and station promotion announcements to read into and out of the music and the commercials, I decide I won't double as engineer Monday night.

Monday, 10:30 p.m.: I report to the Big 610. Turi Ryder is busy getting listeners to call in and sing songs in pursuit of some Pierre Cardin sunglasses. Ryder, a frisky brunette who looks about as old as my yearbook, runs a pretty loose show. The only way to go up against TV, the station figures, is to offer more than the hits. So Ryder is a "personality," with her own silly sound effects tapes and even her own assistant, a young college grad who says his goal is to be "on air" someday. At 11:00 p.m., however, Turi will be the engineer. I'll sit opposite her, with my own microphone controls and time clocks, so that I won't talk over the vocals.

On the air at 11:06, I deliver my opening and immediately talk over the vocal. My voice is revved up; it's high and urgent, and it's not mine at all. Not only is my voice disembodied, the whole show is. High on adrenaline, I have no idea what song is playing or where the time clock is. Ryder guides me through the flood of elements and helps trigger instant decisions. It's hard to pay attention to the phones. My niece calls. A radio groupie calls. He's doing a KFRC poster, he says, and wants to incorporate me—me and my one, whole hour—into it.

Since I don't have the added pressure of running the board, Ryder encourages me to come up with a contest. I devise a quick quiz, but lose sight of KFRC's phone numbers. No matter. Loyal listeners know. The first caller, Leo, has the right answer: "Hey Paula." The second caller is a breathless woman who says she jumped out of her bathtub to get to the phone. And with the wrong answer at that. We put the winner on the air. Now not only do I have to talk to the guy, but I have to remember to get him to say "KFRC" when I ask him what station's worth saving a button for. As a listener, I hate it when DJs do that. As a DJ, it's just a dirty job.

From there, it's on to more commercials, more music, and more bloopers. At mid-hour, my voice drops to a conversational, almost human, level, and I have to remember to get back into character. By hour's end, I'm wiped out. I appreciate, in a different way than I did as a kid, what Top 40 DJs go through. On FM, I was cruising. Here, I'm hugging the wall. Now I understand the excesses. And, now that I'm one of them, I go right out to North Beach and have a couple of drinks with my fellow jocks. Hey—tomorrow morning the boss is critiquing my stint.

Dave Sholin is a program director of the new school. No phone calls to the jocks, just occasional memos and a monthly meeting in which he plays back a random hour and goes through it, stop set by stop set. He spots the tension in my voice, skips charitably over the mistakes (but asks how they happened), notices a missing "KFRC" after a "610" and explains why, in a contest, I should avoid saying "if you're the winner." The word "if," he says, "implies that you could also be the loser." He laughs at my jokes and praises the way I punch out the call letters. Listening to isolated segments of the tape, to those rare seconds that are free of error, I have to agree: I do sound like a Top 40 jock—or at least as if I had been doing this, if only in my head, for 20 years. At meeting's end, Sholin has a surprise. He asks if I want to do an occasional weekend shift. For real. My head swirls with pride, and then with visions of incessantly flashing red and white lights.

I think I need a drink.

Epilogue: A couple of weeks later Sholin calls again. The latest ratings are in, and KFRC's dwindling numbers indicate a near-total desertion by young people to FM. So the station is changing call letters and switching from Top 40 to Top '40s and '50s: Sinatra, Cole, Fitzgerald. The scream is over.

—GQ, October 1986

THE GAWK 'N' ROLL

HALL OF FAME

For *Hickory Wind,* my book about Gram Parsons, I hired a researcher and general assistant, Holly George-Warren, who was working part-time for my agent in New York when she wasn't pursuing her own writing career and playing, on occasion, with the all-women polka-rock band Das Furlines. Within a few years, she'd been published in numerous magazines, co-wrote a book (*Musicians in Tune*) and became the editor of Rolling Stone Press. Besides developing and overseeing book projects for the magazine, she edited the annual printed program book for the Rock and Roll Hall of Fame induction ceremonies, the Rock Hall having been Jann Wenner's baby. And she would call on me to contribute to the program. I wrote pieces on the radio pioneer Tom Donahue, the Jackson 5, and George Harrison. Payment was a ticket to the induction dinner.

In 2001, I wrote a piece on James Burton, the great guitarist, and attended the dinner and a couple of post parties. With no need to write about it, I allowed myself to be what I was at heart: a fan of the music and the people who made it. Back at my office at *Gavin,* I decided to write about just that. You can't be a detached reporter all the time. And maybe I never was one. For this one night, at least, I had left the notebooks and tape recorders to others.

It was a night for gawking. For six hours—and four or five more, if you had the connections and the stamina to attend the parties after the show—the Rock and Roll Hall of Fame induction dinner and attendant bashes, in and around the Waldorf-Astoria in New York, kept your head spinning.

I never schmoozed more in my life . . . from six o'clock with Jerry Blavat, the prince of Pittsburgh Top 40 radio of the '60s—"the Geator with the Heater, the Boss with the Hot Sauce" . . . to well after midnight, when I met Paul Shaffer at Phil Spector's annual post-induction bash.

In between were the legendary Spector himself (for you young ones, he produced a heap o' hits back in the day, including just about everything you know by the Righteous Brothers, the Crystals, the Ronettes, Darlene Love, and that musical gem by Ike & Tina Turner, "River Deep, Mountain High"). Hanging with Sir Phil was Nancy Sinatra, and next to them was Robert Shapiro, who you recall from the O.J. Simpson defense team. Gee, did he think the O'Jays were being inducted? (You know: "They smile in your face, then they take your place, the back stabbers . . .")

There was Keith Richards, who was at *Rolling Stone* Publisher Jann Wenner's table. I hadn't seen Keef since covering a Stones tour in Hawaii in the early '70s, but he granted me an interview when I wrote my book, *Hickory Wind*, on country-rock pioneer Gram Parsons. Richards and GP were tight. After only nine years, it was nice to have a chance to say thanks for the chat. And, just a seat away, there was Paul Allen, the Microsoft billionaire and rock fan who's the main force behind the other rock museum, the new Experience Music Project in Seattle.

They all were part of a warm evening of tributes, many of them from younger to older generations. It was Mary J. Blige who brought on the great—and I mean that literally—Solomon Burke. Ricky Martin inducted the late Ritchie Valens and did a medley of Ritchie's hits, including "Come On Let's Go," "Donna"—the slow-dance classic—and of course, "La Bamba." Some people at my table, mostly media people, grumbled that it should've been Los Lobos performing but, hey, this induction is now a VH1 TV show, and bookings are clearly driven by demographics. Thus, Moby wondered, aloud, what he was doing assigned to induct Steely Dan.

Plus (and thus) there was 'N Sync to induct Michael Jackson. There was Marc Anthony for Paul Simon. David Grohl and Taylor Hawkins of the Foo Fighters introduced and jammed with Queen. Kid Rock brought on

Aerosmith, calling them the greatest rock 'n' roll band in American history, which annoyed a few more of the media people.

There were a couple of peer-to-peer inductions. The Flamingos, for example, were inducted by Frankie Valli. And Keith Richards took care of the two sidemen who were inducted: Johnnie Johnson (Chuck Berry's piano player) and James Burton.

For most fans, the highlight was the music. Michael Jackson was the only party pooper. He needed a cane to climb onstage, explained that he broke his foot, and that he couldn't dance. ("Sing!" I cried out, but he wouldn't budge, thus dashing all hopes I had for a show-ending jam with him and Aerosmith on "Moonwalk This Way.")

Solomon Burke, whose girth will back him up any time he claims to be twice the man that anyone else is, triumphed on his hit, "Cry to Me." The enigmatic Steely Dan, who decided that, instead of giving an acceptance speech, they'd take questions from the audience, performed "Black Friday." Aerosmith did a sweetly emotional and hard-rocking medley spanning 30 years, with Kid Rock joining them on both vocals and turntables, and with Steve Tyler doing his best Mick Jagger right in front of the real Keith Richards.

The traditional climax is the all-star jam. After various inductees returned to the stage, sometimes with surprise guests—Melissa Etheridge here, Dion there—Solomon Burke came back onstage, with James Burton, Keith Richards, and Robbie Robertson on guitar, and Paul Shaffer's CBS Orchestra blasting away on "Everybody Needs Somebody to Love." Burke kept pointing to people in the front of the stage and calling them up. Pretty soon there were a dozen fans up there dancing and getting their pictures taken with these Hall of Famers.

That's a fan's moment. This fan's moment came a bit later, at Phil Spector's party at a nearby Italian restaurant. There, at a back table, I met two surviving members of the Flamingos. That's the vocal group who had the hit "I Only Have Eyes for You," back in 1959 or so, when I was a kid digging Top 40 on KEWB-Oakland/San Francisco. It was the sweetest of love songs, right up there with such doo-wop standards as "Sincerely" and "In the Still of the Night."

A fellow old-fogy rock writer saw me getting autographs from the Flamingos. "You're really a fan, aren't you?" he said. For too many years, I hid that fact. I never asked to have pictures taken with people I interviewed and never asked for autographs, for which, in today's eBay world, I constantly kick myself.

I worked hard, through the years, to maintain an objective distance. But tonight was not a night for distance. Tonight, I was a fan—and proud of it.

—*Gavin*, **March 30, 2001**

A BANQUET

ON A
PING-PONG
TABLE

Table tennis in a Chinese pioneers's house, Peking, 1973.

As **I said** in my introduction to the Cheech & Chong article, that early 1972 piece afforded me my first opportunity to let it be known that, despite my surname, I was, in fact, a Chinese-American. I continued to write articles over the years, at *Rolling Stone* and elsewhere, about personal matters (the culmination being my memoir, *The Rice Room,* published in 1994) and Asian-American issues. A few samples follow, beginning with this one, an item for a column.

From the beginning, one of *Rolling Stone's* models of journalism and style was *The New Yorker.* Jann Wenner, assigning me my first personality profile—of the singer-songwriter Dino Valente—instructed me specifically to look at a few profiles in that magazine, and to see how the reporting of details added to personality sketches. Like *The New Yorker, Rolling Stone* allowed its writers time and space—time (as much as a biweekly publishing schedule could afford) to work on an article and more space than most magazines—except, perhaps, for *The New Yorker* itself. A piece by Tom Wolfe, Joe Eszterhas, or Dr. Hunter S. Thompson could roll past the 10,000-word mark and towards the 15,000-word range. And that could be Part One.

In 1972, Wenner and his editors decided to create a new column, one that would collect items of news, humor, and trivia centered on San Francisco, the city the magazine called home; items that might be written by any correspondent and presented without bylines.

And, to make it as obvious as possible that we were appropriating *The New Yorker's* "Talk of the Town" column, *Rolling Stone* called its new column "On the Town" and—take this, Eustace Tilley!—topped it with a pen-and-ink sketch of a bespectacled dandy facing a cityscape. A post-'60s version, but a dandy nonetheless.

Although my responsibilities already included collating and writing most of another column—"Random Notes"—I went "On the Town" at least once, when I heard about a dinner being held for a team of Ping-Pong players from China. This was in April 1972, only two months after President Richard Nixon went to China and began talks about normalizing relations between the United States and the People's Republic of China. The dinner was hush-hush; I learned of it only hours before the first "gam-bei" toasts. I sensed a story—or, at least, an item.

Our lone Chinese editor has attended plenty of Chinese banquets in his day, but none quite like the one last week at Rickey's Hyatt House in Palo Alto, near Stanford University. For one thing, they served stuffed chicken breasts, peas, and chocolate eclairs. For another, the guests of honor were the world champ Ping-Pong team from the People's Republic of China. And for yet another, the hosts were 500 people—420 of them Chinese—democratically but very carefully chosen by a quickly assembled committee representing 180 groups. Plenty of poor people from Chinatown; plenty of older folks who wept openly at the sight of the first Communist Chinese to set foot in this, the land of Rickey's Hyatt Houses and piano bars.

Red flags overwhelmed the Kuomintang's protest group at the airport as the team arrived for a country-club rest after three weeks of matches and exhibitions. Now, at dinner, the crowd cheered the first outwardly political statement to be issued in America by the team, by its leader, Chuang Tse-tung:

"Cordial greetings from the people of the motherland to our overseas compatriots [Chinese immigrants to the US] . . .

"Through self-reliance, under the leadership of Chairman Mao and the Communist Party of China," he said in Mandarin, "the living standards of our people are constantly rising, and China's influence in the world is building—especially since the proletarian cultural revolution."

At a reception, the lone Cantonese-speaking team member signed autographs and told matronly Chinese women and their husbands how China and her people—their relatives—were progressing. He chatted enthusiastically; they smiled through 22 years of hidden tears. For two decades, San Francisco's Chinatown, the largest Chinese community in the world outside China, has been ruled—financially and politically—by Nationalist China, through the Kuomintang. And so it was that a company of rock-hard security agents kept watch on this trip to the Bay Area, eyes darting while Chuang sang a lilting Communist song to his 500 hosts, while they all sang "The East Is Red," and while they cheered the welcoming speaker as he surprised Chuang with a hug. The Yellow Peril was out of the closet.

One member of the welcoming committee was Min Yee, the former *Newsweek* reporter now helping edit a new Chinatown paper, the *Journal*. "It's fantastic," he kept saying. "Some people saw San Francisco getting neglected out of fear of the Kuomintang, so we got 200 groups together and cabled the team. Then we sent a delegation down to Los Angeles and convinced them we could handle the security. It's just fantastic, you can make up anything you want and quote me."

—*Rolling Stone*, **May 25, 1972**

After only a couple more columns, "On the Town" disappeared. I see that, an issue or so later, a new column appeared: "Dope Notes." But that one also didn't last much longer than a joint.

LARRY CHING

TILL
THE END
OF TIME

*Larry Ching and
Ben in studio, 2003*

As **I get older,** the line between reporter and participant gets blur-rier. And I'm not talking about vision. For reasons I won't get into here—mainly because I get into them in this article—I took on the role of a record producer. And, having done that, I also had to become a pub-licist, a promoter, and a salesperson, for the first time since one memorably ex-cruciating summer when I tried to sell encyclopedias (and sold not one set).

To support the CD I produced—or, more accurately, to spread the word on the performer on that recording—I wrote press releases and biographies, the kind of hype I've been receiving for decades, and shot them off to all the media contacts I knew. And many I did not.

The response was gratifying, and the end results were . . . well, you'll have to read for yourself, but they weren't exactly predictable.

As part of the marketing effort, I pitched an article to the *San Francisco Chronicle,* which, in recent years, had continued to call on me for articles on a freelance basis. Just like that, I had a piece in the paper's Sunday magazine about the CD, which I'd entitled *Till the End of Time.* And when *Paste,* the mu-sic magazine, approached me about possibly deigning to write for it, despite its ten-cents-a-word pay scale (shades of early . . . and not so early! . . . *Rolling Stone*!) I offered, and they accepted, this piece about my experiences as a rookie record producer.

As a reporter for *Rolling Stone* and other publications, I've spent more than a few hours in recording studios, watching artists, producers, and engineers turning musical performances into permanent records. From sessions with Ray Charles and Paul Simon, to Jefferson Starship and Fleetwood Mac, to Linda Ronstadt and Crosby, Stills & Nash, I've been in a position to pick up numerous pointers on how to produce a decent album.

But I almost always focused on the musicians, on the swirl of activity— or the mind-numbing boredom—that was part of the process of record-making. Even when my profile subjects were producers, like Peter Asher (Linda Ronstadt, Bonnie Raitt, James Taylor, 10,000 Maniacs) and Richard Perry (Harry Nilsson, Carly Simon, Diana Ross), I'd pay more attention to their personalities than to the nuts and bolts of record production. Of course, being content as a note-taking behind-the-scenester, I had no plans to ever produce a record of my own.

Then, last spring, that changed. I found myself in a situation of wanting a certain recording made, and of knowing that if I didn't do it myself, right then, it would most likely never happen and a lot of good music would never be heard.

The artist was no rocker. Larry Ching, age 82, was a flat-out crooner, and, as a featured vocalist at Forbidden City, an all-Asian nightclub that flourished near San Francisco's Chinatown in the '40s and '50s, he was billed as "The Chinese Sinatra." (But that was just hype, a way to help non-Chinese customers identify with the performers. There was also a "Chinese Sophie Tucker" and a "Chinese Fred Astaire.") Unlike Sinatra, Ching had a sweet tenor voice, imported from his native Hawaii and a perfect fit for love songs like "Embraceable You" and "Prisoner of Love." As Arthur Lee notes in his book, *Picturing Chinatown*, "Ching had a full repertoire of songs and, with a range of several octaves, could ad-lib others at a moment's notice."

After Forbidden City closed in the early '60s, Ching became a truck driver. Outside Asian nightclubs, there wasn't exactly a demand for Chinese pop vocalists. Ching still loved to sing, and would make appearances whenever he was asked. But for many years, that silk-sweet tenor of his went largely unheard. That is, until 1989, when he appeared in *Forbidden City USA,* Arthur Dong's fine documentary about the club and the performers who smashed through racial and social barriers and stereotypes to be entertainers.

When I co-emceed the film's premiere, I met Larry and heard him sing. His voice transported me back to the pop music I'd enjoyed as a kid in the pre-rock '50s. In the film, he spoke about dealing with racism, even from audience members. During the war, soldiers and tourists would call him "Chinaman" and "slant-eye," and he sometimes had to be restrained from jumping off the stage to confront them. "I had to accept it," he told me. "If I didn't, I wouldn't stay in the business."

Fascinated by his story, I began thinking about getting him on record. I wanted to preserve that voice of his, and to have his music available to whoever might want it, and to others lucky enough to come along and discover it. Larry readily agreed. But I was always juggling jobs with books and other distractions, and never got around to it.

With the film's release, Larry began singing on occasion, at weddings, fundraisers, and senior centers. We met again in November of 2002, at a celebration of the DVD edition of *Forbidden City USA.* Once again, I was emceeing; once again, Larry sang. At 82, he was still sounding fine, but he was also clearly slowed. Encouraged by members of his family and aware that time wasn't exactly on our side, I decided to get him into a studio. I shared my idea with John Barsotti, a veteran record producer and professor of audio engineering at San Francisco State University. Without a moment's hesitation, he volunteered his studios and his services. Suddenly, I was a record producer.

I met with Larry and his pianist George Yamasaki to decide on songs to record, obtained the licenses, and called up two ace session players, standup bassist Dean Reilly and drummer Jim Zimmerman, whose credits range from Carmen McRae to Elvis Presley. Both had played with Larry on his occasional gigs, and both were delighted to take part for modest, if not minimum, wages.

As soon as Barsotti could get us into the studio at San Francisco State we gathered, on a Sunday afternoon in February. Larry's and George's wives showed up to calm their husbands' nerves. Aside from a few demos he cut back in the '40s, Larry had not been in a recording studio; nor had Yamasaki, an immigration attorney by trade.

Laura Allan, a singer-songwriter friend, shot the session on video and offered an extra set of professional ears. One of Barsotti's students served as assistant engineer. Up in the control room, I sat alongside the professor, grateful that, between the two of us, we had one real producer. I kept track of the takes, tossed in thoughts here and there, and popped into the studio once in awhile, mainly to check on Larry and occasionally to make a suggestion or two about his delivery of a line or the tempo of a song. He'd nod and do whatever the hell he wanted to.

Jane Ching, his wife, had been worried about his getting through the session. He had Alzheimer's, she told me, and was losing his short-term memory. But song lyrics? He had them down cold. With Yamasaki positioned near him, offering familiar support, and with the solid backing of Zimmerman and Reilly, Larry nailed the first several tunes on the first take. Within about three hours of recording, we completed 12 tracks, including a downright swinging "All of Me," a plaintive "Prisoner of Love," and a gorgeous "Hawaiian Wedding Song."

By contemporary standards, that's supersonic, but it almost wasn't fast enough. Because the school building had to be shut down by 8:30 p.m., I had to push to get in all 12 songs. When Larry began to tire, and to make mistakes, I conferred with Barsotti to see if we could use technology to fix or mask the errors, rather than put Larry and the band through additional takes. Just often enough, we could.

"Wow," Larry said afterwards, with a sigh. "That's the hardest work I've ever done."

Next came mixing and mastering, which Barsotti did at his funky but up-to-date garage studio at his home south of San Francisco. There, he deftly removed unbecoming sounds like lip-smacks, overly audible breathing, and a sigh of relief—or, in one instance, a loud "whoosh"—at the end of a take. Barsotti did what he could to camouflage the mistakes we didn't have time to correct at the session. And, after only about 20 tries, I came up with an order for the dozen songs, plus the four demos Larry made in the '40s. They were on scratched-up acetate disks and a reel-to-reel tape, but Barsotti rescued them by getting rid of about 100,000 bits of noise that had accumulated over six decades.

Finally, in the first week of May, the last tweak was made and we had a master for a CD. By then I'd written liner notes, and Tom Gericke, a long-time buddy and television graphics designer, had done the CD package. I researched CD manufacturing and settled on a Canadian company that offered a price of just over a buck a disc, including a barcode.

I got my shipment in late May. Disaster. Because of a printing error, Larry's name had been left off the cover. I couldn't wait for a complete re-order, so I plowed ahead with getting copies out. Having heard how next-to-impossible it was to deal with distributors—and to get paid by them—and knowing that Larry was mostly a local story, I chose to go with a handful of online sites and Asian-focused stores in San Francisco, including the book-shop at the Chinese Historical Society of America museum in Chinatown.

Publicity is a cinch when you have an angle—which we did. We had an 82-year-old artist, a star from a storied, all-Asian nightclub from the '40s, making his first CD. The producer was this guy from *Rolling Stone*. Using my media contacts, I got stories in several newspapers and on radio, television, and the Internet. And reviews were warm and generous. "If you dig nostalgia," wrote Wayne Harada, the veteran pop critic at the *Honolulu Advertiser,* "you'll find treasures and pleasures aplenty." With help from some very creative friends, I built Larry a Web page of his own, complete with audio samples and videos from the session.

June 2003 was Larry's month of glory. He did a round of interviews, and then, on June 25, he was surrounded by family, fans, and fellow Forbidden City alumnae at a listening party at the Chinese Historical Society museum. Mayor Willie Brown proclaimed that day "Larry Ching Day" in San Francisco. On June 30, his CD actually made the Top 200 in Amazon. com's sales rankings for a few wonderful hours.

A few nights later, Larry Ching died of a brain aneurysm. Family members and friends were stunned, of course, but they couldn't miss the bittersweet timing. Emerald Yeh, a local television news anchor who was my co-emcee at that film premiere in 1989, wrote: "The timing could not have been more ideal. You let him soar from the world with joy and a sense of being appreciated, as well as a chance to relive the height of his career."

Larry's wife told one television reporter, "He went out with a bang." And she told me, "It was like he had a checklist. And he'd just checked off the last item."

Just one thing, she said. Larry was worried about my having put my own money into the CD, and about whether I'd recoup. On the eve of his death, as it turned out, *Till the End of Time* hit the break-even mark.

Check.

—*Paste*, **February-March 2004**

CYCLING THROUGH CHINA

AND GOING HOME

Kate Jackson and Chinese children

O **nly a year** or so after leaving *Rolling Stone,* I got an assignment that had nothing to do with rock music, and I literally had the time of my life. In the spring of 1982, Charles Jennings, a film producer based in Portland, Oregon, contacted me about a television documentary he was planning. His idea was to organize an all-star group of entertainers to go to China, where, in recognition of the Chinese people's primary mode of transportation, they would ride bicycles from town to town, stopping at various communes, schools, and villages to perform for the people, spreading cheer and American goodwill.

Would I like to accompany the troupe and write about the three-week adventure? Jennings thought I'd have no problem placing an article with a major magazine. In the meantime, I'd get a trip to Hong Kong and China with total access to the entertainers.

Things aren't always as they appear. Shortly before our departure, I learned that the entertainers were mostly B- to D-listers, headed by Kate Jackson, a B-plusser who'd been one of Charlie's Angels, Broadway hoofer Ben Vereen, and veteran actor Lorne Greene. What these performers were going to do for the Chinese audiences, I had no idea.

But, soon, I'd have to come up with a few. On the flight from Los Angeles to Hong Kong, Jennings told me that he hadn't engaged a scriptwriter, although he himself could write. Was I interested in switching gears? Given that the story was now a possibly tougher sell to magazines—the other cast members included a former Harlem Globetrotter, a magician, and a mime—I quickly agreed.

As things turned out, my rewards from the trip had little to do with either writing for the show or with marketing a story to a magazine. I published this piece about those rewards in *Pacific,* a travel magazine published in Hong Kong by the American Express Company. Coincidentally, the cover of the issue in which my article appeared, an overhead photograph of a beach in Santa Monica, California, was shot by Baron Wolman. He was *Rolling Stone's* first chief photographer.

The first time I was in China, the Communists were on their way. Canton, in the southeast, was one of the last cities to fall to the Red Army, and my mother figured that she could sneak in one more visit with her mother before the country's doors slammed shut.

And so, in the summer of 1948, while Mao's troops pressed southward from the Henan Province they'd just conquered, my mother, my sister, and I took a Presidential liner to China. I remember the sweetness of egg custard tarts in Hong Kong and the stench of the streets of our family's village in Guangdong Province. That's it. But then, I was only three.

In subsequent years, I not only forgot that trip; I forgot I was Chinese. There was pressure in school to be as "American" as possible, even though at home our parents spoke nothing but Cantonese. In school, we were taught all about the menace of Communism in Russia and China. "Red China," we were told, was this country with four times the population of ours, all under the spell of a demigod named Mao, all marching toward a goal of world domination.

Our parents told us more personal horror stories. We had, in fact, made it into and out of China in the nick of time. The next year, all of China was "liberated." To my parents, it meant total chaos. The *goong chon ong,* as they called the Communists, were monsters who pillaged villages and stripped people of their freedom as well as their land and their goods. We were always sending money to our family, but the *goong chon ong* went through all incoming mail. We never knew if our relatives got it.

As China closed itself off from the rest of the world, we found ourselves shut off from the rest of our family. For 30 years, family meant distant cousins, people we ran into at wedding banquets, any descendants from our village, anyone with the surname Fong.

Last year, I got the chance to go back to China. The idea, the TV producer said, was a show called *Cycling through China*. A group of American entertainers—chief among them Kate Jackson, Ben Vereen, and Lorne Greene—would bicycle through the Kwangtung Province (now Guangdong) toward the city of Canton (Guangzhou), where they'd do a free concert for the masses. Was I interested in going along?

I managed to say "yes" before the shakes overtook me. I couldn't wait. Since 1948, a few things had changed, you see.

My parents had come around about what Mao had done for, as well as to, China. The United States and China had played Ping-Pong. Doors had been opened. At home, I began a series of interviews with my parents to learn about their past, using an interpreter to get around our lifelong language barrier. I got interested again in being Chinese.

And now, we—our group of 40 entertainers and crew—were in Macao, on our way to China. At 5:00 a.m., I was up in my hotel room peering out into the predawn darkness of Macao. The plumbing made strange noises, little blips and beeps, as if there was a video game wired into the sink. But that's not what had me up. I heard the first crows of some distant roosters. "And so it begins," I thought. "The countdown to China."

I knew I was being melodramatic, but everything was skewed. I was here to do a job, but I had another, equally vital mission: to find my parents' home villages.

Only a few days before, I'd huddled with my parents, who armed me with letters, photographs, and instructions—in case I was able to break away from our group. Given my itinerary, Mom and Dad couldn't be sure when I'd be closest to their villages. They'd written to our remaining kin there, but they'd made it clear that nothing was certain. As we had said goodbye, they didn't need to tell me how important it was for me to make contact, to be the first among my generation to go home.

Now, a day or so into China, I was in the bustling town of Shiqi looking at a nostalgic piece of pastry. It was a custard tart. Two local women watched while I fumbled through my Chinese currency and offered to buy me one. I declined, but on my first words, they laughed loudly at my halting, clumsy mix of Cantonese dialects. It was a dead giveaway, they said, as to where my parents were from.

I could hardly believe my luck. I told them that I was hoping to find my mother's village in the Kai Ping (Hoi Ping in Cantonese) region. I showed them a photo of my father's brother, age 85. My dad hadn't heard from him in ten years, had received no response to letters and money, had no idea whether he was dead or alive. The women read the town name off the back of the picture and consulted with some other people who'd gathered around. One of them swore that the village was closer to Shiqi than to Guangzhou. They pointed to a shack across the street, near our tourist hotel. A small sign in English read, "Cars for Hire."

There, my pidgin Chinese worked its sympathetic charm, and another friendly woman pulled out a map and pinpointed Kai Ping. It would be a three-hour drive. From there, it would be another four hours north to rejoin our group in Foshan, and I had to allow time for the driver to get back to Shiqi by mid-evening. For the taxi and the driver's 12-hour day, I'd pay US$125.

At our hotel in Shiqi, the head clerk on our floor reminded me that most people in China don't get to travel. "Three hours away?" she asked. "That's *far!*" My visit, she made it clear, was something special, and she happily dove into it. She called the one telephone to be located in the village and had my family alerted. She confirmed my parents' instructions to buy chicken, pork, and red paper with which to pay my respects to deceased members of our family. She suggested buying candy and simple toys for kids, and taught me how to pronounce my aunts' and uncles' names. In a land still torn apart by that civil war of long ago, she intrinsically understood the importance of re-forging and of maintaining family connections.

At 8:00 a.m. the next morning, my interpreter, Sero, and I climbed into our car—a blue, no-frills Toyota. As we hit the rocky road (most all roads in China, paved by hand, are rocky), I recalled the talks I'd had with my parents.

They'd described their childhoods, their living conditions, their parents, their ambitions, my father's move to the United States by way of Manila, and his arranged marriage to my mother. Dad said that his home was so small that he and a brother had to sleep in a nearby ancestral hall. My mother didn't have it any better. Her main memories were of the universal dream around the village: to escape to America, to the land of the golden mountains.

I learned a lifetime's worth of information from those talks with my parents. Still, their recollections were black-and-white sketches, at best.

Our car hurtled over what passed for highways, crossed rivers on ferries, rolled past peasants, water buffalo, and rice paddies, past women hauling wood wagons loaded with coal and carrying garlic trees; overtook bicycles weighed down with straw, produce, and sugar canes, slapping bike bells and weaving their way past horn-blowing buses and rumbling mini-tractors; blurred past construction workers on bamboo scaffolding everywhere. And China took shape. It's a country of basic truths. In one village, I asked a young woman what she did for a living. "Work," she replied.

We made our way into the town of Chikan, and the portraits my parents had drawn vanished into the dusty air, replaced by the reality of people, deeply lined and tanned, going about their business in a small China town. Many stood idly around in front of decayed buildings; others hawked goods—sugar canes, peanuts, garlic, greens, and roasted meats—along the streets. At the sight of our car (motorized vehicles are available only to licensed farmers and for official use), people stopped and stared.

Sero, whose own family is from a nearby village, turned to me. "Your cousin's going to be a star for a month," she said, "between you coming here from America—and the car." It was my cousin's son who greeted us at our designated meeting spot and guided the driver to my aunt's house. A flash: he spoke just like my parents. Even as we made the final few turns, the cynic in rue remembered what others had warned me about: overseas Chinese returning home are often mobbed by villagers, counterfeit cousins hopeful of a gift of a few dollars each.

When I walked through the door of this small, two-floor house and into the dark front room, all doubts were displaced. On the wall facing me was a large framed photograph of my grandmother, the same photo I'd seen as a child in Oakland. Along another wall were several long frames holding montages of pictures, one of them devoted to my immediate family. There we were—in grade school, graduating high school, getting married—our life histories hanging on a wall in a dusty little town in southern China. I looked around at the anxious, smiling faces before me, and realized that I had more than wedding banquet-cousins.

Almost casually, with handshakes, I was introduced to my relatives. Throughout my visit, I was never sure which of three women was my aunt, and which of the other people gathered around were in-laws, and who was whose brothers, sisters, and kids. I was dazed. The reporter in me wanted to take notes on everything, and to ask questions. The human being in me kept me quiet, made me what they expected: a good, obedient son, here to visit from America.

Over tea, we talked mostly about the family. My aunt and uncle wanted to see my parents again. "Why don't you come to America?" I asked, and they laughed at my naïveté. Aside from money considerations, Chinese are rarely allowed outside their cities, let alone overseas. "Their letters and those pictures," my cousin said, indicating the wall, "that's how we stay in touch. We look at them every day and think about you." A few minutes into our visit, I realized that my interpreter didn't have much to do. Every bit of Chinese I ever knew seemed to be coming back, pitiful little scraps that they were. Language barrier? What barrier?

On a quick tour of the house, I got the feeling I was in a cave. The kitchen, like most kitchens in China, is open-air, which takes care of ventilation, but not rainstorms. Between the kitchen and front room is a small area set aside for worshipping departed relatives. Upstairs are several simple bunks in a common bedroom. It's a Spartan life, and it confirms what my parents always told me about China. My family members said they were happy to have this house. And, they added, they have it because we sent money over the years, and they got it.

I wanted to locate my father's brother. My aunt told me that he was alive, even though they hadn't seen him in some time. With my cousin accompanying us, we took a short ride, then traversed a narrow farmland road into my father's village. It was much smaller than my mother's, the homes all squat, low brick buildings fronted by dirt yards.

In a dark shack, more a hovel than a house, we found my uncle sitting on a rumpled, straw-matted wooden bed. I looked around. So this was my father's birthplace. Dirt floors, mud-brick walls, no electricity, no windows. Now I understood just why he had to escape to Manila as a teenager to seek a better life. Any place would have been a better life.

It took my uncle several minutes to comprehend my visit, to grasp the fact that the son of his brother had suddenly materialized. I told him I was happy to see him, on behalf of my father, and asked if he had a message for him. Feebly, he responded, "Send some money." My cousin spoke with some of his neighbors, who'd quickly gathered around the doorway, and learned that my uncle had received mail—and money—from my parents, but was no longer mentally or physically able to write back. Now, they said, he needed to buy food and medicine.

I'd dispensed most of my cash to my mother's relatives; now I emptied my pockets and left feeling terrible that I hadn't brought more.

As much as China has accomplished, and however content so many of the people seem to be, life for others is still a bowl only half-full. China has expended a lot of vitriol at the United States, at our running dog, capitalist imperialists. But the Chinese, like people all over the world, need money. That's why the government opened the door to Westerners and has kept it open despite the Reagan administration's constant slaps—and why we were doing a television show then.

On our ride out of the village, I asked my cousin about life since liberation. She shrugged. "It's pretty good," she said, but with a distinct lack of conviction. At her mother's house, the family seemed to hold back from discussing their lives since 1949. The fact that the taxi driver was sitting nearby, sipping tea, may have had something to do with it. Even though I'd traveled freely, without even getting permission from any authorities, my family—and they were by no means alone—felt the constant presence of the *goong chan ong.*

Suddenly it was time to say goodbye. From the front seat my cousin looked back, visibly sad for the first time since our visit, and asked that I come again soon.

Promises were made and, from outside the car, she reached in with the first real emotion of the day. Our hands met and clasped. Hers clung to mine for a long moment—just in case promises couldn't be kept. We finally let go, brushed back tears, and had a last look at each other.

In a strange way, I felt like I was leaving home. Wenda Fong, a Los Angeles woman on the trip as a producer, put it well. She was looking around a primitive commune, then turned to me and said, with a quiet sigh: "There but for fortune go I. . . ." Ahead, I had a job to do, write material for the TV show, words for Kate Jackson and Lorne Greene to read. And in Foshan, the Seven Star Crags, the Emperors' Hot Springs in Conghua, and Guangzhou—

there was a lot of China left. But, in a sense, I'd seen all I wanted. As my roommate had said blissfully one morning on his return from a park where dozens of people did their Tai Chi exercises every dawn: "I found China."

In Shiqi, groups of teenage boys wore satin-like jackets emblazoned "Rider Fellas." In Guangzhou, college students gathered around David Talbott, head of World Pacific Pictures, and asked: "Who was John Lennon?" They'd read a paragraph or so in the China press, so they knew he was important. "But who was he?"

In a Dong Fang hotel discotheque in Guangzhou, which caters to Westerners with color television sets and a Xerox machine downstairs, the only album endlessly played was *The Stars on 45's,* Donna Summerizing Beatles hits. China is also finding America, but at its own pace.

Onstage at the Sun Yat-Sen Memorial in Guangzhou, Vereen and company wrapped up the tour with a televised concert for the masses. After all the Americans had performed, and after the Chinese had done a few songs and the traditional lion dance, led by the same kind of lion that used to visit our restaurant in Oakland's Chinatown during the Chinese New Year's of the '50s, Lorne Greene bade China farewell. He talked about connections.

"Our visit has been far too short," he concluded. "But among friends, visits always are. Until the next time, may the bridges we have built stand strong, and may our lions always dance together."

Greene read that to several thousand people gathered in a park in Guangzhou, but those words, truth be known, were written for a few folks in Kai Ping.

—*Pacific,* June 1984

BARRY, MY BROTHER . . .

On the night of June 26, 1972, I was up late, which was the norm in those days of multi-tasking at *Rolling Stone*. This particular night, I was editing a book. The magazine made deals with various publishers for paperback anthologies of articles, and Wenner would give various editors a chance to do some extra work for some extra money. But I was feeling gloomy that Monday. A few days before, my long-distance romance had ended, and now I'd poured myself into work, writing an obituary of Clyde McPhatter, rolling a few "Random Notes" through my typewriter, and, wading through a collection of *Rolling Stone* Interviews.

Half an hour after midnight, I got a call with the news that my brother Barry, who'd just turned 29 and was two years older than me, had died of gunshot wounds at his apartment in the Sunset District.

The case remains unsolved after more than 30 years. Fearing for my safety, my parents forbade me from looking into the case, as any reporter would do. And so I left it alone. But, of course, it would not leave me alone. One night in 1984, for no particular reason, I began writing about the loss. It was just a list of things that had happened since his murder, things that had changed, odd things that I did. Sometime later, I showed it to one of my editors at the *Chronicle* and she asked to publish it. Soon, the editor at *Parade* saw it and suggested that I expand the piece for a national audience.

Yes, I thought. I do want people to know about Barry. As my dear friend Gordon Lew, publisher of the Chinatown paper *East West,* eulogized: "Barry's death is not a common death. His death could be a turning point."

———

It was nearly 13 years ago that I last saw Barry, my older brother. He came by my apartment in San Francisco with some food from our parents across the bay in Oakland. We sat around and chatted, and it struck me as ironic. We lived in the same town, but now that we were well established in our careers—he, at 29, was a probation officer and youth worker; I, at 27, was a magazine editor and writer—we saw very little of each other.

Barry had just returned from Lake Tahoe, where he had taken Dad for Father's Day. They had won a couple hundred dollars. He smiled. "That kind of makes up for what happened at my apartment," he said.

Someone had broken in a couple of days before, he said, but had taken only a few antique rifles and guns. His fine collector's swords and jade pieces, a TV set, stereo equipment, cameras, skis, and a bike all had been left alone. Barry shrugged, mystified.

I asked about Chinatown. These were troubled times, and that part of San Francisco abounded with gangs and violence. Barry had taken a leave of absence from his probation work to become director of a youth center there. He said he wanted to do something for "his people." And, though frustrated by the conflicts, he told me he wanted to stay just a little longer.

I started complaining about our parents. I was still going through a mildly hippie phase and (how absolutely American) had had a fight with them over the length of my hair. Barry was no stranger to estrangement from our folks. After all, we had both, in our ways, rebelled against the strict, traditional Chinese upbringing we'd had.

Barry was dating girls who weren't Chinese, and he had studied not law or medicine, which most Chinese parents seemed to encourage, but criminology. Still, he had worked hard at the family restaurants, he had gone to the University of California at Berkeley, and he was always available to help our parents—who don't speak or write English—do various chores. In short, he was a good "number one son," so important to the Chinese family structure.

And now he was sounding just like one, as he counseled me with words I hadn't heard from him before. "Just be patient," he said. "Just go along with them. They're the way they are, and the best thing to do is to give in a little."

Barry sounded like a young man who had come home not only to Chinatown but also to his identity. He was telling me that I should understand the Chinese way. I remember thinking that he didn't sound like the Barry I had grown up with.

A few days later, the edgy mysteries of our last visit somehow crystallized even as our lives were suddenly shattered.

At about 11:30 p.m. on June 26, 1972, Barry was shot down in front of his apartment. The next morning, the front-page story began: "A brilliant and respected youth worker has become the tenth known victim in a series of Chinatown gangland slayings." Barry, it was made clear, was not a member of any gang himself. There were, reportedly, two assailants; the case was never solved. Although I was a journalist, I couldn't investigate; my parents forbade me from getting involved.

And I was bound to obey. After all, as Barry had just reminded me, I am, more than anything else, a Chinese-American.

Don't get me wrong. Our family is American, and not without a bit of struggle. My father, born in a village of dirt-floor hovels in Guangdong Province in southeast China, slept on wooden planks, using bricks for pillows, and dreamed of doing better. As a teenager, his dreams turned to America, and he labored through his teenage years in Manila, saving money and eventually buying official papers bearing a non-Chinese name that made it easier for him to enter the United States.

My mother was born in another Guangdong village. She has one dominant memory of her life as a young girl. "What I wanted most was to come to the United States," she once told me. "I heard that life was much, much better than in the village."

It was, but it took much hard work. And it resulted in a dual identity for their five children. Growing up and going to school, we knew we were American, but we spoke Cantonese at home as well as English; in the evenings, we went to "Chinese school."

Our parents, understandably, clung to the ways of the country they had left behind; their work, they said, did not afford them the time to learn good English, and so we would have to accommodate them. Besides, they said, we should not forget that we were, first and foremost, Chinese. As such, we had different priorities. The understanding—once we were old enough to understand—was that, just as they had sacrificed for us, we would sacrifice for them.

The obligation begins with work. If the family has a business, the child automatically is part of that business. Our family business was the restaurant. I was raised in the New Eastern Cafe in Chinatown, Oakland. At age eight, I was shelling prawns and stripping snow peas. As soon as I could take an order and carry a dish, I was a waiter.

Through our high school years and into college, Barry and I worked at various restaurants almost every evening, weekend, and summer. We missed out on any semblance of social life. We stayed up late to squeeze in our homework. We covered for each other for the very occasional night off. We were often angry and frustrated, but business was such that we couldn't afford any overhead, and there was no use complaining.

"Party? What for? Plenty of time to have fun later—when you grow up." Then, having grown up: "When you get married."

I didn't escape until I became an editor on my college daily newspaper at San Francisco State and had to move across the bay. And even then, I felt guilty about not being at the restaurant.

In the end, there is no real escape from one's heritage. Thinking back, we saw beyond the boredom and frustration and came to appreciate what we got. We learned to be responsible. And, although there are few outward displays of affection in Chinese families, we earned our parents' respect for sticking by them.

The stuff of lower-class life—cardboard swords, paper bags as baseball gloves, cardboard boxes on fences for basketball—may have been embarrassing then; now, it serves to remind me that my parents didn't have much while raising five children. All they had were our futures.

And, in Barry's case, they were robbed even of that. Thirteen years later, all they have of him are bittersweet anniversaries—on May 8, of his birth; on June 26, of his death. And, of course, memories.

But I have something more. For 13 years, there have been few days when I haven't thought of Barry. And though the pain has lessened over those years, there are indelible thoughts and images, not connected as much with my brother as with his death.

Whenever I think of him, he is still my older brother; somehow, right now, he is ageless yet perennially two years older than I. He is wiser. He has kept me forever younger.

In the aftermath of his murder, I was numbed. I witnessed the major events of that summer in a warped daze. I remember thinking of Barry missing the high drama of the Watergate hearings. I thought just of him when the terrorists struck at the Munich Olympics.

I remember acting irrationally. I collected and devoured newspaper stories about gangs. Reading the articles, I stopped at every name, wondering. I watched crime shows on TV and lived vicariously through the likes of Peter Falk, whose "Columbo" always managed to nail the killer, and of Charles Bronson, whose various characters made it their personal mission in life to exterminate the scum of the earth. I've never wanted anything more than answers and justice.

But, yes, sometimes, lost in the celluloid vigilante heroics of a Bronson or Clint Eastwood, I thought about the sweetness of revenge.

I looked on people as possible surrogate older brothers. I remember the brother of a girlfriend. A roommate. But that was just wistful non-thinking. I came to realize that, by Chinese tradition, I was now the older brother of the family, and I had obligations and responsibilities, among them not to dwell on the past.

Still, I think of Barry almost every day. Anything will trigger it: talking with any member of the family, hearing or reading the name "Barry," any trip into or through the neighborhood where he last lived, a glimpse of an antique sword in a store window, a song by Elton John called "Daniel" (". . . my brother, you are older than me, do you still feel the pain?").

I was unable to listen to Bach, especially to pieces that were on one of Barry's favorite albums, *A New Sound from the Japanese Bach Scene.* We played it at his wake. With the turntable unattended, the record played repeatedly, so that *Minuet in G, Air on a G String,* and other melodies got embedded in my mind—a soundtrack of our loss.

Since then, whenever I come across those compositions, I have to tune out or walk away.

Our family was never religious, but after Barry was gone, I found myself looking into the heavens and talking with him, with his soul. I did—

and do—this usually on visits to the Mountain View Cemetery, high over Oakland. The talk is easy, loving, sometimes eloquent, in a balanced, yin-yang way. I tell him the news of the family, the ups and downs, and I think about how he might fit in, might affect those events. Sometimes, standing at Mountain View, I believe he still does.

Barry's death ultimately inspired the bridging of a lifelong language barrier between my folks and me. With help from a family friend, I was able to interview them about their lives in China, their courtship by mail, and the beginnings of our family in Oakland. I still haven't asked them about Barry. If he enters my mind almost every day, he must enter theirs almost every hour.

The family of any victim of senseless, sudden death knows that it isn't easy being a survivor. But all one can do is survive and look for what lessons there are.

After years of disinterest in my identity as a Chinese, I had occasion to visit China two springs ago, and I immersed myself in that country. I visited my parents' villages and met relatives I never knew I had. On their walls, I saw framed photos of myself and the rest of our family. We are forever connected.

And, in China, in a moment of paying respects to deceased family members, I of course thought of Barry.

I remember thinking about him on the ferry from Hong Kong to Macao, our gateway into China. I felt as if I'd somehow taken him to China with me, to a home he'd never seen. On the deck, my fellow travelers were dancing joyously to a song by the Doobie Brothers. In my head, another tune fought through the disco beat; a tune I'd been resisting for years. As we spotted the mountains of China in the distance, the tune took hold in my consciousness. It was a quiet little thing by Bach. And it was really quite lovely.

—*Parade*, **April 21, 1985**

I received many letters, responding to both the *Chronicle* and *Parade* pieces from people expressing condolences, reminding me of the universality of loss. The director of the Chinatown Youth Center wrote to say that it was carrying on Barry's work. Friends of his shared still-vivid memories.

Gail Katagiri, Barry's girlfriend, who was with him that night, wrote and said that she'd never found it easy to talk with me about him. Sometimes, she said, words just didn't seem necessary. "Last night," she continued, "I was munching dinner with KDFC playing in the background. Now I was thinking more seriously about contacting you . . . then the strains of Bach's *Air on a G String* came from the speakers. (Never could understand how such a delicate melody has such an unexpected name.) It was suddenly very difficult to swallow, and not because of the chiles in the Malaysian curry."

Barry, she continued, "forever changed my view of death and life, making me more accepting of the former and more appreciative of the latter. I feel that he tried to teach me that our existence here is tenuous, but that we shouldn't unnaturally shy away from death. I believe he knew that his own death was impending. When the doorbell rang on June 26, I will never forget the solemn gleam in his eyes as he touched the handle of his antique sword and said, 'I'd better take this with me; you never know.'"

And, typed on a sheet of stationery imprinted with the image of a bus—its destination, FURTHER—I got this:

Dear Ben:

I always read your stuff when I come across it. Never felt the need to comment before. But the piece today in *Parade* made me weep.

It was the part about Bach. When my son Jed was killed a year ago we heard that the local symphony was going to play a little tribute for him and Lorenzo, his black buddy that was also done in by the wrestling [team] van accident, so Faye and I attended. The piece was *Air on a G String.*

Then, a few months ago, we were invited to attend the Oregon-Oregon State match. Traditional wrestling rivals, although Oregon was going to get slaughtered, the team still decimated like it was. It seemed necessary that we go, if only to show the assistant coach who had been driving the van that there were no hard feelings. Besides, it's our family tradition; we have always wrestled. I lettered three years at Oregon. Jed's older brother, Zane, wrestled for them. My brother, Chuck, wrestled for Oregon State. I didn't relish the event, but I knew that all our family would feel obliged to go. It was an affair of state for us Keseys.

On the drive over to the campus, feeling very blue and still battling despair, I turned on the radio. *Air on a G String* was playing. I began to feel better. I could feel that big strong hand of Bach reaching out of the dark to grip my shoulder, trying to reassure me that not only was I going to make it, but so was ol' Jedder.

Ol' J.S. was in on things, see, and he guaranteed it!

Thanks for the piece. It's nice to know we've got strong people battling for us, on both sides of the river.

L'chaim,

Ken Kesey

BEING ALMOST FAMOUS

Terry Chen and Ben

When I met Sheryl Crow for the first time in 2002, for an interview, we seated ourselves in a banquette at the Grand Café in downtown San Francisco and, before I could get off a prescripted ad lib to, you know, break the ice, she leaned over and said, "So, what was it like? Was *Almost Famous* accurate?"

And when I was in Los Angeles—Beverly Hills, actually—one afternoon that same year, I ran into Jon Lovitz, "The Liar" on *Saturday Night Live* circa the mid-'80s. "So," he said in that insinuating voice of his, "did you know that I was once married to Sheryl Crow?" No—actually, he asked pretty much what she did, adding that he couldn't imagine being portrayed in a major motion picture by another actor.

Celebrities—people who actually *are* famous—realize that it's highly unlikely that they will ever be a real-life character in a movie. And, like everyone else, they want to know what it feels like to go through that experience.

Thus, this story. Once it became known that Cameron Crowe, whose last movie had been the smash hit *Jerry Maguire,* was making a more-or-less autobiographical film about his adventures as a young—very young—writer for *Rolling Stone* magazine in the '70s, and that I was going to be a character in the movie, I could sell any number of stories. I did one for the *San Francisco Chronicle,* after Terry Chen, the actor who played me, came to town to visit—and, mostly, to observe—me. I wrote a short piece for *MOJO.* And I wrote about assorted adventures surrounding the movie in my bloggy column at www.asianconnections.com. For example, Crowe, Patrick Fugit (who played the Crowe character), and Kate Hudson were supposed to attend the San Francisco preview of *Almost Famous,* after their rounds of press interviews, but had to fly off to Seattle. By chance, Chen, who I'd begun calling my "Mini-Me," had come to town to see the film. So we wound up hosting the screening and schmoozing at the party afterwards.

The schmoozing continues. Not long ago, I was in Cincinnati with Tim McGraw, the country superstar. Time was tight, as it always is these days for celeb interviews. But he couldn't resist telling me that the video set piece that he and his band produced for their last concert tour was based on a scene from *Almost Famous.* And by the way, he added, "What WAS that like?"

What a difference a movie makes.

Cameron Crowe is into details. On the set of *Almost Famous,* which traces his own beginnings as a teenage rock journalist, he's directing a scene depicting a *Rolling Stone* editorial meeting when he trots over to where I'm standing to check a detail about one of the writers we worked with years ago.

"Did Chet Flippo cover the Who tour in 1973?" he asks. "I'm not sure," I reply, "but I do know one thing: we always called him 'Flippo,' and not 'Chet.'" Immediately, the name is changed.

I'm on the set because I'm portrayed in the movie. Back in 1973, I was an editor at *Rolling Stone* and met this gangly kid, Cameron, at a Rolling Stones concert. He said he'd like to write for the magazine. He didn't tell me then that he was 15 years old (and already enrolled at San Diego City College), but said that he had written for an underground paper, *The San Diego Door.* I gave him his first assignments for *Rolling Stone* and within a year he'd profiled Yes, Poco, Deep Purple, and Van Morrison, and he'd scored a cover story—on the Allman Brothers. There were questions about me assigning major stories to a teenager, but the quality of Cameron's work was response enough. Besides, several of our editors were amused—even proud—to have such a young guy, with fresh enthusiasm for the rock scene, writing for us.

Terry Chen is costume as Ben in Almost Famous

When he set out to make a movie about those times, he cast a young actor from Vancouver, Terry Chen, to play me. On the set, Chen (looking eerily like me a quarter-century ago) came up to ask how, standing in the hallway, I might place my hands on my hips, how I might adjust my eyeglasses. I admitted I had no idea how I touched my glasses a quarter-century ago. I also thought, "Who could possibly care?" But I remained silent. For a film, I knew, details were everything.

On my way to the set in downtown Los Angeles, I passed the building whose exterior had been decorated to resemble the front of our old San Francisco offices. A set designer had called a month before to quiz me on the MJB Coffee sign in front of the building. I'd described its colors, and the numbers "625" that identified our building on Third Street. And now, here they were on a warehouse building on Figueroa, in L.A.

Cameron's need to get it right has its limits. Although the film is clearly autobiographical, he created a fictional band (called Stillwater) as an amalgam of artists he traveled with back in the day. The models, he says, are Led Zeppelin, the Allman Brothers, and the Eagles. And, while he searched high, medium, and low to cast look-alike actors to portray editor Jann Wenner, writer David Felton, and me, he himself hides behind an actor (newcomer Patrick Fugit) who looks nothing like the younger Crowe, and then gives him the name William Miller!

On the set, Cameron told me that it was tough enough doing such a personal piece, that to have to give direction to an actor who looked like his 15-year-old self, named Cameron, would have been too much.

"I'm still not prepared to talk about this—the family stuff," said Crowe, whose mother (portrayed by Frances McDormand) understandably disapproved of her son wading into the gritty rock underworld. But he had to make the film. "I love personal stories. Every time a director does a personal story, like Truffaut with *The 400 Blows*—it's my favorite."

Almost Famous is very personal. And, like Cameron Crowe himself, it's cheerful, charming, and smart. Although it's difficult to see him topping his last film, the Oscar-winning *Jerry Maguire,* with a smaller (albeit $60 million) film featuring marquee names no bigger than McDormand (*Fargo*), Billy Crudup (*Jesus' Son* and *Without Limits*), and Kate Hudson (*200 Cigarettes*)—he does it.

Set in 1973, *Almost Famous* shows what the rock scene was like back then, and how it was to be a writer, trailing and covering the bands, seesawing between the highs of the music (on stages, on planes and buses, and in hotel and green rooms) and the lows of being a reporter, an outsider—"the enemy," as Stillwater calls Crowe's character.

The film has its requisite time-warped jokes (one manager advises Stillwater, "You've got to take what you can, when you can, while you can . . . because if you think Mick Jagger will still be out there trying to be a rock star at age 50, you're sadly, sadly mistaken"), but manages to be timeless. The focus, when all is said and seen, is on a sweet kid, a passionate rock fan who, on his first writing assignment and road trip, learns about family—the one at home in San Diego and the one he encounters with the band—about love, and about loyalty. Yes, there's an acid scene, and yes, there's a bit of sex, and some onstage concert footage—but Crowe has made a rock film that encompasses drugs and groupies without the clichéd cartoon scenes we've seen in a dozen other period films. There's no dwelling on anything. There's no full song, no drawn-out getting-high-on-pot scene. Crowe's achieved something special because, like his spiritual mentor Billy Wilder, he came to screenplays (in 1981 with *Fast Times at Ridgemont High*) with a reporter's ears, instincts, and training.

And, yes, because he's into details, there are authentic on-the-road, backstage, and onstage moments, so real that I identified more often with the Crowe character than with my own. There really was nothing quite like the sensation of running along with a rock or pop act—a Stones, a Dylan, a Jackson 5—down coliseum corridors and into an arena illuminated only with the energy of 30,000 fans, then standing at one side of the stage, absorbing it all—the performance, the response, the aftermath—into a notebook and tape recorder, and, finally, meeting an inflexible deadline of right now.

Crowe, who apparently kept every single note and piece of memorabilia he gathered during his rock 'n' roll years, scores with true, true moments: the boredom of life on the road and on the bus, broken up by groupies, card games, and the occasional spontaneous sing-along; the conflicts between treating rock 'n' roll as art and as commerce; and, on the writer's side, the frustrations of losing promised interviews to a musician's whims. When William gets one too many "Go aways" from behind a hotel room door, he flips an unseen bird, rages silently, and finally collapses into tears. It's a moment with which many rock journalists will identify.

Watching the scene, I felt guilty. Back in 1973, sending Cameron off to chase after Crosby, Stills, Nash & Young and Rod Stewart and so many others, I never thought much about his age, and what it meant to him—and his family—for him to be plunged into the world of sex, drugs, and rock 'n' roll. As an editor, all I cared was that he was a good writer willing and able to score important articles for us.

On screen, that's pretty much how I appear. Some overly protective family and friends have said that I come off too "mean," and that Crowe didn't portray my more flippant side. This is true. I was more than a hard-nosed editor. I was on the road half the time, chasing stories along with Cameron and all our other bylines. I had a radio show on Sundays. If memory serves, I even had a girlfriend. But what really peeved some friends about the movie was the depiction of me as humorless (forget clueless). I have, in fact, been known to cause laughter—on the phone, onstage, and elsewhere. I'm not good at remembering such moments. Fortunately, they sometimes get chronicled.

For example, at the 2000 South by Southwest music conference in Austin I sat on a panel about music writing, where Jaan Uhelszki reminisced about a nightmarish 1970s interview with Jimmy Page. While Uhelski had tried to pepper the Led Zeppelin ax-slinger with questions, Page had simply refused to acknowledge her presence, meeting every query with silence. Finally, Uhelszki realized that she was supposed to address each of her questions to the publicist, who would then relay them to His Pageness.

Here's a report about the panel from the *Austin American-Statesman:*

> "What do you think of the new album?" Uhelszki asked the flack.
>
> "She wants to know what you think of the new album," the flack asked Page, and so it went for the duration of the interview.
>
> "I should have strangled him," Uhelszki told the 50 or so people gathered in the Convention Center's San Jacinto Room.
>
> "Actually," said old-line *Rolling Stone* writer Ben Fong-Torres, "you should have strangled the publicist, and then *she* should have strangled Jimmy Page."

Panel moderator Evan Smith laughed so hard no one could hear his cell phone ring.

Both friends and strangers continue to ask about the accuracy of some of the details in *Almost Famous*—and I've had to say no, I wasn't fooled over the phone into thinking Crowe was older; I'd met him twice in Los Angeles before receiving samples of his writing. No, that first assignment wasn't for a $1,000 cover story that was dumped because the subject disputed the quotes, but for a $60 piece about a country-rock band, Poco, that was fine. Lester Bangs, the late and legendary critic who serves as Crowe's mentor and rails against the rock establishment—including *Rolling Stone*—actually wrote about 100 record reviews for the magazine. And he didn't spend all his time on the phone counseling Cameron-the-young-rock-writer. And no, Cameron never described any article of his to me as a "think piece." I probably would've hung up on him.

But here's the deal: it's a movie. There's also a DJ, named Alice Wisdom. She's based on a real-life radio hero of Crowe's. Except that the real DJ was a man, Gabriel Wisdom. All of us—Gabriel, Lester, the groupies, the rock band, *Rolling Stone,* and I—served a purpose. We had a role: to help Crowe tell his story. So, yes, it's partly fiction, partly fact.

For me, it's true enough.

—CMJ New Music Monthly, **November 2000**

INDEX

A

acid, xvii, 31, 38, 136, 137, 195

acid rock, 127–128, 134

Adler, Lou, 46

Aerosmith, 200–201

After Bathing at Baxters, 27

Agnew, Spiro, 7, 155

Ahern, Brian, 68, 70

Airplane House, 26, 40

Aldrich, Ronnie, 50

Alexander, Shirley, 52

All Music Guide books, 157

Allan, Laura, 210

Allen, Paul, 200

Allen, Steve, xviii

Allman Brothers, 231

allmusic.com, 66, 157

Almost Famous, 2, 229–234, 237

Altman, Joey, 185, 187

A&M label, 16, 18

Anderson, Ian, 118

Anderson, Signe, 26–27, 28, 135

Anderson, Walter, 75

Andrews, Colman, 184

Anthony, Marc, 200

Apollo Theater, 51

Arias, Olivia, 168

Arthur's Discotheque, 16–17

asianconnections.com, 230

Atlantic Records, 62

Avalon Ballroom, 136

The Avengers, 17

B

Back Burners Blues Band, 183–187

Bad Songs, 144

Balin, Marty, 26–27, 33, 36, 40, 134

Ballard, Hank, 121–126

the Band, 55–59, 116

Bangs, Lester, 234

Barbato, Nancy, 151

Barbwires, 184, 185, 188

Barry, Dave, 144–145

Barsotti, John, 209–211

Batson, Paula, 129–130

Beatles

    compared to Rolling Stones, 84

    Harrison, George, 94, 114–115,

        165–169

    Lennon, John, 91, 92, 94, 102

    McCartney, Paul, 91–94

    Starr, Ringo, 94

Bell, Madelene, 16

Bennett, Tony, 149

Berry, Chuck, 122, 136

Big Brother & the Holding Company, xv,

    22, 23

Billboard charts, 121–123, 151

biography, author, 237

Blackwell, Chuck, 19

Blavat, Jerry, 200

Blige, Mary J., 200

Blind Faith, 5

blog, author's, 230

Bloodstone, 51

Bloomfield, Michael, 136

Boarding House, 78, 79, 119

Boccucci, Dante, 185

Boone, Rob, 185

Boone, Steve, 186

Booth, Henry, 124

BIOGRAPHY

Ben Fong-Torres joined *Rolling Stone* magazine as an editor and writer shortly after graduating from San Francisco State University. At *Rolling Stone,* he wrote dozens of cover stories and won the Deems Taylor Award for magazine writing. He has written for a wide variety of publications and has published five books, including *Not Fade Away,* his first compilation of favorite articles, and *Hickory Wind,* a biography of Gram Parsons. His upcoming book is titled *The Doors By the Doors.* Fong-Torres is also an Emmy award-winning broadcaster and writes the radio column for the *San Francisco Chronicle.* In 2000, he was depicted in the Cameron Crowe film *Almost Famous.*

PUBLICATION CREDITS

Grateful acknowledgment is made to the following for permission to reprint previously published material:

CMJ New Music Monthly: The following article was originally published in *CMJ New Music Monthly:* "Being Almost Famous"

GQ: The following articles were originally published in *GQ:* "Michael Nesmith Shakes the Monkee from His Back," "Why Linda Ronstadt Spent Valentine's Day Alone," "Hank Ballard's Fistful of Hits," "Lou Reed: The Prince of Darkness Lightens Up," "My Hour in the Top 40 Hot Seat"

Gourmet: The following article was originally published in *Gourmet:* "Rhythm 'n' Whites"

Parade: The following articles were originally published in *Parade:* "Steve Martin: More than Just a Pretty Face," "Paul McCartney: 'What I Meant Was . . .'", "Sheryl Crow: 'I'm Where I'm Supposed to Be,'" "Barry, My Brother . . ."

Paste: The following article was originally published in *Paste:* "Larry Ching: Till the End of Time"

People: The following article was originally published in *People:* "Sinatra: Night and Day"

Rolling Stone Magazine: The following articles were originally published in *Rolling Stone Magazine* and are © 2005 *Rolling Stone.* All rights reserved: "Supersession: Crosby, Stills, Nash & Young," "Joe Cocker Is Not a Mad Dog," "Janis: The Scene in Larkspur," "Grace Slick and Paul Kantner: The *Rolling Stone* Interview," "Cruisin' with Cheech & Chong," "Al Green: 'I've Got to Be Free, and Then I Can Sing,'" "The Band with Dylan: 'It's Right On the Dot,'" "Lounging with the Wicked Mr. Pickett," "Emmylou Harris: Whole Wheat Honky Tonk," "Land of the Dead: San Francisco, Where It All Began," "A Banquet on a Ping Pong Table"

San Francisco Chronicle: The following articles were originally published in the *San Francisco Chronicle:* "Groupies of the '80s: Still Grabbin' for the Stars," "A Mind-Blowing Array of Music: The Summer of Love," "George Harrison: A Love-Haight Relationship," "Al Green, Soul Savior," "The Night Rock 'n' Roll Woke Nobody"

PICTURE CREDITS